MODERN
FRENCH POETS

MODERN FRENCH POETS

Selections with Translations
A Dual-Language Book

EDITED BY

WALLACE FOWLIE
James B. Duke Professor of French
Duke University

841

DOVER PUBLICATIONS, INC.
NEW YORK

ॐ

ACKNOWLEDGMENTS

THE BIOGRAPHICAL notices on Max Jacob and St.-John Perse have appeared in *Poetry*, as well as the translation of Perse's poem, *Et vous, mers*. Part of the introduction (*Legacy of Symbolism*) first appeared in *Yale French Studies*. Acknowledgment is also made to *Poetry*, *Yale French Studies*, and *The New Republic* for permission to reprint some passages from the essays and the translations.

Published in Canada by General Publishing Company, Ltd., 30 Lesmill Road, Don Mills, Toronto, Ontario.

Published in the United Kingdom by Constable and Company, Ltd., 3 The Lanchesters, 162–164 Fulham Palace Road, London W6 9ER.

This Dover edition, first published in 1992, is an unabridged and slightly corrected republication of the work originally published under the title *Mid-Century French Poets*, Grove Press, New York, 1955.

Manufactured in the United States of America
Dover Publications, Inc., 31 East 2nd Street, Mineola, N.Y. 11501

Library of Congress Cataloging-in-Publication Data

Modern French poets : selections with translations : a dual-language book / edited by Wallace Fowlie.
　　　p.　　cm.
Originally published: Mid-century French poets. New York : Grove Press, 1955.
Includes bibliographical references.
ISBN 0-486-27323-7
　　1. French poetry—20th century—Translations into English. 2. French poetry—20th century. I. Fowlie, Wallace, 1908–   . II. Fowlie, Wallace, 1908–   Mid-century French poets.
PQ1170.E6M572　1992　　　　　　　　　　　　　　　92-19215
841'.9108—dc20　　　　　　　　　　　　　　　　　　CIP

CONTENTS

INTRODUCTION

Legacy of Symbolism

EVER SINCE THE RICH PERIOD OF SYMBOLISM, in fact, ever since the work of the two leading forerunners of symbolism, Nerval and Baudelaire, French poetry has been obsessed with the idea of purity. To achieve poetry of a "pure state" has been the persistent ambition of a century of literary, and specifically, poetic, endeavor. This ambition is to create poetry that will live alone, by itself and for itself. In a very deep sense, it is poetry of exile, narrating both the very real exile of Rimbaud from Charleville and from Europe, and Mallarmé's more metaphysical exile within his favorite climate of absence. In this effort of poetry to be self-sufficient and to discover its end in itself, it has appropriated more and more pervasively throughout the span of one hundred years the problems of metaphysics. As early as Nerval, who actually incorporated the speculations of the 18th century *illuminés,* poetry tried to be the means of intuitive communication between man and the powers beyond him. Nerval was the first to point out those regions of extreme temptation and extreme peril which have filled the vision of the major poets who have come after him.

This search for "purity" in poetic expression is simply a modern term for the poet's will of all ages to break with daily concrete life, to pass beyond the real and the pressing problems of the moment. Poets have always tended to relegate what may be called "human values" to novels and tragedies or to their counterparts in earlier literary periods. Poetry is the crossroads of man's intelligence and imagination, from which he seeks an absolute beyond himself. That is why the term "angelism" has been used to designate the achievement and the failures of the modern poets, especially those of Rimbaud and Mallarmé. Baudelaire called the poet, "Icarus," and Rimbaud called him "Prometheus, fire-stealer." The progressive spiritualization of modern art in all its forms is its leading characteristic. It brings with it a mission comparable to that of the angels, and also a knowledge of pride and defeat which, strikingly, are the most exact characteristics of some of the great poetic works of our day. Defeat of one kind is in Mallarmé's faun and in his *Igitur.* Claudel, in discussing *Igitur,* called it a "catastrophe." Defeat of another kind is in the long literary silence of Rimbaud, after his 20th or 21st year. And still of another kind, there is defeat in most of the poetry of the surrealists who found it impossible to apply their poetic theory rigorously to their actual poems.

The example of Mallarmé's art was never considered so fervently and piously as during the decade 1940-1950. His lesson is the extraordinary penetration of his gaze at objects in the world, and the attentive precision with which he created a world of forms and pure relationships between the forms. His will to abstraction isolated the object he looked at and his will of a poet condensed the object into its essence and therefore into its greatest power of suggestiveness. The object in a Mallarmé poem is

MODERN FRENCH POETS / INTRODUCTION

endowed with a force of radiation, with a force that is latent and explosive. The irises, for example, in *Prose pour des Esseintes*, have reached a "purity" from which every facile meaning has been eliminated. Such flowers as these come from the deepest soil of the poet's consciousness and emotions. They retain in their "purity," exempt as they are from all usual responses, the virtue of their source in great depths and dreams. Their purity is their power to provoke the multiple responses of the most exacting readers, those who insist that an image appear in its own beauty, isolated from the rest of the world and independent of all keys and obvious explanations. Whatever emotion, whatever passion was at the source of the poem, it has been forgotten in the creation of the poem. Poetry makes no attempt to describe or explain passion—that is the function of the prose writer, of the novelist; rather the object or the image is charged with the burden of the literal experience. The image becomes the experience, but so changed that it is no longer recognizable.

The metaphor is an image endowed with a strange power to create more than itself. Mallarmé's celebrated sonnet on the swan caught in the ice of a lake, *Le vierge, le vivace et le bel aujourd'hui,* illustrates this power of a metaphor to establish a subtle relationship between two seemingly opposed objects in the world: a swan and a poet. The relationship is not stated in logical specific terms, but it is implied or suggested or evoked by the metaphor. The reader's attention is fixed on the swan, as it is almost never fixed on an ordinary object in the universe. This attention which the metaphor draws to itself becomes something comparable to a spiritual activity for the reader, as it had once been for the poet. His consciousness is contained within the metaphor. When the metaphor is an image of a sufficiently general or collective meaning, it becomes a myth, not merely establishing a relationship with another object, but translating some aspect of man's destiny or man's nature. It is often difficult to draw a clear distinction between a metaphor and a myth, as in the case of Mallarmé's swan, who testifies to a basic human struggle and defeat.

Today, in the middle of the century, sixty years after his death, Rimbaud's fame is higher than ever and the influence of the poetry is felt everywhere. Editions of his work multiply each year. More than 500 books about him have been written in all languages. Perhaps never has a work of art provoked such contradictory interpretations and appreciations. One hears of his legend everywhere, and underneath the innumerable opposing beliefs, one continues to follow the legend of a genius who renounced his genius to embrace silence and conceal whatever drama tormented him. He was the adolescent extraordinarily endowed with sight and equally endowed with speech, but with the advent of manhood he deliberately desisted from the prestige of letters and a poet's career. The period of wonderment about his life and his flight from literature is just about over now. In its place, the study of the writings themselves is growing into its own, and it is obvious that their mystery far exceeds the actual language of the writings. With Mallarmé's, it forms the most difficult work to penetrate, in French poetry, and the most rewarding to explore because for both of them, poetry was the act of obedience to their most secret drama.

The work of Rimbaud is far more knowable than his life, but in his case especially, the one cannot be dissociated from the other. The example of his human existence has counted almost as much as the influence of his writing. Breton named him a surrealist by his life, and Rivière named him the supreme type of innocent. Although it must, in all justice, be noted that Breton modified his earlier view and called Rimbaud an apostate, one who renounced his discoveries and called them "sophisms." Nerval's suicide and Lautréamont's total disappearance would please the surrealists more than Rimbaud's final choice of another kind of life than that of poetry.

Rimbaud's example will remain that of the poet opposing his civilization, his historical moment, and yet at the same time revealing its very instability, its quaking torment. He is both against his age and of it. By writing so deeply of himself, he wrote of all men. By refusing to take time to live, he lived a century in a few years, throughout its minute phases, rushing toward the only thing that mattered to him: the absolute, the certainty of truth. He came closest to finding this absolute in his poet's vision. That was "the place and the formula" he talked of and was impatient to find, the spiritual hunt that did not end with the prey seized. Rimbaud's is the drama of modern man, as critics have often pointed out, by reason of its particular frenzy and precipitation, but it is also the human drama of all time, the drama of the quest for what has been lost, the unsatisfied temporal existence burning for total satisfaction, for total certitude. Because of Rimbaud's universality, or rather because of poetry's universality, the Charleville adolescent can seemingly appropriate and justify any title: metaphysician, angel, voyou, seer, reformer, reprobate, materialist, mystic. The poet, as Rimbaud conceived of him, is, rightfully, all men. He is the supreme savant. The private drama of one boy, which does fill the poignant pages of *Une Saison en Enfer*, is always deepened into the drama of man, tormented by the existence of the ideal which he is unable to reach. And likewise, the pure images of *Les Illuminations*, which startle and hold us by their own intrinsic beauty, were generated and formed by a single man in the solitude of his own hope to know reality.

To the role of magus and prophet for the poet, so histrionically played by Victor Hugo, was substituted the role of magician, incarnated not solely by Rimbaud, (whose *Lettre du Voyant* of 1871 seems to be its principal manifesto) but by Nerval and Baudelaire, who preceded him, by his contemporary Mallarmé, and by his leading disciples, the surrealists, thirty years after his death. This concept of the poet as magician dominates most of the poetic transformations and achievements of the last century. The poem, in its strange relationship with witchcraft, empties itself of much of the grandiloquence and pomposity of romanticism. The poet, in his subtle relationship with the mystic, rids himself of the traits of the Hugoesque prophet and the vain ivory-tower attitude of a Vigny. This emphasis on the poet as the sorcerer in search of the unknown and the surreal part of his own being has also caused him to give up the poetry of love, or especially the facile love poetry of a Musset. Except for the poems of Eluard (and a few pages of Breton), there has been no love poetry in France since Baudelaire!

The modern poet in France has become the magician, in accordance with the precepts of Mallarmé, or a visionary, in the tradition of Rimbaud, by his willful or involuntary exploration of dreams and subconscious states. He prefers, to the coherence and the colors of the universe which the romantics celebrated, the incoherence and the half-tones of the hidden universe of the self. There they have learned to come upon thoughts and images in their nascent form, in their primitive beginnings before a conscious control had been exercised over them. The *vert paradis* of the child's world, first adumbrated by Baudelaire, is the world which the modern poet has tried to rediscover. To descend into it brought about a divorce between the poet and the real world around him. The world of childhood and innocence is so obscured in mystery and has been so outdistanced by the gadgets of adulthood, that to return there, a system of magic, a new series of talismans, has to be invented. The richest source of the poet turned out to be the subconscious, precisely that in himself which had not been expressed. The pride of the romantic poet and the somewhat melodramatic solitude he so often created for himself unquestionably helped him later to discover the new regions of his spirit. The historical period of romanticism is seen more and more clearly to be the preparation for the far richer periods of symbolism and post-symbolism when the poetic word is understood in terms of its potential magic and the symbol in its power of exorcism.

The critical writings of Baudelaire, Mallarmé and Valéry are as important as their poetry. They discovered, as if for the first time, some of the oldest laws of poetry. What Racine did in the 17th century for the ageless laws of tragedy, Baudelaire did in the 19th for the ageless laws of poetry. He saw the constraints of rhythm and rhyme to be, not arbitrary, but imposed by a need of the human spirit. A great line of poetry combines a sensual element with an intellectual vigor and Valéry marvelled at the delicate equilibrium which poetry established between them. This very equilibrium was defined by the modern poet as the witchcraft, or the incantation of the word, which no other kind of word possesses. Poetry is not, therefore, the art of obstacles and rules, but the art of triumph over obstacles, the art whose beauty is accomplished by the enveloping of obstacles and the transcending of adventure, brutality, love, sorrow. Modern poetry will one day be described as the revindication of the profoundest principle of classicism where the most universal problems of life are transcribed in a style of language that has reached a high degree of enchantment. The most obscure mysteries of the French language, and of language in general, were explored by Rimbaud, in his seeming anarchy and disorder, and by Mallarmé, in his seeming abstractions and absences. The poetry toward which they were moving, almost without fully realizing it, and which they almost reached, was poetry which would have sung only of itself. Claudel and Valéry, in their time and in their acknowledged role of disciples, realized more acutely than Rimbaud and Mallarmé the perils of such an attainment, and they willfully diverted poetry from anarchy or verbal alchemy to a religious celebration of the universe, and from the dream of poetic purity to a celebration of the intellect.

Just as the moment when poetry might have become an abnegation or a defeat, it was redefined by Claudel as a conquest of the universe. Claudel's method, the new freedom of poetic expression developed by Léon-Paul Fargue, the new strength of poetic enumeration and breath discovered by St.-John Perse, helped to close off the danger which poetry courted in the writings of Rimbaud and Mallarmé. If with Mallarmé, poetry stopped being essentially a lofty mode of expression, it became in the subsequent poets what it had been only partially with Mallarmé: an instrument of knowledge, an art in the service of the human spirit utilized in order to reach a higher degree of domination and knowledge of self. Cubism, surrealism, existentialism, have been some of the successive chapters in this same quest dominated by poetic experimentation. One of the most recent episodes is *lettrism*, revealed by Isidor Isou in his book, *Introduction à une nouvelle poésie et à une nouvelle musique* (Gallimard, 1947). This criticism of language, remarkably youthful in its violence and boldness, will in time be rightfully attached to Rimbaud's revolution. Older thinkers in France today, men like Rolland de Renéville, Thierry Maulnier, Jean Paulhan, Jules Monnerot, Roger Caillois, Maurice Blanchot, have devoted the major part of their work to inquiries into the meaning and the scope of poetry. Their investigations and elucidations are varied, but they all agree on seeing poetry as one of the extreme "experiments" of modern times. The basis of their important works is in their several interpretations of symbolism, in their effort to analyze the indifference of the symbolist toward the world, his narcissism, and the closeness he came to a destruction of poetry by itself. They are the major critics who have seen the poetry of post-symbolism in France, the poetry that has been published between 1900 and 1950, as the reconstruction of poetry.

Because of the extreme solitude of the poet, spoken of by Baudelaire and poignantly epitomized in the life story of Rimbaud, and because of the extreme detachment from the world exemplified in the art of Mallarmé, poetry almost ceased being the full creation that it really is, that of a word which bears in itself the very substance of man. The past fifty years have witnessed a return of poetry to the joys and sufferings of man. This has represented a revindication of the complete freedom of poetry, after the dizzying lessons of magic and abstractions, of Rimbaud's alchemy and Mallarmé's purity. The act of constructing a poem has helped the poet to construct himself. The miracle of poetry has always been the conferring of a new life on that which already has life. By means of the word, designating signs in the physical world, the poet creates a world which is eternal. The lucidity with which the modern poet has learned to do this would probably not have developed without the examples of Baudelaire and the two major poets who succeeded him.

A poem is a marriage between expression and meaning. In order to compose the poem, the poet has to question everything all over again, because a successful poem is a new way of seeing and apprehending something which is familiar. This is Mallarmé's profoundest lesson and it seems now to be fully incorporated in the contemporary poetic consciousness. The poet's power of questioning the universe is essential. His capacity to be amazed at what he beholds is his sign. Without it, his poem will never be the revelation it should be, the revelation to himself and to his readers of what his questioning glance has resurrected, illuminated and understood. In order to be amazed, the poet has to practice a freedom which is unusual, because it is related to everything: the physical world, morality, mythology, God. The practice of this freedom insures what we may best call the poetic response to the world and to everything in it. This is vigilance, attentiveness, lucidity: all those disciplines which are impossible to define but which the artist needs in order to achieve his work.

Since 1940, French poetry has drawn its themes more directly from the tragic quality of contemporary events: blood, catastrophe, hope, than it did in the periods of Baudelaire or Mallarmé. And yet this poetry is far from being a *reportage* or direct transcription. The lesson taught by Mallarmé that there is no such thing as immediate poetry is to such a degree the central legacy of modern poetry, that the younger poets move instinctively toward the eternal myths, like that of Orpheus, which are just beyond the event, the first reactions and the first sentiments. The myth is man's triumph over matter. It is his creation of a world drawn from the world of appearance. It is the world of poetry we are able to see and comprehend far more easily than the real world. This process was once called inspiration or enthusiasm by the Greeks. The modern poets prefer to call it the alchemy or the quintessence of the word. The part of poetry has always come from a new ordering of the real, a new arrangement of ordinary words and common phrases created as a means to hold on to the real and contemplate it. This was the fundamental belief of symbolism which has continued to our day and by which the modern poet denies that poetry is an arbitrary convention. Rather it is an enterprise of the human spirit, directed toward the living words of speech, or rather toward that invisible world which provides words with their life. Between the object and the symbol, there is a distance to be covered, an experience to be explored which is the very act of poetry: the imposition of order on words.

The Generations

AT THE TURN of the mid-century, French poetry is still fully engaged in one of the richest periods of its long history. Its roots are essentially in symbolism and in the achievements of poetry between *Les Fleurs du Mal* of Baudelaire (1857) and the death of Mallarmé (1898). Especially in France the creative spirit has always been fully conscious of its heritage, of its belonging to the past, of its role destined to continue and perfect a tradition. During the past fifty years, the youngest and the oldest poets have been proud of the fact that the art of poetry has enjoyed an extraordinary prestige. The wealth of modern French poetry and its high quality have jealously preserved this prestige. More than the novel and more than drama, poetry has continued to renew itself. Only perhaps the realm of literary criticism has been productive to a similar degree, and the most vital books of criticism have considered the problems of poetry and poets.

The half-century has been dominated by four major writers, all born around 1870, only one of whom is still living, and who have reached now the status of classical writers. Two of these are prose writers: Proust and Gide; and two are poets: Valéry and Claudel. Their common background was symbolism. They were initiated into literature by the stimulation, the achievements and the manifestoes of symbolism. Each reacted to symbolism in his own way and according to his own purposes. They are the most illustrious members of the oldest generation still writing in 1950. In a certain sense the 20th century did not begin until 1914. The first decade was still very much a part of the 1890's. These four writers had begun writing and publishing by the literal turn of the century, but recognition of their importance did not come until soon after the First War, about 1920.

Mallarmé and Rimbaud are the greatest poets of the symbolist period, although, paradoxically, neither one is purely representative of the symbolist creed. Mallarmé was guide, director and high priest of the movement, but his poetry far transcends the doctrine and the art of the lesser poets. Rimbaud repudiated a literary career, and had no direct influence on symbolism, although he wrote between 1869 and 1875. To a far lesser degree, the example of Verlaine counted also in the symbolist period. His was the poetry of the heart and pure sentiment, a tradition maintained, for example, by Francis Jammes (1868-1938) who belongs to this first generation of 20th century poets. Even more isolated from the central evolution of French poetry, stands Charles Péguy (1873-

MODERN FRENCH POETS / INTRODUCTION

1914), celebrated for his deeply religious poetry on Notre Dame de Chartres and for his *Mystère de la Charité de Jeanne D'Arc* (1910).

But the combined examples and influences of Mallarmé and Rimbaud have proved more permanent and more vital than any others in the 20th century. The word "purity," a concept with which modern poetry is permeated, is associated primarily with Mallarmé, with the doctrine he expounded on Tuesday evenings for so many years (1880-1898) in his apartment on the rue de Rome. There his most brilliant disciple, Paul Valéry (1871-1945) listened in his early twenties to Mallarmé's conversations on poetry. The leading symbols of Mallarmé's purity: his virgin princess Hérodiade; his faun, more interested in his own ecstasy than in the nymphs; his swan caught in the ice of the lake,—all reappear, changed but fully recognizable, in the leading symbols of Valéry's poetry: his Narcissus, the contemplation of self pushed to its mortal extreme; his Jeune Parque and his marine cemetery. *La Jeune Parque*. which may well be Valéry's greatest poem, composed during the war years (1914-17), reflects in no way the event of the war. This poem, with the major poems of Mallarmé, with *Les Illuminations* of Rimbaud and the early prose pieces of Gide, treat so pervasively the theme of solitude and detachment that they create a new mythology of poetic purity and human absence. It is poetry anxious to live alone for itself and by itself. It is poetry of exile, written outside of the social sphere. It bears no relationship to a society or to a world which might be comparable to the bond between the poetry of Racine and the monarchy of Louis XIV.

Rimbaud, in his own way, is as profound an example as Mallarmé of this separation of poetry from the immediate world. The experience of the *bateau ivre* was not only an exploration of exoticism and of the unknown, it was also an extreme lesson in the exile which is solitude. After writing his poetry of exile, Rimbaud lived in exile in the deserts and cities and mountainous regions of Abyssinia. The same need for voyage and solitude was felt by Paul Claudel (born in 1868), who has always claimed Rimbaud as his master in poetry, as the writer who revealed to him the presence of the supernatural in the world. Rimbaud's greatest ambition was to move beyond literature and poetry, and this has been realized to some degree by Claudel, whose vocation as poet has always been subordinated to his role of apologist of Catholicism. The entire universe is the site of the Christian drama for Claudel. The form of his *verset* is reminiscent of the rhythms in *Les Illuminations* and *Une Saison en Enfer*. He continues Rimbaud's Dionysian turbulence, whereas Valéry, in his more chastened, more classical style represents, with Mallarmé, the Apollonian tradition of French poetry.

Rimbaud's experience of exile becomes Claudel's knowledge of solitude (*Faites que je sois comme un semeur de solitude . . .*) and the act of the poet for both of them is comparable to the secret act of the magus or the magician. Poetry for Rimbaud, as it had been for Baudelaire before him, is witchcraft. He is hallucinated and his poems are illuminations. The way is opened toward the surreal. Rimbaud's real disciples are not the symbolists of the 80's and 90's, they are the surrealists of 1925-1935. But Claudel, who was over eighty in 1950, was the first to understand and appropriate Rimbaud's lesson on poetry. His *Cinq Grandes Odes* of 1911 and his *Poèmes de Guerre* of 1922, treat the universe as the communication of God to man.

The second generation of poets were those men born at the end of the century. On the whole, they participated in the experience of the First World War much more directly than the generation of Valéry and Claudel. In fact, some of the most gifted writers of this generation lost their lives in the war: Apollinaire, Alain-Fournier, Psichari, and Péguy (although Péguy was slightly older and belongs more strictly to the other generation.) This group of writers, particularly in the years after the War, demonstrated a changed attitude toward the role and the activity of the writer. The poet was for them a far less exalted being than he had been for Mallarmé and Rimbaud. The excessive intellectualism and aestheticism of the late symbolist period were drastically modified and diminished. The experience of the war and the rise of the cinema were only two of the many new forces which were shaping the younger poets at that time. *La Nouvelle Revue Française*, founded in 1905 by Copeau, Gide and Schlumberger became, during 1920 and 1940, an organ of great influence and subjectivity. It was almost a literary chapel, exclusive as such groups tend to be, but intelligent and judicious in its power. Its editor, Gaston Gallimard, was responsible for the publication of most of the major literary texts during that time.

The oldest figures of this second generation were Max Jacob and Léon-Paul Fargue, both born in 1876. They had begun publishing their poetry long before the war, but their influence was felt after the war. They and the younger poets following them no longer exemplified a distinct influence of either Mallarmé or Rimbaud. Such influences were combined in them. Stylistic traits, for example, of Verlaine and Laforgue, are as present in their writing as characteristics of Mallarmé and Rimbaud. They were both friends of painters and musicians, and participated actively in the avant-garde movement in France. They were both (especially Fargue) poets who wrote of Paris. Jacob died first, in the German prison of Drancy, in 1944, just before the end of the war. Fargue survived the war, and died in 1947.

By his creation of a style of poetry distinctly modern, Guillaume Apollinaire, born in 1880, occupies a more significant place in the development of French poetry than either Jacob or Fargue. His influence is apparent in the writing of Blaise Cendrars (born in 1887) who is a greater prose writer than a poet, and who illustrates the non belle-lettristic approach to writing. His autobiography of 1945, *L'Homme Foudroyé*, is written in the prose of a poet.

Surrealism was the most significant literary movement in France between symbolism and existentialism. It flourished especially in the decade 1925-35, and attracted many of the younger poets of that period, most of whom are still living. Reverdy, born in 1889, was as closely allied to symbolism as to surrealism. Tristan Tzara, born in Rumania in 1896, was the founder of the Dada movement, in collaboration with Jean Arp and Hugo Ball, in Zurich in 1916. Dadaism was the immediate forerunner of surrealism. The leading spirit and theorist of surrealism was André Breton (born in 1896) who ever since the Second World War has made attempts to revive surrealism as an organized movement. But most of the poets who at one time or another adhered to the tenets of surrealism are today writing poetry that is no longer strictly surrealist. Breton himself and Benjamin Péret have remained closest to the beliefs and practices of orthodox surrealism. Péret took part in the Civil War in Spain, and has been living in Mexico since 1942. He was perhaps the best satirist of the group, the closest spiritual descendant of Alfred Jarry, whose *Ubu-Roi*, of 1896, was a major text for the surrealists. Some of the purest of the surrealist poets have died: Crevel (1900-1935), whose suicide was interpreted as an act of heroism; Desnos (1900-1945), a victim of a German concentration camp; Artaud (1895-1948), who spent the last nine years of his life in an insane asylum. Others have continued only intermittently with the writing of poetry: Soupault (b. 1897), Leiris (b. 1905), and Georges Hugnet (b. 1906) who was active in Les Editions de Minuit, the publication of the Resistance. Aragon, born in 1897, became the best known Resistance poet, but by that time he had broken all ties with surrealism. The greatest poet from surrealism is Paul Eluard who is actually the oldest of the entire group since he was born in 1895.

To this list, which is not exhaustive, of the major French poets associated with surrealism, should be added many other names of poets who wrote during the same decade, and who have continued to write since, but who had no formal connection with any literary school or movement. The contribution of Jules Supervielle (b. 1884) is distinguished and abundant, although his best books seem to have been written before the Second World War. Jouve (b. 1887) in recent years has grown into a poet of great influence. His universe of catastrophe is described in poetry of a lofty Christian inspiration. Since 1940, St.-John Perse (b. 1887) has lived in the United States where he wrote *Exil*, one of the profoundest poetic statements on the war. Jean Cocteau (b. 1892) has written poetry intermittently throughout his career. He remains one of the most gifted poets of his generation, even if the signal success in his other genres: theatre, cinema, criticism, has somewhat detracted from his position as poet. One of the most independent modern poets, Henri Michaux (b. 1899), has enlarged the domain of poetry. He was discovered in 1941 by Gide whose fervent criticism introduced him to a wider public than he had known. Audiberti (b. 1899) is as well known in the fields of the theatre and the novel as he is in poetry. He is the most highly endowed rhetorician of the new poets. The torrential flow of his lyrics and his purely verbal virtuosity give him a distinctive place among his contemporaries. With Aragon, Prévert (b. 1900) is probably the most widely read of the French poets. More important than his poetry is his writing for the cinema. *Les Visiteurs du Soir* and *Les Enfants du Paradis* are two of his outstanding successes. René Char, born in 1906, is one of the best poets of the south. He first allied himself with surrealism and has always retained in his subsequent poetry the boldness and profusion of imagery one associates with surrealism. He was a maquis captain in Provence at the end of the war and has written movingly in his poetry of his war experience.

The third and youngest generation of poets writing in France at the turn of the mid-century is more dramatically allied with action, with the war and the Resistance, than the poets of the other two generations. Sartre defined the new literature as being "engaged" (*la littérature engagée*), and this term applies to the poetry of this generation so directly concerned with the actual circumstances and events. The greatness of Jouve (who chronologically belongs to the previous generation) brilliantly illustrates this use of the immediate event in poetry. Pierre Emmanuel (b. 1916) has written generously of his admiration for Jouve and of the influence which Jouve's poetry has had on his own. One of Emmanuel's noteworthy achievements is the vigor he has given to poetry of a well-defined subject matter. His mingling, for example, of the Orpheus theme with the redemptive power of Christ is in one of his early works, *Le Tombeau d'Orphée*, where the mystery of man is not separated from the mystery of the exterior world.

The ambition of this youngest generation has been, in general, to recall the poet to reality, after the long experimentation of poetry with language, with the symbol, with the hieratic role of the poet. The new writer has felt a greater desire for communication, for immediate communication, we should say, with the reader. On the whole, he is less subjective than the earlier poets. He appropriates the common basis of world events and world problems for his verse. This tendency was already visible in the poetry of Eluard, of Supervielle and of Michaux. The earliest poetry of Patrice de la Tour du Pin (b. 1911) was published in 1932 and seemed to prophesy the advent of a very great poet. His 600 page *Somme de Poésie* has not justified these hopes, but the work illustrates the ambition of discovering for the modern age a common body of metaphysics.

Existentialism, as a literary movement, has not developed any poets, with the possible exception of Francis Ponge, on whose work Sartre himself has written a long essay. Although Ponge was born in 1899, his first important publication was in 1942, *Le Parti Pris des Choses,* a poetic work of great rigor and objectivity, and one completely lacking in any subjective lyricism. In describing an object: a pebble, for example, or a piece of bread, Ponge can also write as a moralist, as a contemporary La Fontaine.

Robert Ganzo, born in 1898, and therefore a contemporary of Ponge, also attracted for the first time serious attention in the 1940's. A skillful meticulous technician, his poem *Domaine* is a remarkably achieved poem on a jellyfish as symbol of the poet's conscience reflecting all appearances. Although Raymond Queneau, born in 1903, has written principally and prolifically in the domain of the novel, he is also a poet. His central preoccupation with language, with what he considers a needed revolution in language, places him very centrally among the poets. His influence is wide, exceeded only by the more massive influence of a writer like Sartre. By advocating the reintegration of the vitality of spoken language, each book of his is a "stylistic exercise." His powers seem to be tricks with words and in the freedom of composition he practices, he is often reminiscent of surrealism with which he was in fact at first associated. His writing mingles all the contemporary scenes: the suburbs, the "zone," the movies, autocars, but his distortions of caricature are suffused with what is an essentially poetic atmosphere.

It is impossible to mention all the poets born since 1900 or just before. We have already referred to Patrice de la Tour du Pin and Emmanuel. Henri Thomas (b. 1912) is as spontaneous and youthful in his writing as Maurice Fombeure (b. 1907) who maintains in his verse elements of the refrain, the *chanson,* a certain shrewd peasant-like quality, not absent from Apollinaire who still is in France the leading modern poet of this style. Luc Estang (b. 1911) recalls persistently the art of the symbolists. Jean Cayrol (b. 1911) is almost prophetic in his use of the great myths of humanity and in his preoccupation with the spiritual. By many, and especially by Breton, Aimé Césaire (b. 1913) is considered the first major colored poet in French. He lives in Martinique. Not until after the Second War was his poetry discovered in France. Breton has acclaimed him as one of the legitimate heirs of surrealism, by reason of the violence and richness of surrealism, and by his spirit of revolt against an unjust society. Alain Borne (b. 1915) in company with Patrice de la Tour du Pin and Luc Estang, represent the Catholic tradition in recent French poetry. The Catholicism of Loys Masson, born also in 1915, is perhaps less orthodox. A poet from l'Ile Maurice, Malcolm de Chazal, has recently been discovered by Jean Paulhan who has for many years exercised a very powerful role of literary critic and judge in the house of Gallimard. In 1947, the lyric play, *Les Epiphanies*, by Henri Pichette (b. 1924) was a marked success for the experimental theatre and for the talent of one of the youngest poets.

These, then, are some of the most representative of the three generations of French poets writing at the turn of the mid-century. During the tragic years of the war and the German occupation of France, the poets reached a larger audience than usual. At the grave moments of history humanity is wont to turn to its poets in order to reconsider man's fate, to understand more profoundly the relationship of man with the universe, and to enjoy the poetic word as the expression of the ideas by which men live. The last generation is the most difficult to judge. There are signs in it of impatience and haste, but its poetry has in common with the poetry of the two preceding generations the visible influence and even domination of the same gods of modern French poetry: Rimbaud and Apollinaire, especially, and then the less visible but always present influence and examples of Baudelaire and Mallarmé.

Forerunners:
Nerval 1808-1855
Baudelaire 1821-1867

Symbolists:
Mallarmé 1842-1898
Verlaine 1844-1896
Rimbaud 1854-1891

In the symbolist tradition:
Jammes 1868-1938
Claudel 1868-
Valéry 1871-1945

Oldest generation in the 20th:
Péguy 1873-1914
Jarry 1873-1907
Fargue 1876-1947
Jacob 1876-1944

Second generation:
Apollinaire 1880-1918
Supervielle 1884-
Jouve 1887-
Perse 1887-
Reverdy 1889-
Cocteau 1892-
Artaud 1895-1948
Eluard 1895-1952
Tzara 1896-

Breton 1896-
Aragon 1897-
Soupault 1897-
Ganzo 1898-
Péret 1899-
Michaux 1899-
Ponge 1899-

Born since 1900:
Crevel 1900-1935
Desnos 1900-1945
Prévert 1900-
Queneau 1903-
Leiris 1905-
Hugnet 1906-
Char 1906-
Senghor 1906-
Fombeure 1907-
La Tour du Pin 1907-
Estang 1911-
Cayrol 1911-
Thomas 1912-
Césaire 1913-
Borne 1915-
Masson 1915-
Emmanuel 1916-
Pichette 1926-
Chazal
Isou

MAX JACOB

THE EARLY YEARS of the century in Paris prepared the artistic movement which flourished especially in the period between the two wars. They were years of anecdotes and friendships and discoveries which quickly grew into legends. Max Jacob was one of these legends. His Montmartre period was as simple and as fantastic as any legend. He belonged integrally to those epic years which invented cubism and other fabulous products we accept today as historical familiar works of art. Three figures especially presided over the first years of the century which has just now reached its mid-way mark: Guillaume Apollinaire, one of the truly great poets of France, who died on the day of the Armistice, 1918; Pablo Picasso, still living in Paris and already recognized as the genius of the century; and poverty-stricken

Max Jacob, who was to remain poor all his life, famished for lyricism and food, and who was to die in early 1944, in the German concentration camp of Drancy, because he happened to be born a Jew.

His art was created in the midst of friends and poverty, in the rue Ravignan. It is a style very much his own, without pretension, a kind of improvisation both learned and childish. A combination of poetry, satire, sarcasm, popular lyrics, parody. Yet it is writing of exceptional beauty and delicacy, comparable in a way to the music of Satie, an art stripped of almost all literary effects, save those of sentiment and wit. Max Jacob preserved the joy of his period, when he was seen everywhere in Paris. A small man with a monocle, who had countless friends and who disguised the poverty of his life by selling his manuscripts and his gouaches. He performed all trades, from that of a store clerk to a secretary, and always with a characteristic sly humor and verboseness. One wonders about his buffoonery when he was alone. Did it drop from him then, like an actor's cloak?

He met Picasso in 1901. They lived together for a while in a kind of famished bohemianism. Picasso was Max's first admirer. "You are the only poet of the times," he used to say to him. The painter finally settled down, independently, at No. 13, rue Ravignan. Jacob was at No. 7, in a sunless room where a smoking lamp used to burn night and day. Max's one luxury was fresh flowers which he kept in a small blue glass vase, won by a friend at some street circus on the boulevard de Clichy. To economize, he would prepare his own meals. On the wall he kept nailed up a sign: *Ne jamais aller à Montparnasse* ("Never go to Montparnasse"). One evening Picasso took him to the Austin Fox bar on the rue d'Amsterdam, near the Gare St. Lazare, where he introduced him to a heavy-set fellow whose pleasant face was crowned with reddish hair. It was Guillaume Apollinaire, who became a brother artist of Max and Picasso. No. 13, rue Ravignan turned into an artistic center where the "bande Picasso" counted, among others, the painter Juan Gris and the art critic André Salmon. They used to go often to Frédé's (the Lapin Agile) whose Burgundian wife served them wine gratuitously. Francis Carco was one of the last comers to the group. They used to read the Fantômas stories and even formed a *Société des Amis de Fantômas* (S.A.F.).

The first episode which was to lead Max Jacob to his conversion occurred on the 7th of October, 1909. He returned from the Bibliothèque Nationale and entered his room on the rue Ravignan. There he saw on one of his watercolors hanging on the wall a vision of Christ. He has described this revelation in a justly celebrated page in his book, *La Défense de Tartufe*. Before being received into the Catholic Church, he had to wait six years. He was baptised on February 18, 1915, "Cyprien-Max Jacob," in the presence of Picasso, whom he had chosen godfather. His rich vein of buffoonery and his comic genius, which Cassou has compared to Molière's, were not altered by this conversion. Like the mediaeval juggler of Notre Dame, Max never took off his bells, even in the presence of the crucifix. The tone of his art remained essentially the same. Like Satie, Jacob is a combined humorist and mystic. His art is an affront to the languorous, the plaintive, the serious in art. He initiated a vogue of punning in poetry which many subsequent poets have profited from. His bleak satire of the French bourgeoisie has caused him, with some justice, to be compared with the painter Rouault.

In June, 1921, he moved to Saint Benoît-sur-Loire, close to an ancient Benedictine church. Save for a few interruptions, he lived there until he was taken to Drancy, in 1944. He became a well known and well loved figure in the small town. As his religious life deepened, he grew in charity and humbleness. He rose very early to write a meditation before serving the first mass. Young poets found their way to Saint Benoît. His correspondence was voluminous. Max Jacob became an indefatigable proselytizer.

From the beginning of the German Occupation, he was placed under suspicion by the Nazis, who forced him to wear the yellow star of his race. As soon as the news reached his friends in Paris, in February, 1944, that Max had been arrested, they used every means to obtain his release. When his death, on March 5th, was announced, it was received with consternation and indignation. He was 68, an old man who spent most of his time on his private devotions and who had no political affiliations whatever. Like

Lorca and Saint-Pol-Roux, Max was one of those men killed by the war simply because they were poets.

Jacob was born into a Quimper family of the *petite bourgeoisie*, became an esthete of the rue Ravignan, and ended his life as a kind of hermit at Saint Benoît-sur-Loire. Less gifted than Apollinaire, he has nevertheless exerted an important influence on young French poets. In his *Cornet à dés* (1917) he has left some of the finest prose poems in the language, and in the preface of the book, a significant theory of the form of the prose poem.

His poems are never perfected works of art. They are close to being ways of producing a poetic state or awareness in the reader. Their parody intent is almost always perceptible. The music of his verse is irregular and often irritating in its eccentricities. Superficially his poetry would seem to be largely composed of commonplaces, of witticisms, of gossip about the *faits divers*. But the deeper, more total effect of his poetry is one of exceptional suppleness in verbal expression, of infinite metamorphosis. In a way, he is a poet for poets. The work of such poets as Cocteau, Maurice Fombeure and Jacques Prévert would perhaps not be exactly what it is without the example of Max Jacob.

The Catholicism of his poetry mingles heaven and hell, angels and demons, with a resolute boldness that is totally unlike the Catholic poetry of Jammes, Péguy, Claudel. The piety of his books is as startling and unconventional as the piety of his real life. It would be as false to call him a saint as it would be to call him a real clown or a pure humorist. He is somewhere in between the saint and the clown, in his will to humble and deprecate himself, on the one hand, and in his genius as a mime, on the other hand, whereby he multipled his roles without effort.

The younger group of poets in France today, who just before the war, read for the first time Rimbaud's *Saison en Enfer* and Lautréamont's *Chants de Maldoror*, read also, as one of their principal books of poetic initiation, Jacob's *Cornet à dés*. Many of them knew him personally and paid him visits at Saint Benoît-sur-Loire. They remembered he had been a close companion of Apollinaire and had known Verlaine. He talked endlessly with them about the artistic period at the beginning of the century when poets lived as poets should. Picasso's affection for him never diminished. The painter did all he could to save his friend's life in the last tragic months. About 1936-37, Max Jacob began taking on the proportions of a celebrity. During the first year of the war, in June 1940, the new periodical *Confluences* courageously published poems of Jacob, and welcomed among its contributors Gertrude Stein, who was under as much suspicion as Jacob. Since his death, his fame has continued to grow, with endless testimonials and posthumous publications.

More clearly than ever he is seen today to be the type of modern mystic who reveals himself by means of a burlesqued fantasy in which he can permit himself every form of adventure, even the love of God. He is an example of the man who is embarrassed by having come upon a profound part in his own being, whose face bears the inwardly turned expression of the clown. The center of the world is his heart, but it beats so faintly that he never listens to it. His own heart is hostile and foreign to himself. This modern clown's heart is the source of the new poignant fantasy created by Jacob, and which can be rediscovered today in the paintings of Marc Chagall, where donkeys, violins, angels and roses form patterns whose beauty is the incongruous, and in the nightmares of Donald Duck, where the universe is pulverized.

The fantasy of Max Jacob, when taken over by a master, becomes an act of tremendous dynamism, as in the paintings of Rouault. The religious theme dominates the new circus school. Cocteau's letter to Maritain is its manifesto, and the writings of Max Jacob form one of its most authentic testimonials. The complaint of Laforgue's Pierrot and Jarry's *Ubu Roi* of 1897, helped to consecrate the break with the "poetic" subjects of symbolism and instituted the new tragic fantasy of the circus, where the real spectacle is always performed before God.

Jacob's life was the prodigal son's. His art resembles the buffoon's, without being it too literally, in which disorder is a saving grace. Rimbaud had revealed the new creed in his sentence, *Je finis par trouver sacré le désordre de mon esprit.* ("I came to realize that my mind's disorder was sacred.") To the generation of Mallarmé, interested in the symbolism of objects, succeeded the generation of Max Jacob, men born between 1870 and 1880, who turned their interest to the symbolism of man and found themselves involved in a circus exhibitionism. Max Jacob became the most histrionic of his generation. He changed from bohemian to mystic, from Montmartre to Saint Benoît-sur-Loire, and then changed back from saint to sinner, from the cell to the Lapin Agile. The clown's vocation is partly angelic. He causes laughter through understanding the source of joy and through enacting the innocency of man.

Selected Bibliography of Max Jacob

1912 *Les Oeuvres Burlesques et Mystiques de Frère Matorel*, illustré par Derain, Kahnweiler.
1917 *Le Cornet à dés*, chez l'auteur.
1919 *La Défense de Tartufe*, Société littéraire de France.
1921 *Le Laboratoire Central*, Au Sans Pareil.
1922 *Art Poétique*, Emile-Paul.
1925 *Les Pénitents en Maillots Roses*, Kra.
1937 *Morceaux Choisis*, Gallimard.
1945 *Derniers Poèmes*, Gallimard.
1947 *Max Jacob: Poètes d'aujourd'hui*, No. 3, Seghers.

on Jacob

Billy, André, *Introduction à Poètes d'aujourd'hui*, No. 3.
Cahiers du Sud, No. 273, 1945, *Passage de Max Jacob*.
Fabureau, *Max Jacob, son oeuvre*, Ed. de la Nouvelle Revue Critique, 1935.
Hell, Henri, *Max Jacob*, Fontaine.
Rousselot, Jean, *Max Jacob L'Homme qui faisait penser à Dieu*, Laffont, 1946.

Hamletism
(from *Art Poétique*, 1922)

Man is a venerating animal. He venerates as easily as he purges himself. When they take away from him the gods of his fathers, he looks for others abroad. The 19th century invented the worship of genius. To avoid ridicule, or as a guarantee, people were careful to worship only dead or dying geniuses. The pious dress up their cults or their divinities. Beethoven's head, Mephistopheles' goatee, and Hamlet's tights have received ecclesiastical honors. I beg you not to speak of a genius who resembles physically Messrs. Racine or La Fontaine. . . . Modern geniuses, knowing the conditions of the contract for admiration, make one with their barber. Beethoven's head has served as model for economists, great philosophers, actors. Mephisto's goatee is used rather by amateur geniuses and reporters. Hamlet's tights have warmed many poets under their suits for more than sixty years. The conviction that several poet friends of mine have undressed Hamlet in order not to take him any longer as a model prompts me to publish the following reflections . . .

I once knew in a family of the high Parisian industrial world a young boy who seemed to have only one goal in life, that of terrifying by fits of madness his excellent mother and his young sister who was just beginning to play easily her scales and arpeggios on the piano. "Yes or no, Marcel, do you want some soup?"—And Marcel would answer, "I think there are also some spider webs in the absolute." His father raised his head, his mother, her shoulders, the girl, her mouth. During the dinner Marcel would run to the wall, then to a chair, and make the gesture of catching a fly and throwing it into the gravy, with charming mannerisms. Today Marcel is a stockbroker, a music lover and divorced. When I published my first verse, about 1905, I was acquainted with poets already celebrated. One of them continuously employed in his discussions the manners of Marcel and used them to mark the distance between a genius such as he was and his disciples. It appears that one night this behavior stopped some prowlers whom respect didn't stop when they met the wandering *littérateur*. I see this great poet from time to time. I wonder why age, wars and a few disillusions have modified his language.

Here are the words I propose to describe such an original manner of speech: hamletism, hamletic, to hamletize, hamletomane, hamletomania, to dehamletize. And here are some examples of their use.

Hamletism is an unsuspected way of expressing profundity of thought or of implying. Hamletic poets are rare. We only know hamletomanes.

Hamletomaniacs infest the insane asylums. It would be erroneous to claim genius for them.

Intoxication and the use of narcotics develop hamletomania. The war of 1914 dehamletized avant-garde literature.

"The language you attribute to Shakespeare's Hamlet," someone said to me, "is not his as much as it is that of the court jesters in romantic plays. The language of Fantasio in Musset."

—Objection, please. Allow me to say that I have already answered this. Posterity attributes to a hero it knows by name the great deeds of others it doesn't know, and to an immortal genius the innovations of forgotten creators, because of the fact that man, being a venerating animal, in order to venerate further, adorns his idols even at the expense of truth. Let us keep the word "hamletism" even if the author of Hamlet is not the inventor of the thing. But I plead with you not to confuse hamletism with obscurity in general. What is obscure is not hamletic, and what is hamletic is not necessarily obscure. The hamletic may be non-obscure. Obscurity may be hamletic when it is humorous and willfully bent on astonishing. Modern poetry may appear obscure, but it is not hamletic. Modern poetry is objectified but the essence of hamletism is its subjectivity. The first is mad at not being understood. The second would be mad if it were understood. The modern poet explores the associations of ideas and harmonizes them into the scene of cities, countrysides and customs. The hamletic is preoccupied solely with inciting belief in its own genius. The hamletic would be a lyric writer and the modern poet an epic writer. Newspapers are sometimes conceived with national poetry, but hamletic poetry is chamber poetry. I do not know what national poetry is, but modern poetry is world poetry. The distinction between the poets of 1900 and those of 1910, has not been made in the light of what I am calling, perhaps for the first time, "hamletism."

Frontispice

Oui, il est tombé du bouton de mon sein et je ne m'en suis pas aperçu. Comme un bateau sort de l'antre du rocher avec les marins sans que la mer en frémisse davantage, sans que la terre sente cette aventure nouvelle, il est tombé de mon sein de Cybèle un poème nouveau et je ne m'en suis pas aperçu.

Le Cornet à dés

Les Vrais Miracles

Le bon vieux curé! après qu'il nous eût quitté, nous le vîmes s'envoler au-dessus du lac comme une chauve-souris. Il était assez absorbé dans ses pensées pour ne pas même s'apercevoir du miracle. Le bas de la soutane était mouillé il s'en étonna.

Le Cornet à dés

La Rue Ravignan

"On ne se baigne pas deux fois dans le même fleuve," disait le philosophe Héraclite. Pourtant ce sont toujours les mêmes qui remontent! Aux mêmes heures, ils passent gais ou tristes. Vous tous, passants de la Rue Ravignan, je vous ai donné les noms des défunts de l'Histoire! Voici Agamemnon! Voici madame Hanska! Ulysse est un laitier! Patrocle est au bas de la rue qu'un Pharaon est près de moi. Castor et Pollux sont les dames du cinquième. Mais toi, vieux chiffonnier, toi qui, au féerique matin, viens enlever les débris encore vivants quand j'éteins ma bonne grosse lampe, toi que je ne connais pas, mystérieux et pauvre chiffonnier, toi, chiffonnier, je t'ai nommé d'un nom célèbre et noble, je t'ai nommé Dostoiewsky.

Le Cornet à dés

La Révélation

Je suis revenu de la Bibliothèque Nationale; j'ai déposé ma serviette; j'ai cherché mes pantoufles et quand j'ai relevé la tête, il y avait quelqu'un sur le mur; il y avait quelqu'un! il y

Frontispiece

Yes, it fell from the nipple of my breast and I did not see it. As a boat comes out from the rock cave with the sailors without the sea quivering in the least, a new poem fell from my breast of Cybèle and I did not see it.

Real Miracles

The good old priest! After he left us, we saw him flying over the lake like a bat. He was so absorbed in his thoughts that he didn't even see the miracle. The bottom of his cassock was wet. He was surprised at that.

Ravignan Street

"You don't bathe twice in the same river," said the philosopher Heraclitus. Yet always the same ones pass by. At the same time each day they go by sad or happy. You who walk on Ravignan Street, I have given you names of the dead in history! This is Agamemnon! There is Madame Hanska! Ulysses is a milkman! Patrocles is at the bottom of the street while a Pharaoh is near by. Castor and Pollux are ladies on the sixth floor. Old ragman, you who, in the bewitched morning come to take away the yet living debris, when I am putting out my good fat lamp, you whom I don't know, mysterious poor ragman, I have called you a noble and famous name: Dostoievsky.

The Revelation

I came home from the library. I laid down my briefcase. I looked for my slippers and when I raised my head again, there was someone on the wall. There was someone. There was someone on the red wallpaper. My flesh fell to the ground! I was stripped by lightning! Oh! that imperishable moment! truth! tears and joy of truth! unforgettable truth! The Body of God

avait quelqu'un sur la tapisserie rouge. Ma chair est tombée par terre! j'ai été déshabillé par la foudre! Oh! impérissable seconde! oh! vérité! vérité! larmes de la vérité! joie de la vérité! inoubliable vérité. Le Corps Céleste est sur le mur de la pauvre chambre! Pourquoi Seigneur? Oh! pardonnez-moi! Il est dans un paysage, un paysage que j'ai dessiné jadis, mais Lui! quelle beauté! élégance et douceur! Ses épaules, sa démarche! Il a une robe de soie jaune et des parements bleus. Il se retourne et je vois cette face paisible et rayonnante. Six moines alors emportent dans la chambre un cadavre. Une femme qui a des serpents autour des bras et des cheveux, est près de moi.

L'Ange: Tu as vu Dieu, innocent! tu ne comprends pas ton bonheur.

Moi: Pleurer! pleurer! je suis une pauvre bête humaine.

L'Ange: Le démon est parti! il reviendra.

Moi: Le démon! oui!

L'Ange: Intelligence.

Moi: Tu ne sais pas le bien que tu me fais.

L'Ange: Nous t'aimons, paysan. Consulte-toi!

Moi: Ravissement! Seigneur! Je comprends, ah! je comprends.

La Défense de Tartufe

Visitation

Ma chambre est au fond d'une cour et derrière des boutiques, le No. 7 de la rue Ravignan! tu resteras la chapelle de mon souvenir éternel. J'ai pensé, étendu sur le sommier que quatre briques supportent; et le propriétaire a percé le toit de zinc pour augmenter la lumière. Qui frappe si matin?—Ouvrez! ouvrez la porte! ne vous habillez pas!—Seigneur!—La croix est lourde: je veux la déposer.—Comment entrera-t-elle? la porte est bien étroite.—Elle entrera par la fenêtre.—Mon Seigneur! chauffez-vous! il fait si froid.—Regarde la croix!—Oh! Seigneur! toute ma vie.

A M. Modigliani Pour Lui Prouver que Je Suis un Poète

Le nuage est la poste entre les continents
Syllabaire d'exil et que les Océans,

is on the wall of my poor room! Why? O Lord! Forgive me! He is in a landscape, one I drew years ago. What beauty, what elegance and gentleness in Him! Look at his shoulders and the way he holds himself. He's wearing a dress of yellow silk with blue ornaments. He turns around and I see his calm radiant face. Then six monks carry a corpse into the room. A woman, with snakes around her arms and in her hair, is near me.

The Angel: Innocent one, you've seen God! You don't understand your happiness.

I: Let me cry! Let me cry! I am a poor human animal.

The Angel: The demon has gone. He will come back.

I: Yes! The demon!

Angel: Intelligence.

I: You don't know the good you do me.

Angel: Peasant, we love you. Look into your heart!

I: Joy, O Lord! I understand, I understand.

Visitation

My room is at the back of the courtyard and behind some shops. Number 7, rue Ravignan. You will always be the chapel of my eternal memory. I was thinking, stretched out on the mattress supported by four bricks. The owner made an opening in the zinc roof to increase the light. Who is knocking so early? —Open up! open the door! don't get dressed!—My Lord!—My cross is heavy. I want to put it down.—How will it come in? the door is so narrow.—It will come in through the window.— Lord, warm yourself, it's cold.—Look at my cross!—Yes, Lord, for always!

To Modigliani To Prove to Him that I Am a Poet

The cloud is the post office between continents
The spelling book of exile which the oceans,
Condemned by hell to fight in tears
Will not spell out on the polish of space.

Condamnés par l'Enfer à se battre en pleurant
N'épèleront pas sur le vernis de l'espace.
Le noir sommet des monts s'endort sur les terrasses
Sillons creusés par Dieu pour cacher les humains
Sans lire le secret du nuage qui passe
Lui ne sait pas non plus ce que portent ses mains
Mais parfois lorsque son ennemi le vent le chasse
Il se tourne, rugit et lance un pied d'airain.
J'étais, enfant, doué. Mille reflets du ciel
Promenaient, éveillé, les charmes de mes songes,
Et venaient éclipser l'étendard du réel.
Au milieu des amis, enseignés par les anges
J'ignorais qui j'étais et j'écrivais un peu.
Au lieu de femme un jour j'avais rencontré Dieu
Compagnon qui brode mon être
Sans que je puisse le connaître.
Il est le calme et la gaîté
Il donne la sécurité
Et pour célébrer ses mystères
Il m'a nommé son secrétaire
Or pendant les nuits je déchiffre
Un papier qu'il chargea de chiffres
Que de sa main même il écrit
Et déposa dans mon esprit.
Dans l'aquarium des airs vivent les démons indiscrets
Qui font écrouler le nuage pour lui voler notre secret.

Le Laboratoire Central

Il Se Peut

(à Georges Auric)

Il se peut qu'un rêve étrange
Vous ait occupée ce soir,
Vous avez cru voir un ange
Et c'était votre miroir.

The black top of the mountains falls asleep over the terraces
Furrows ploughed by God to hide men
Without reading the secret of the passing cloud
He doesn't know either what his hands bear
But at times when his enemy the wind chases him away
He turns around, roars and hurls a bronze foot.
As a child I was gifted. Awake, thousands of lights
From the sky moved the charms of my dreams
And came to eclipse the banner of the real.
In the midst of friends, taught by angels
I didn't know who I was, and I used to write.
One day, rather than a woman, I met God
The companion who embroiders my being
Without my knowing him.
He is peace and happiness
He offers security
And to celebrate his mysteries
He has named me secretary.
So during the night I decipher
A paper he covered with figures
Which he writes with his own hand
And placed in my mind
In the aquarium of the air live indiscreet demons
Who collapse the cloud to steal from it our secret.

It May Be

It may be that a strange dream
Seized you tonight,
You thought you saw an angel
And it was your mirror

Dans sa fuite Eléonore
A défait ses longs cheveux
Pour dérober à l'aurore
Le doux objet de mes voeux.

A quelque mari fidèle
Il ne faudra plus penser.
Je suis amant, j'ai des ailes,
Je vous apprends à voler.

Que la muse du mensonge
Apporte au bout de vos doigts
Ce dédain qui n'est qu'un songe
Du berger plus fier qu'un roi.

Le Laboratoire Central

Réponse à l'Apparition

La description est assez belle,
L'édredon rouge à la fenêtre
et tous ces buissons de prunelles,
la foire! la foire à ses pieds
les ponts, la rue, les marronniers,
mais, je vous en prie, par pitié
effacez à la sandaraque
Dieu passant derrière les baraques.
Etant partout, Dieu n'est pas là
et fût-il un jour quelque part
il choisirait un autre endroit
que ménageries et bazars
de profils, de faces, de dos
et votre nom sur calicot!
A cet homme d'humeur amère
qui se plaint de sa mère
de ses amis et frères, soeurs
Dieu aurait fait si grand honneur!
La description est assez belle:
les maisons blanches sous les hêtres
rivière en ville, noir aux fenêtres!
mais de la tête jusqu'au coeur
l'écrivain fut un imposteur.

In her flight Eléonore
Undid her long hair
To rob the dawn
Of the sweet object of my desire.

You should think no longer
Of some faithful husband.
I am the lover, I have wings
I will teach you to fly.

May the muse of falseness
Bring to the end of your fingers
That scorn which is but a dream
Of the shepherd prouder than a king.

Reply to the Apparition

The description is fine enough,
The red quilt at the window
and all those bushes of sloe,
the fair! the fair at his feet
the bridges, the street, the chestnut trees
but, I beg you, for pity sake,
rub out with sandarac
God passing behind the booths.
Being everywhere, God is not there
and if one day he were somewhere
he would choose another place
than menageries and bazaars
of profiles, faces, backs
and your name on calico!
To that man of sulking mood
who complains about his mother
his friends and brothers, sisters
would God have paid such respect!
The description is fine enough:
the white houses under the beech trees
river in the city, black at the windows!
but from his head to his heart
the writer was an imposter.

La Pluie

Monsieur Yousouf a oublié son parapluie
Monsieur Yousouf a perdu son parapluie
Madame Yousouf, on lui a volé son parapluie
Il y avait une pomme d'ivoire à son parapluie
Ce qui m'est entré dans l'oeil c'est le bout d'un parapluie
Est-ce que je n'ai pas laissé mon parapluie?
Il faudra que j'achète un parapluie
Moi je ne me sers jamais de parapluie
J'ai un cache-poussière avec un capuchon pour la pluie
Monsieur Yousouf vous avez de la veine de vous passer de para-
    pluie.

Les Pénitents en Maillots Roses

Amour du Prochain
à Rousselot

Qui a vu le crapaud traverser une rue? c'est un tout petit
homme: une poupée n'est pas plus minuscule. Il se traîne sur les
genoux: il a honte, on dirait . . . ? Non! il est rhumatisant, une
jambe reste en arrière, il la ramène! où va-t-il ainsi? il sort de
l'égoût, pauvre clown. Personne n'a remarqué ce crapaud dans
la rue. Jadis personne ne me remarquait dans la rue, maintenant
les enfants se moquent de mon étoile jaune. Heureux crapaud!
tu n'as pas d'étoile jaune.

Derniers Poèmes

Rain

Monsieur Yousouf forgot his umbrella
Monsieur Yousouf lost his umbrella
Madame Yousouf, they stole his umbrella
There was an ivory knob on his umbrella
What went into my eye was the end of an umbrella
Didn't I leave my umbrella?
I must buy an umbrella
But I never use an umbrella
I have a dust-coat with a hood for rain
Monsieur Yousouf you're lucky not to need an umbrella.

Love of One's Neighbor

Who saw the toad cross a street? He's a very small man. A doll isn't smaller. He drags himself on his knees. Might you say he's ashamed? No, he has rheumatism. One leg drags behind and he brings it forward! Where is he going? The poor clown comes out of the sewer. No one noticed this toad in the street. At one time no one paid any attention to me in the street, and now the children make fun of my yellow star. Happy toad! you have no yellow star.

LEON-PAUL FARGUE

WITH EXCEPTIONAL PRECOCIOUSNESS Fargue wrote his first poems between the ages of ten and fourteen. Some of these he preserved and published in the collection *Ludions*. His father and uncle ran a factory of ceramics and glass-work, and the poet all his life cherished the concept of the craftsman or the artisan, a love of objects, a respect for the precision of technical terms. His visits as a child to the Natural Museum explain to some degree the fabulous world he created in *Vulturne* and *Visitation Préhistorique*, with their petrified flora and fauna.

Fargue's first collection of poems was published in 1911, when he was thirty-three, but they had been written as early as 1894. At that time they were appreciated by Mallarmé who had been Fargue's English teacher at the Lycée Rollin, in Paris. Fargue was one of the habitués in the last years of the century at Mallarmé's Tuesday evenings on the rue de Rome. *Tancrède* was the title of this first volume and was the name given to a school mate who had inspired Fargue by his elegance and grace. Fargue himself has acknowledged the influence on his work of such poets as Laforgue, Corbière and Lautréamont. There is also visible an influence of Rimbaud in the rhythm of the sentences and in the condensation of the images. His form of writing is markedly independent, an intermediary form between narrative prose and rigorously composed verse. The writing of Fargue is distinguished by its musical effects, by its purely verbal virtuosity.

The first edition of *Poèmes, suivis de Pour la Musique*, appeared in 1919. Here and in all the subsequent volumes of Fargue, there are examples of that art of the genius whose sensibility closely resembles the child's. Everything is an image or a metaphor. Everything is evocative of an earlier period, of a reality which most men lose sight of. The poet willingly turns toward the past and even a very distant past, as that in *Vulturne*, and questions all that is perpetually mysterious for man. He can see back to the creation of the world, and ahead to its dissolution. Throughout this vast space of time he claims the age-old privilege of the poet to explore and to exploit the secret forces of the universe. He wonders about the centuries that have passed and about the last scenes of the world's destruction. But he is also a man of science who knows the precise terms of his subject, who knows the popular songs of his age and the slang of his contemporaries. The ease with which Léon-Paul Fargue evokes the past and the present, and the vigor of his style remind one of Rabelais, that other student of the past, whose imagination was unruly.

Until near the end of his life, Fargue was a bachelor, a Parisian who was well known in the literary and artistic circles of the capital. He was a noctambulist who knew the cafés of Paris, its taxis and hotels as well as anyone. He was born in the section of the Halles, on the rue Coquillère. Not until he was thirty, did his father marry the poet's mother. This was a secret sorrow for the boy as he was growing up, which he referred to almost never, and which gave him a sense of being rejected. Yet, there were happy memories of childhood, and a deep devotion to his parents. He was an excellent student (his philosophy teacher was Henri Bergson, at the Lycée Henri IV), but he did not enter the Ecole Normale. Poetry became the center of his life.

After the last years of Mallarmé's Tuesday gatherings (1895-98), Fargue spent his evenings in the literary cafés in Paris, at the *Chat Noir,* for example, in Montmartre, during its richest period, 1895-1910. He was an intimate friend of the composers of those years: Maurice Ravel, Florent Schmitt, Stravinski, Satie. Some of his poems have been set to music by Ravel, Schmitt, Satie and Auric. He was among the early enthusiasts of the Ballets Russes at the Châtelet. His unerring taste in painting helped to introduce Cézanne and other impressionists, and later he became a good friend of Picasso and Braque. In the literary world those whom he saw the most frequently were Valéry-Larbaud, Gide, Louys.

The death of his father was a great sorrow in Fargue's life and he returned to it constantly in his poetry: *Aetenas, Depuis il y a longtemps.* He joined ranks with the surrealists for a while and published in their *Littérature.* But he never remained associated with any one group. The literary magazine, *Commerce,* was founded in 1924, and Fargue became its director. It was distributed by Adrienne Monnier, in her bookstore on the rue de l'Odéon, an important meeting place for writers, where Fargue saw Gide, Valéry and Joyce. In 1932 Fargue was elected to the Académie Mallarmé. By this time he was well known in Paris as the vagabond bachelor, courted by the most brilliant and witty ladies of the capital.

Most of his friends believed he lived in bars and taxis. At the period of *Le Boeuf sur le Toit,* around 1922, he saw there Auric, Picasso, Ravel and even Proust infrequently. That was the moment celebrated for the piano acrobatics of Wiener and Doucet. His legend of vagabond poet and noctambulist is well substantiated by his writings in Paris, by his remarkable knowledge of life in Paris. The picture of Fargue that is best remembered is the poet seated before the pile of saucers at Lipp's or the Deux Magots, late at night. There he appeared at his best: witty, cultivated, ironical, and at the same time mysterious and complicated. Official recognition came to him very late, in the year of his death, when he was awarded the Grand Prix de la Ville de Paris. He had by then married the painter Chériane. Much of his time during his last years was given to newspaper columns, to magazine articles and to radio addresses. His first attack of hemiplegia occurred in April 1943. The regime of illness created a new life for him to which he adjusted with admirable courage and fortitude.

Fully half of his writings is devoted to Paris. His pieces on St. Germain, on the Ile Saint-Louis, on the railroad stations and the faubourgs are lyric-realistic prose poems where, underneath comic metaphors and concetti, one can sense a deep sadness. His language at all times is musical and supple. His use of enumeration and analogy is reserved but always exhilarating. Fargue's poetic style is comparable to that developed by Michaux and Audiberti, and, to some extent, to the style of Giraudoux. The delicate tenderness of these four writers never exists without some element of anguish, some degree of distrust. The poet's dream turns ironical, as it once did with Laforgue.

Selected Bibliography of Fargue

1918 *Poèmes*, suivis de *Pour la Musique*, Gallimard.
1928 *Banalité*, Gallimard.
      Vulturne, Gallimard.
1930 *Sous la Lampe*, Gallimard.
1939 *Le Piéton de Paris*, Gallimard.
1941 *Haute Solitude*, Emile-Paul.
1942 *Refuges*, Emile-Paul.
1946 *Méandres*, Ed. du Milieu du Monde.
1947 réédition de *Poèmes*, suivis de *Pour la Musique*, Gallimard.
1950 *Léon-Paul Fargue: Poètes d'Aujourd'hui*, No. 19, Seghers.

on Fargue

Blanchot, Maurice, *Faux Pas* (Fargue et la Création Poétique) Gallimard.
Chonez, Claudine, Introduction à *Poètes d'Aujourd'hui*.
Renéville, Rolland de, *Univers de la Parole* (La Poésie de Fargue), Gallimard.

. . . Mais c'est le soir seulement que le quartier enfile son véritable costume et prend cet aspect fantastique et sordide que certains romanciers ont su rendre de chic, comme on dit, et sans risquer le voyage. Le soir, quand les rapides semblent prendre leur vitesse dans le coeur même de Paris, quand les jeunes sportifs se rassemblent devant les boutiques d'accessoires pour automobiles et se mettent à parler vélo ou plongeon, quand les matrones consentent à lâcher leur mari pour une partie de cartes entre copains et que les cinémas s'emplissent selon une cadence que l'on retrouve à la consultation gratuite des hôpitaux, alors la Chapelle est bien ce pays d'un merveilleux lugubre et prenant, ce paradis des paumés, des mômes de la cloche et des costauds qui ont l'honneur au bout de la langue et la loyauté au bout des doigts, cet Eden sombre, dense et nostalgique que les soldats célèbrent le soir dans les chambrées pour venir à bout de l'ennui solitaire. C'est aussi la Chapelle nocturne que je connais le mieux et que je préfère. Elle a plus de chien, plus d'âme et plus de résonance. Les rues en sont vides et mornes, encore que le cri des trains de luxe lui envoie des vols de cigognes. . . . La file indienne des réverbères ne remplace pas la disparition de cette accumulation de boutiques qui, de jour, rend le quartier comparable à des souks africains. L'arrondissement tout entier trempe dans l'encre. C'est l'heure des appels désespérés qui font des hommes des égaux et des poètes. Rue de la Charbonnière, les prostituées en boutique, comme à Amsterdam, donnent à l'endroit un spectacle de jeu de cartes crasseuses. Des airs d'accordéon, minces comme des fumées de cigarettes, s'échappent des portes, et le Bal du Tourbillon commence à saigner de sa bouche dure. . . .

. . . Bien que je n'y habite pas en ce moment—mais j'y retourne à chaque instant pour y retrouver mes chers fantômes, et j'y reviendrai peut-être un jour, honteux et repentant—je tiens ce que j'appelle mon quartier, c'est-à-dire ce dixième arrondissement, pour le plus poétique, le plus familial et le plus mystérieux de Paris. Avec ses deux gares, vastes music-halls où l'on est à la fois acteur et spectateur, avec son canal glacé comme une feuille de tremble et si tendre aux infiniment petits de l'âme, il a

. . . Only in the evening does my part of the city put on its real costume and appear in that fatalistic and sordid style which certain moralists have been able to paint without a model, as they say, and without risking a visit. In the evening, when the express trains seem to gather their speed in the very heart of Paris, when young fellows meet in front of shops for automobile parts and begin to talk about their bicycles or their driving, when matrons agree to liberate their husbands for a game of cards with other men, and when the movie houses fill up in a regularity you can find in hospitals on days of free examination, then La Chapelle is really a miraculous land both gloomy and seductive, a paradise for the poor, for hoboes and hefty fellows whose honor is on the end of their tongues and whose loyalty is on the end of their fingers, a dark Eden, dense and nostalgic which soldiers celebrate at night in their barracks in order to overcome their lonely boredom. I know La Chapelle best at night and I prefer it then. It has more charm, more soul, more resonance. Its streets are empty and mournful while the shriek of the pullman trains releases its flock of storks. . . . The Indian file of street lamps doesn't replace the disappearance of the number of shops which by day make the section look like African markets. The entire ward is drenched in ink. It's the time of desperate shouts which make men equal and make them poets. Rue de la Charbonnière, where the prostitutes on exhibit, as in Amsterdam, give the place the appearance of a filthy pack of cards. Accordion tunes as thin as cigarette smoke, come out from the doors, and the Tourbillon Dancehall begins to bleed from its hard mouth. . . .

. . . Although I don't live there now—but I constantly go back to see my beloved ghosts, and perhaps one day I'll go back, ashamed and repentant—I consider what I call my part of the city, namely the 10th ward, the most poetic, the most intimate, and the most mysterious in Paris. With its two stations, tremendous cabarets where you are both actor and audience, with its canal glazed like a poplar-leaf and so tender in the tiny recesses of the soul, it has always given my heart and my steps their strength and sadness.

toujours nourri de force et de tristesse mon coeur et mes pas. . . .

. . . Pour moi, le dixième, et que de fois ne l'ai-je pas dit, est un quartier de poètes et de locomotives. Le douzième aussi a ses locomotives, mais il a moins de poètes. Mettons-nous d'accord sur ce mot. Point n'est besoin d'écrire pour avoir de la poésie dans ses poches. Il y a d'abord ceux qui écrivent, et qui constituent une académie errante. Puis il y a ceux qui connaissent ces secrets grâce auxquels le mariage de la sensibilité et du quartier fabrique du bonheur. C'est pourquoi je pare du noble titre de poète des charrons, des marchands de vélos, des épiciers, des maraîchers, des fleuristes et des serruriers de la rue Château-Landon ou de la rue d'Aubervilliers, du quai de la Loire, de la rue du Terrage et de la rue des Vinaigriers. A les voir, à leur sourire en courant sur le trottoir gravé de fatigues, à demander des nouvelles de leurs filles, à voir leurs fils soldats, je me sens réjoui jusqu'aux écrous secrets de mon vieux coeur sans haine.

Le Piéton de Paris

Saint-Germain-des-Prés

. . . La place Saint-Germain-des-Prés, qui ne figure pas dans le laïus adressé aux Yougoslaves et aux Ecossais par le speaker du car de Paris la nuit, est pourtant un des endroits de la Capitale où l'on se sent le plus "à la page," le plus près de l'actualité vraie, des hommes qui connaissent les dessous du pays, du monde et de l'Art. Et ceci même le dimanche, grâce à ce kiosque à journaux qui fait l'angle de la place et du boulevard, une bonne maison bien fournie de feuilles de toutes couleurs.

Hantés, on ne sait trop pourquoi, par le souvenir des Ecoliers qui se flanquaient des trempes, et souvent avec les Bourgeois, dans le Pré-aux-Clercs, aux Halles, rue Brisemiche ou rue Pute-y-Muce, les chapeliers ou marchands d'articles de bureau des environs ont à coeur de venir prendre un bain intellectuel, à l'heure de l'apérituf, le long des librairies qui se mettent en boule ou des terrasses qui gazouillent comme un four à frites. La place en effet vit, respire, palpite et dort par la vertu de trois cafés aussi célèbres aujourd'hui que des institutions d'Etat: les Deux

. . . For me, the 10th—and how many times have I said so!—is the neighborhood of poets and locomotives. The 12th also has locomotives, but it has fewer poets. Let's agree on that word. You don't need to write to have poetry in your pockets. There are first those who write and who make up an itinerant academy. Then there are the men who know those secrets because the marriage of their sensitivity with the neighborhood creates happiness. That is why I grace with the noble title of poet: cartwrights, bicycle dealers, grocers, market gardeners, florists, locksmiths on the rue Château-Landon, rue d'Aubervilliers, quai de la Loire, rue du Terrage and rue des Vinaigriers. When I see them and smile at them as they hasten along the sidewalk, heavy with fatigue, when I ask about their daughters and when I see their soldier sons, happiness spreads through me to the cockles of my old beaming heart.

Saint-Germain-des-Prés

. . . The square of Saint-Germain-des-Prés, which isn't referred to in the speech addressed to the Jugoslavs and Scots by the guide of the Paris sight-seeing bus at night, is however one of the spots in the capital where you feel most "in the know," closest to the real names, to the men who know the real workings of the country, of society and of art. And this even on Sunday, thanks to the newspaper stand which forms the angle of the square and the boulevard, a good house well supplied with papers of all colors.

Haunted for some reason or other by the memory of students who used to fight, and often with the bourgeois, in the Pré-aux-clercs, in the Halles, rue Brisemiche or rue Pute-y-Muce, the hatters or stationers of the neighborhood want to come to take an intellectual bath, at the apéritif hour, along the book stores which curl up or along the sidewalks which sputter like frying potatoes. The square really lives, breathes, emotes and sleeps thanks to the three cafés as famous today as state institutions: the Deux Magots, the Café de Flore and the Brasserie Lipp, each of which has its high functionaries, its managers,

Magots, le Café de Flore et la Brasserie Lipp, qui ont chacun leurs hauts fonctionnaires, leurs chefs de service et leurs gratte-papier, lesquels peuvent être des romanciers traduits en vingt-six langues, des peintres sans atelier, des critiques sans rubrique ou des ministres sans portefeuille. L'art et la politique s'y donnent la main, l'arriviste et l'arrivée s'y coudoient, le maître et le disciple s'y livrent à des assauts de politesse pour savoir qui payera. C'est à la terrasse des Deux Magots, celle d'où l'on peut méditer sur les cendres de Childebert ou de Descartes qui furent déposées dans l'Abbaye, qu'un comitard assez mal décapé me fit un jour une courte esquisse de la vie parlementaire: "Un député est un électeur qui gagne à la loterie, un ministre est un député qui améliore sa situation." Formule élastique, et qui peut aussi bien s'appliquer à la vie de tous les jours.

Le café des Deux Magots, devenu "des deux mégots" pour les initiés, depuis que l'on a cessé de demander au patron des nouvelles de son associé, est un établissement assez prétentieux et solennel où chaque consommateur représente pour son voisin un littérateur, où des Américaines presque riches, presque belles, mais pas trop propres et la plupart du temps pompettes, viennent bâiller et se tortiller devant les derniers surréalistes, dont le nom traverse l'Océan s'il ne dépasse pas le Boulevard. Par sa large terrasse, si agréable à la marée montante des matins ou à la descente du crépuscule d'été, par la cherté de ses consommations, les plus chères de Paris, le café des Deux Magots est fort recherché des snobs, qui trouvent que le Dubonnet à cent sous ne constitue pas une dépense exagérée pour qui veut assister à l'apéritif des écrivains modernes. . . . Chaque matin, et la chose a déjà passé la terrasse, Giraudoux y prenait son café au lait et y recevait les quelques amis qui ne pourraient plus le saisir de la journée. A une heure du matin, les garçons commencent à pousser les tables dans le ventre des clients nocturnes, qui ne sont plus que de braves bourgeois du sixième arrondissement, à balayer sur leurs pieds, à leur envoyer des coins de serviette dans l'oeil. Une demi-heure plus tard, les Deux Magots ferment comme une trappe, sourds au murmure suppliant de deux ou trois Allemands qui stationnent devant la boutique, attirés là par les quarante ans de vie littéraire et de boissons politiques du lieu. Quelques minutes

its hack writers who may be novelists translated into 26 languages, painters without studios, critics without a magazine, or statesmen without portfolios. Art and politics join company, the arriviste with the one who has arrived sit at the same table, the master and the disciple compete in rounds of politeness to see which will pay. It was on the sidewalk of the Deux Magots, the one where you can meditate on the ashes of Childebert or Descartes who were interred in the Abbey, where an ill-cleaned individual gave me one day a brief sketch of Parliamentary life: "A deputy is an elector who wins the lottery, a minister is a deputy who betters his position." A supple formula, which can also apply to daily life.

The Café des Deux Magots (two apes), grown into "des deux mégots" (two butts) for the initiate, since they've stopped asking the owner news of his associate, is quite a pretentious solemn institution where each customer symbolizes a writer for his neighbor, where American women, almost wealthy, almost beautiful, but not very clean and usually a little drunk, come to yawn and swing their hips in front of the last surrealists whose names are known on the other side of the ocean even if they haven't crossed the boulevard. Because of its wide sidewalk, so agreeable to the rising tide of the mornings or to the descent of summer evenings, and because of the high cost of its drinks, the dearest in Paris, the Café des Deux Magots is patronized by snobs who feel that a glass of Dubonnet for five francs isn't an exaggerated expense for some one who wants to watch the apéritif habits of modern writers. . . . Each morning, and this news has already gone beyond the sidewalk, Giraudoux used to take his coffee there and talk with the friends who couldn't reach him the rest of the day. At one in the morning, the waiters begin to push the tables into the stomachs of the night clients who are simply the good bourgeois of the 6th ward, to sweep under their feet, and poke ends of napkins into their eyes. A half-hour later, the Deux Magots closes up like a trap door, deaf to the soft supplications of two or three Germans stationed before the establishment, attracted by the forty years of literary activity and political drinks of the place. A few minutes later, the Café de Flore, that other lock-gate of the crossroads, already bleary-eyed, curls up also.

plus tard, le Café de Flore, autre écluse du carrefour, l'oeil déjà miteux, se recroqueville à son tour. . . .

. . . Tantôt, c'est Monzie, qui déclenche son feu à répétition d'idées aiguës; c'est Léon Bérard, qui est un seigneur et le plus "attique" de nos ministres; c'est Daniel Vincent, qui aime les poètes et dit si bien les vers, avec son air farouche et sa grosse moustache; c'est Marcel Abraham, qui vient de son ouvrage et qui va nous parler de l'Encyclopédie. Quelque autre jour, c'est la Comtesse de Toulouse-Lautrec, dont les entrées sont "sensationnelles"; c'est Derain et sa garde, composée de dessinateurs et de modèles; c'est lady Abdy ou le bon Vergnolle, architecte à tous crins, socialiste A.P.L.G., qui accompagne, avec Emmanuel Arago, disert et souriant, la belle Marquise de Crussol. Et parfois André Gide est là, qui dîne seul.

Le Piéton de Paris

Voici Tants d'Années!

Voici tant d'années! Gérard de Nerval partit dans la nuit pour aller revoir une figure de vierge. . . .

Hier soir chantaient nos voitures le long du fleuve tout fêlé de lumière. . . .

Départs! Vos chants et vos odeurs. Huées et plaintes des trains qui rêvent. Un couple tout noir sur un quai sonore. . . .

On accueille un train de banlieue rempli de fanfares. . . .

Mais le train pour nous refait son histoire. . . .

Il crie les fanaux qui ont l'air si tristes.

Il crie les paysages traversés à tour de bras. Des gouffres pris de biais dans un grand bruit frais sur des ponts de fer qui grincent des dents. . . . Une halte encore où sonnent des voix lourdes, où tout le silence assiège les vitres.

Mais un autre train perce en cris noirs. . . .

Une aube au coeur serré se lève.

La nuit a séché les pleurs de la veille et consacré les solitudes. . . .

Sous le ciel pommelé que traverse un ange, de petites maisons

. . . Sometimes, it's Monzie releasing his rapid fire of penetrating ideas; or Léon Bérard, who is a lord and the most "Attic" of our statesmen; or Daniel Vincent, who likes poets and recites poetry very well with his wild manner and heavy moustache; or Marcel Abraham coming from work and who will talk about the Encyclopedia. . . . On another day, there is the Countess Toulouse-Lautrec whose entrances are "sensational"; or Derain with his guard, composed of designers and models; or Lady Abdy or friendly Vergnolle, an architect with flowing mane and socialist who, with smiling and talkative Emmanuel Arago, comes with the beautiful Marquise de Crussol. And sometimes André Gide is there, dining alone.

So Many Years Have Gone!

So many years have gone! Gérard de Nerval left at night to see again a virgin face. . . .
Last evening our cars sang along the river all cracked with light. . . .
Departures! Songs and smells. Shouts and complaints of trains dreaming. A couple, all dark, on a resounding platform. . . .
They're welcoming a suburban train filled with a brass band. . . .

But our train relives its history. . . .
It cries out the head-lights which seem so sad.
It cries out the landscapes cut through with all its might. Chasms caught at an angle in a great fresh noise over iron bridges grinding their teeth. . . . Another stop where heavy voices sound out, where silence besieges the windows.
But another train pierces in black cries. . . .
A sad-hearted dawn rises up.
Night has dried the tears of the vigil and blessed the solitude. . . .
Under the dappled sky which an angel crosses, small isolated houses still sleep, sensitized by the morning twilight. . . .
A cock of Caldecott spits out a poppy!
Men ploughing relax their gestures of labor and, with their

isolées dorment encore, affinées par le crépuscule matinal. . . .

Un coq de Caldecott crache un coquelicot!

Des laboureurs défont leurs gestes de travail, et la main sur les yeux, regardent. . . . Des bêtes au pacage tournent lentement, d'un mouvement de rite, d'un air sacré. . . .

Les rivières sont encore toutes bleues d'ombre avec une écharpe de brume. La fumée du train s'embûche dans les bois humides comme une poursuite de fantômes. . . .

Un village avec les bâches d'une fête qui s'installe, s'envole . . . .

Des choux bleus tournent leur bonne face de Quasimodos saouls de lune. . . .

On brûle de petites gares naïves avec leur intimité pâlotte, l'horloge au centre, les employés qui sont du pays, leurs paniers pleins de volaille crieuse, et les trains d'intérêt local qui attendent. . . .

Et puis, plus tard—les maisons d'une vieille ville rouge et noire jouent à saute-mouton dans les rochers. Les voilà qui font la haie et qui regardent par-dessus le fleuve parce que j'embrasse ton doux visage dans le médaillon de la vitre. . . .

Au Pays

Un nom, Cromac, nous fait parler
D'un golfe sombre. . . . O mort d'amour,
Sois moins triste d'avoir pleuré
Pour d'autres noms, pour d'autres jours

Où tu étais comme l'aveugle,
Qui regarde du rouge sombre
Et joue avec ses mains grattées
Sur le vieux banc de son enfance. . . .

Comme l'aveugle, lorsqu'il songe
Et bougonne, et que son coeur gronde
Contre la beauté au corps tiède
Qui le regarde, toute en larmes. . . .

hands over their eyes, look out. . . . Animals at pasture turn slowly, in a ritual movement, as if sacred. . . .

The rivers are still blue from shadow with wisps of fog. The train smoke is ambushed in the wet woods like a pursuit of ghosts. . . .

A village with the canvases of a carnival being installed, flies away. . . .

Blue cabbages turn their kind Quasimodo faces drunk with moonlight. . . .

They burn small innocent stations with their pale friendliness, the clock in the center, the employees who are native, their baskets full of shrieking fowl, and the local trains waiting. . . .

And then, later—the houses of an old red and black town play leap-frog over the rocks. There they are making a hedge and looking over the river because I kiss your sweet face in the center inset of the window. . . .

Home

A name, Cromac, makes us speak
Of a dark bay. . . . O death of love,
Be less sad for weeping
Other names, other days

Where you were like the blind man
Looking at the dark red
And playing with his scratched hands
Over the old bench of his childhood. . . .

Like the blind man, when he dreams
And grumbles, and when his heart
Scolds the warm bodied beauty
Watching him, in tears. . . .

Cromac. The House under the branches
Whose window with flower eyes
Separated her long white hands
Gently, noiselessly, over your heart. . . .

Cromac. La Maison sous les branches,
Dont la fenêtre aux yeux en fleurs
Ecartait ses longues mains blanches,
Doucement, sans bruit, sur ton coeur. . . .
              Poèmes suivis de *Pour la musique*

A Saint-Germain

A Saint-Germain-des-Prés, avec ses trois cafés, ses magasins
sérieux, spacieux, indifférents à la rue et devant lesquels on ne fait
pas la queue pour entrer, avec son kiosque bien rembourré, ses
banques tristes, son square toujours dans l'ombre, ses orfèvres et
son vaste atelier de photographie, qui semblent recruter leur clien-
tèle dans le Rouergue, à Saumur, à Vitré, en Suisse; à Saint-Ger-
main-des-Prés, où s'opposent et se marient le raffinement intel-
lectuel et la plus pure mélancolie du bourgeois non encore evolué,
je suis la plupart du temps grisé par la simple sensation d'exister,
par la certitude honnête de jouer un rôle, non pas providentiel,
mais solide et actuel, qui tourne rond, dans la vraie vie de Paris.
J'y ai des amis qui ne sont pas les mêmes chez Lipp, à Flore ou aux
Deux-Magots, qui ne sont pas seulement l'achiviste paléographe,
le romancier, l'acteur ou le président de commission, mais des
artisans, des simples, des passants, le marchand de dixièmes,
le bouif, le plombier. . . .
    Dirai-je que j'ai vu là Picasso, Gaston Leroux, Carco, Girau-
doux, des officiers de marine, le musée Guimet, toutes sortes
d'académies, Aragon, Saint-Ex, Gertrude Stein, le pétrole, les
affaires, le sport, Rainer Marie Rilke . . . je n'en finirais pas. J'y
vois surtout ma vie, mes dîners hâtifs chez Lipp, où l'on attend
aujourd'hui le retour du Münster et du cervelas rémoulade; j'y
vois mes articles jetés sur le papier à l'heure où l'on commençait
à balayer sous les pieds des clients, mes retours de Pleyel ou de
Gaveau, des petites stations mélancoliques mais remplies que l'on
fait devant une consommation avant de rentrer chez soi. J'ai dans
ma boîte à souvenirs des odeurs de pardessus, des passages de
chiens sous les tables, des bruits de soucoupes mêlés à des chutes
de ministères, des colères d'horloges, des rires de jolies femmes

At Saint-Germain-des-Prés, with its three cafés, its serious stores, spacious and indifferent to the street and where you don't wait in line to go in, with its stuffed newspaper stand, its sad-looking banks, its square always in the shade, its goldsmiths and large photographic gallery, which seem to recruit their clientele in Roumergue, Saumur, Vitré, Switzerland; at Saint-Germain-des-Prés, where are opposed and joined intellectual refinement and the purest melancholy of the not yet evolved bourgeois, I am most of the time intoxicated with the simple sensation of existing; with the honest certainty of playing a role, not providential but solid and real, turning in a circle, in the true life of Paris. I have friends there who are not the same at Lipp's, at Flore, at the Deux Magots, who aren't merely the paleographer, the novelist, the actor or the broker, but artisans, simple beings, passers-by, the fellow who sells lottery tickets, the plumber. . . .

Do you want me to say that there I saw Picasso, Gaston Leroux, Carco, Giraudoux, naval officers, the Guimet museum, all kinds of academies, Aragon, Saint-Exupéry, Gertrude Stein, petroleum, business, sports, Rainer Maria Rilke . . . there's no end. Especially I see there my life, my hasty dinners at Lipp's where today they're expecting the return of Münster cheese and Saveloy with the sharp sauce; I see my articles consigned to paper at the moment they begin to sweep under the feet of the habitués, the times on the way home from Pleyel or Gaveau, those brief stops, sad but rewarding you make in front of a drink. In my memories I have smells of overcoats, dogs passing under the tables, noises of saucers mingled with government collapses, the wrath of clocks, laughter of pretty women fallen there like feathers of turtle doves, rounds of theories which were to fix or upset everything, handshakes confused with a distraught and peaceful state of mind, inflated, whispering, warm and almost salutary, which is like the mind of the highest steeple.

Beloved Saint-Germain-des-Prés, where adventurous failures and artistic scatterbrains have the exceptional chance of sipping their glass of brandy between a prince of the intellect and a movie villain, under the knowing and vaguely desperate eyes of those

tombées là comme des plumes de tourterelles, des rondelles de théories qui devaient tout arranger ou tout chambarder, des poignées de main qui se confondent toutes en une sorte d'état de conscience tumultueux et doux, gonflé, murmurant, tiède et presque salutaire, qui est comme un esprit de clocher supérieur.

Cher Saint-Germain-des-Prés, où les ratés de l'aventure et les hurluberlus de l'Art ont la chance exceptionnelle de pouvoir siroter leur verre de chasse-brouillard entre un prince de l'esprit et un voyou de cinéma, sous le regard entendu, vaguement désespéré de quelques-unes de ces jeunes filles modernes à qui Richepin, dans sa fière jeunesse de vagabond rimeur, criait, du haut de sa barbe: "Trop tôt l'adultère!" Rue de l'Abbaye, rue du Dragon, Hôtel Taranne, rue Saint-Benoît, librairies d'art, concierges, lingères et droguistes, marchands de couleurs de la rue Bonaparte, revendeurs, tapissiers, réparateurs de candélabres, de parapluies, de porcelaines, restaurant corse, pharmacies, sorte de potinière où l'on trouvait le temps, au plus teuton du couvre-feu, de s'emporter contre la pensée bourgeoise devant un demi de bière infecte . . . délicieuse parade qui va droit au coeur. C'est là que j'ai bu un dernier verre avec tant de disparus dont le souvenir pèse sur mon âme de toute la légèreté amère et fidèle des morts.

Méandres

modern young girls to whom Richepin, in his proud youth of poet-vagabond, used to say from behind his beard: "It's too early for adultery!" Rue de l'Abbaye, rue du Dragon, Hôtel Taranne, rue Saint-Benoît, art book stores, concierges, seamsters, dry-salters, art dealers on the rue Bonaparte, second-hand dealers, upholsterers, repairers of candelabra, umbrellas, porcelain, the Corsican restaurant, pharmacies, a center of talk where you found the time, at the most Teutonic curfew, to rage against bourgeois thinking in front of a poisonous glass of beer . . . delightful parade speaking to my heart. That is where I drank a last glass with so many departed friends whose memory weighs on my soul with all the bitter faithful softness of the dead.

JULES SUPERVIELLE

THE POETRY OF JULES SUPERVIELLE represents a triumph in verbal simplicity in an age when poetry is not simple. There is a subtle narrative element in many of his poems, and the tradition of modern poetry has not been receptive on the whole to any discursive or story-telling tendency. Most of the modern poets are theorists also, concerned with the metaphysical implications both of poetry and of the act of writing poetry. Here again, Supervielle seems to be outside of the main current. He is perhaps more simply and directly a poet, one endowed, as at birth, with a special gift, and who all his life has been a poet and has written poetry as naturally as he breathes.

Supervielle has spent a good part of his life in Uruguay, although today he lives in Paris. He has always been exhilarated by vast spaces, by seas and pampas. He is a cardiac who has paid an extraordinary attention to his heart condition, not as a hypochondriac, but as a poet intent upon hearing the beating of his heart, on following the flow of his blood, his breathing, and all the physical manifestations of his body's enigma.

His poetry has evolved during the long period he has been writing, but to a slighter degree than with most poets. His earliest verse has some of the favorite words of symbolism and faint traces of Whitman, Laforgue and Baudelaire. By 1925, with his important volume of *Gravitations*, Supervielle had found his own voice which was not to vary in any marked way during the next twenty-five years. It is a poetic voice which seems monotonous until one realizes that its tone and vocabulary match very perfectly the total simplicity of the thought and the imagery. The power of sustaining such exactness of pitch and of mingling so adroitly sensation with sentiment is an accomplishment in itself. The paleness which envelops so much of Supervielle's poetry is due to the inner world he likes best to transcribe: thought and emotion at their birth, the speech of the blood in the veins and the beating of the heart, the land explored by the breath before it leaves the body. His poetry is a reporting on the relationship he bears with his inner physical and psychic self. He has made of himself a tangible presence. To observe this presence he gives all the lucidity his mind possesses, all the attentiveness his spirit is capable of. What he studies is mystery, but the frankest and the most universal mystery there is: that of man in his body and soul, that especially of man in the strange duality of his body and soul. He is one and many at the same time. He is an individual and he is also the dead who return to live in him.

Death is constantly present in the writings of Supervielle and completely freed from any description of horror or threat. She is a companion, ubiquitous, coquettish. Since life is a moving toward death, the poet each minute of time grows more accustomed to this companion, more willing to accept the idea and the conception of his future. To remain a poet, it is important to hold death off and yet at the same time to establish some kind of rapport with her. This is the art of the architect-poet, the builder, which Rilke sensed in his reading of *Gravitations* and which he expressed in a letter to Supervielle of Nov. 28, 1925: "You are a great builder of bridges in space, your arches are as alive as the footsteps of St. Christopher, that great forerunner of bridges and poetry who, by his gait, was one of the first to endow with rhythm the impassable."

For Supervielle the domain of poetry is without limitation. There everything becomes possible. There, what is forbidden to a man in his real life may be achieved by the poet in his creation. Poetry can meet all his wants and supply him with everything he is lacking. It is the art of abundance and plenitude and satisfaction. The poet makes his poem just as God created man, with the tips of his fingers, almost in a state of indifference. Supervielle returns often to the beginnings of the world, to reach in its original simplicity, the genesis of man, and he willingly composes speeches of God to man, and speeches of man to the mysteries he discovers around him, because in such verses he attains the greatest degree of transparency.

Supervielle is more at ease with the primitive fables of the world than with the metaphysical problems of the modern poets. Whatever in the world is harmony, relationship, resemblance holds Supervielle and converts him into an image-maker, a translator of such harmonies. The occurrences throughout the world reach him simultaneously. Supervielle is the giant poet who reaches everywhere at once with his hands and his eyes, as Albert Béguin says in his essay, *Supervielle, poète des deux nuits*. He has rightfully been called the spacial poet, the contemplator of seas, pampas, deserts, heights. The animals he evokes the most often are those associated with plains and vast territories: horses and bulls. There are others, too, for Supervielle has made of Noah one of his favorite fables. *L'Arche de Noé* is a book of stories written by a poet. The pivotal point of the stories, as is also true of many of the poems, is a brief detail. The coming of the flood, for example, is announced by a blotter of a little girl at school which will not dry. Supervielle has the genius of rejuvenating the oldest stories in the world as well as that of recreating the most familiar objects. It is preciosity in its most simple state, quite different from the more profound preciosity of Scève and Mallarmé. Supervielle's is the preciosity of childhood and innocency, which discovers in the midst of the world's disorder a series of metaphors possessing the power of conferring on the world a new order.

Selected Bibliography of Supervielle

1925 *Gravitations*, Gallimard (édition définitive, 1932).
1930 *Le Forçat Innocent*, Gallimard.
1946 *Poèmes 1939-1945*, Gallimard.
1947 *Choix de Poèmes*, Gallimard.
1949 *Oublieuse Mémoire*, Gallimard.
1949 *Jules Supervielle: Poètes d'Aujourd'hui*, No. 15, Seghers.

on Supervielle

Gants du Ciel, revue d'Ottawa. Hommage à Supervielle, 1945.
Roy, Claude, introduction à *Poètes d'Aujourd'hui*.
Sénéchal, Christian, *J. S., poète de l'univers intérieur*, Jean Flory, Paris, 1939.

Thinking About a Poetics
(from *Naissances,* poèmes suivis de
En songeant à un art poétique, Gallimard, 1951)

Poetry comes to me from an ever latent dream. I like to direct
this dream, except on days of inspiration when I have the im-
pression that it directs itself.

I don't like the dream which moves aimlessly. I try to make
it into a substantial dream, a kind of prow figure, which after
crossing inner space and time then confronts outside space and
time. For it, the outside is the white page.

To dream is to forget the materiality of one's body and to
confuse to some degree the outer and the inner world. The
ubiquity of the cosmic poet has perhaps no other origin.

People are sometimes surprised over my marvelling at the
world. This arises as much from the permanency of my dreams
as from my bad memory. Both lead me from surprise to sur-
prise, and force me to be amazed at everything. "Why, there
are trees and an ocean. There are women. There are even beau-
tiful women. . . ."

I was long in coming to modern poetry, in being attracted to
Rimbaud and Apollinaire. I couldn't get over the walls of flame
and smoke which separate these poets from the classics and
the romantics. And if I may make a confession, which is only
a wish perhaps, I hoped consequently to be one of those who
dispersed the smoke in trying not to put out the flame, a con-
ciliator, a reconciler of ancient and modern poetry.

Since poetry had been quite dehumanized, I proposed, in the
tradition and continuity of the classics, to reveal the torments,
hopes and sufferings of a poet and a man today. I remember a
certain preface of Valéry, written for a young poet, André
Caselli. "Don't be dissatisfied with your verses. I have found in
them delicate qualities of which one is essential for my taste, a
sincerity of tone, which is for the poet the analogue of true
pitch for the singer. Keep this *real* tone. Don't be surprised that
it's I who notice it to praise it. There is a tremendous difficulty
in combining this exact sound of the soul with the sacrifice of
art. One needs an enormous amount of art to be really oneself,
really simple. But art alone would never be enough."

There is certainly an element of delirium in every poetic creation but this delirium must be purified and separated from the ineffective or harmful residue. A delicate operation to be carried out cautiously. In my case, it is through simplicity and lucidity that I succeed in confronting my central secrets and in purifying my deepest poetry. I strive until the supernatural becomes natural and flows easily (or seems to), and until the ineffable becomes familiar without ever losing its fabulous source.

At the poet's disposal are two pedals, one clear, permitting him to reach transparency, the other obscure, leading to opaqueness. Only rarely have I pressed on the obscure pedal. If I veil, I do so, naturally, and it is, I believe, the mere veil of poetry. The poet often operates warmly in darkness, but the cold operation has its advantages also. It permits us greater feats because they are more lucid. We know that we shall never have to blush at them one day, as at some passing intoxication and frenzy we no longer understand. I need this lucidity all the more since by nature I am obscure. I don't believe there is any poetry without some confusion at the beginning. I try to bring some light to it without diminishing the power of the subconscious element.

I like the strange only when it is tempered and humanized. I test myself on making a straight line out of one or several broken lines. Some poets are often victims of their trances. They give themselves over to the single pleasure of freedom and never worry over the beauty of the poem. Or to use another image, I might say that they fill their glass to the brim and forget to serve you, reader.

I have seldom had the dread of banality which haunts most writers, but rather that of incomprehension and strangeness. Since I don't write for mystery specialists, I always suffered when a sensitive person didn't understand one of my poems.

The image is the magic lantern which lights up the poets in their darkness. But images aren't alone. There are passages between them which also must be poetry. People have called analysis of poetry anti-poetic, and this is true enough if it is a logical analysis. But there are submerged explanations in the dream world which may be revealed without leaving the realm of poetry.

I don't wait for inspiration to write, and I go half way to meet it. The poet cannot count on the very rare moments when he writes as by dictation. It seems to me he should imitate the scientist who doesn't wait for inspiration in order to work. Science is an excellent school of modesty, if it isn't the opposite, since it trusts the constant value of man and not solely a few privileged moments. How often we think we have nothing to say when a poem is waiting in us, behind a thin curtain of mist, and it's enough to silence the noise around us for that poem to be unveiled.

I do not like a too exaggerated originality (save for a few glowing exceptions like Lautréamont or Michaux), and prefer a less conscious originality like that of our classic writers.

Despite the brilliant examples of some poets who transform words into precious objects, I often write without thinking of words, and I even try to forget their existence in order to enclose more tightly my thought or rather that intermediary stage between thought and dream which gives rise to the poem. By this, I don't mean thinking in poetry but giving in some way its equivalent or nostalgia for it. The sentiment of creating a poem, at least in my own case, I have tried to show in this following passage, in answer to an inquiry of Jean Paulhan in the *Nouvelle Revue Française*. (But it is a state of lyric intoxication which I have seldom felt in its fullness, and one can see in what I have already said that I do not wait for this trance in order to write.) "Inspiration generally is made manifest in me by the feeling that I am everywhere at once, in space as well as in the diverse regions of the heart and mind. The state of poetry then comes to me from some magical confusion where ideas and images begin to live and abandon their forms, either to make advances to other images—in this nearby realm nothing is really far off—or to undergo profound changes which make them unrecognizable. For the mind, then, confused with dreams, opposites no longer exist. Affirmation and negation because a single thing, as well as past and future, despair and hope, madness and reason, death and life. The inner song rises and chooses the words it needs. I give myself the illusion of helping obscurity in its effort toward light while the moving images touch the surface of the paper, calling out in the depths. After that, I know better where I am with myself. I have created dangerous powers and exorcized them. Out of them I have made allies of my innermost reason." . . .

If there is some humanity in my poetry, that is perhaps because my being is enriched with suffering. This dull continual anxiety prevents my poetry from being more brilliant. To suffer in one's body or in one's ideas is to think of oneself, to turn against oneself. To think of oneself is to be poor and stripped of ornament. I have always feared attacking the monsters I feel in me. I prefer to tame them with everyday words which are the most reassuring. (Aren't they the same words which quieted us down after our childish terrors?) I count on their well-tested friendliness and wisdom to neutralize the venom of the strange, which is often the forerunner of panic. The best of my wisdom I owe to the madness I have often had to cure. . . .

I use many different poetic forms: regular verse (or almost), blank verse (with rhyme when it comes), free verse, versicles of rhythmical prose. Preferring what is natural, I never say to myself beforehand that I shall use any one form. I let my poem make its choice. This is not scorn but adjustment of technique. Or rather, a mobile technique fixing on each poem whose song it marries. This permits a great variety of inspiration.

Each poet has his secrets. I have tried to tell you some of mine by unveiling this double who watches us in the dark, and either approves or makes us tear up the paper we have written. But I have said almost nothing about the most important secret, a mystery inhabiting the poet and which he can never completely separate himself from in order to see it from the outside. I hope it has found its place in my poems.

Prophétie
à Jean Cassou

Un jour la Terre ne sera
Qu'un aveugle espace qui tourne,
Confondant la nuit et le jour.
Sous le ciel immense des Andes
Elle n'aura plus de montagnes,
Même pas un petit ravin.

De toutes les maisons du monde
Ne durera plus qu'un balcon
Et de l'humaine mappemonde
Une tristesse sans plafond.
De feu l'Océan Atlantique
Un petit goût salé dans l'air,
Un poisson volant et magique
Qui ne saura rien de la mer.

D'un coupé de mil-neuf-cent-cinq
(Les quatre roues et nul chemin!)
Trois jeunes filles de l'époque
Restées à l'état de vapeur
Regarderont par la portière
Pensant que Paris n'est pas loin
Et ne sentiront que l'odeur
Du ciel qui vous prend à la gorge.

A la place de la forêt
Un chant d'oiseau s'élèvera
Que nul ne pourra situer,
Ni préférer, ni même entendre,
Sauf Dieu qui, lui, l'écoutera
Disant: "C'est un chardonneret."

Gravitations

Prophecy

One day the Earth will be only
A blind space turning,
Mingling night with day.
Under the great sky of the Andes
It will have no more mountains,
Not even a small ravine.

From all the houses of the world
Only one balcony will remain
And from the human map of the world
A sadness without bounds.
From the late Atlantic Ocean
A small taste of salt in the air,
One flying magical fish
Which will remember nothing of the sea.

From a carriage of 1905
(Four wheels and no road!)
Three young girls of that time
Remaining in the form of smoke
Will look out of the window
Believing Paris not far off
And they will smell nothing
But the smell of the sky which catches in your throat.

Where the forest was
A bird's song will rise up
Which no one will place,
Nor prefer, nor even hear,
Except God. When He listens,
He'll say: "It's a goldfinch!"

Coeur

Suffit d'une bougie
Pour éclairer le monde
Autour duquel ta vie
Fait sourdement sa ronde,
Coeur lent qui t'accoutumes
Et tu ne sais à quoi,
Coeur grave qui résumes
Dans le plus sûr de toi
Des terres sans feuillage,
Des routes sans chevaux,
Un vaisseau sans visages
Et des vagues sans eaux.
Mais des milliers d'enfants
Sur la place s'élancent
En poussant de tel cris
De leurs frêles poitrines
Qu'un homme à barbe noire,
—De quel monde venu?—
D'un seul geste les chasse
Jusqu'au fond de la nue.
Alors de nouveau, seul,
Dans la chair tu tâtonnes,
Coeur plus près du linceul,
Coeur de grande personne.
                    Gravitations

Whisper in Agony

Ne vous étonnez pas,
Abaissez les paupières
Jusqu'à ce qu'elles soient
De véritable pierre.

Laissez faire le coeur,
Et même s'il s'arrête.
Il bat pour lui tout seul
Sur sa pente secrète.

Heart

A candle is enough
To lighten the world
Around which your life
Makes its way with muffled step,
Slow heart which grows familiar
And you don't know with what,
Serious heart which contains
In the surest part of yourself
Lands with no leaves
Roads with no horses,
A ship with no faces
And waves with no water.
But thousands of children
Rush out on the square
Uttering such shrieks
From their thin chests
That a black bearded man
—Where did he come from?—
Sent them off with a wave of his hand
To the top of a cloud.
Then, alone, once more,
You feel your way into the flesh,
Heart nearer your shroud,
Heart of a grown-up.

Whisper in Agony

Do not be astonished
Just close your eyelids
Until they are
Of real stone.

Let your heart alone
Even if it stops.
It beats only for itself
On its secret slope.

Les mains s'allongeront
Dans leur barque de glace,
Et le front sera nu
Comme une grande place
Vide, entre deux armées.
      Le Forçat Innocent

Dieu Pense à l'Homme

Il faudra bien qu'il me ressemble,
Je ne sais encore comment,
Moi qui suis les mondes ensemble
Avec chacun de leurs moments.
Je le veux séparer du reste
Et me l'isoler dans les bras,
Je voudrais adopter ses gestes
Avant qu'il soit ce qu'il sera,
Je le devine à sa fenêtre
Mais la maison n'existe pas.
Je le tâte, je le tâtonne,
Je le forme sans le vouloir
Je me le donne, je me l'ôte,
Que je suis pressé de le voir!
Je le garde, je le retarde
Afin de le mieux concevoir.
Tantôt, informe, tu t'éloignes
Tu boites, au fond de la nuit,
Ou tu m'escalades, grandi,
Jusqu'à devenir un géant.
Moi que nul regard ne contrôle
Je te veux visible de loin,
Moi qui suis silence sans fin
Je te donnerai la parole,
Moi qui ne peux pas me poser
Je te veux debout sur tes pieds,
Moi qui suis partout à la fois

Your hands will stretch out
In their barge of ice
And your brow will be bare
Like a large square
Empty, between two foes.

God Thinks of Man

He will have to resemble me,
And I don't yet know how,
I who am the worlds together
With each of their moments.
I want to separate him from all else
And isolate him in my arms,
I would like to use his gestures
Before he is what he will be,
I can see him at his window
But the house doesn't exist.
I feel him, I touch him with my hands,
I form him without wanting to
I give him to myself, I take him away from myself,
How impatient I am to see him!
I watch over him, I delay him
In order better to conceive him.
At times, unformed, you move away,
You limp, into the depths of night,
Or grownup, you climb over me
Until you are a giant.
No look controls me
But I want you visible from afar,
If I am endless silence,
I will give you speech,
If I cannot rest on the ground
I want you upright on your feet,
If I am everywhere at once,
I want to put you in one place,
If I am more alone in my fable

Je te veux mettre en un endroit,
Moi qui suis plus seul dans ma fable
Qu'un agneau perdu dans les bois,
Moi qui ne mange ni ne bois
Je veux t'asseoir à une table,
Une femme en face de toi,
Moi qui suis sans cesse suprême
Toujours ignorant le loisir,
Qui n'en peux mais avec moi-même
Puisque je ne peux pas finir,
Je veux que tu sois périssable,
Tu seras mortel, mon petit,
Je te coucherai dans le lit
De la terre où se font les arbres.

La Fable du Monde

Lourde

à A. Ruano Fournier

Comme la Terre est lourde à porter! L'on dirait
Que chaque homme a son poids sur le dos.
Les morts, comme fardeau,
N'ont que deux doigts de terre,
Les vivants, eux, la sphère.
Atlas, ô commune misère,
Atlas, nous sommes tes enfants,
Nous sommes innombrables,
Toute seule est la Terre
Et pourtant et pourtant
Il faut bien que chacun la porte sur le dos,
Et même quand il dort, encore ce fardeau
Qui le fait soupirer au fond de son sommeil,
Sous une charge sans pareille!
Plus lourde que jamais, la Terre en temps de guerre,
Elle saigne en Europe et dans le Pacifique,
Nous l'entendons gémir sur nos épaules lasses
Poussant d'horribles cris
Qui dévorent l'espace.

Than a lamb lost in the woods,
If I neither eat nor drink,
I want to seat you at a table
With a wife opposite you,
If I am always supreme
Always unknowing of leisure,
Who can do nothing with myself
Since I cannot end,
I want you to be perishable,
You will be mortal, my child,
I will put you to bed in the earth
Where trees are made.

How Heavy

How heavy the Earth is to bear! you might say
That each man has its weight on his back.
The dead, for their burden,
Have only two inches of earth,
The living have the sphere.
Atlas, O common woe,
Atlas, we are your children,
We are without number,
All alone is the Earth,
And yet and yet
Each one must bear it on his back,
And even in sleep, still this burden
Which makes him sigh from the heart of his sleep,
Under a peerless weight!
Heavier than before, the Earth in time of war
Bleeds in Europe and in the Pacific,
We hear it moaning over our weary shoulders
Uttering horrible cries
Which devour space.
But we have to carry it still a bit farther
To make it extend from today to the next day.

Mais il faut la porter toujours un peu plus loin
Pour la faire passer d'aujourd'hui à demain.

Poèmes 1939-45.

Plein Ciel
à Etiemble

J'avais un cheval
Dans un champ de ciel
Et je m'enfonçais
Dans le jour ardent.
Rien ne m'arrêtait
J'allais sans savoir,
C'était un navire
Plutôt qu'un cheval,
C'était un désir
Plutôt qu'un navire,
C'était un cheval
Comme on n'en voit pas,
Tête de coursier,
Robe de délire,
Un vent qui hennit
En se répandant.
Je montais toujours
Et faisais des signes:
"Suivez mon chemin,
Vous pouvez venir,
Mes meilleurs amis,
La route est sereine,
Le ciel est ouvert.
Mais qui parle ainsi?
Je me perds de vue
Dans cette altitude,
Me distinguez-vous,
Je suis celui qui
Parlait tout à l'heure,
Suis-je encor celui
Qui parle à présent,

I had a horse
In a field of the sky
And I plunged
Into the burning daylight.
Nothing stopped me
I moved without knowing,
It was a boat
Rather than a horse,
It was a desire
Rather than a boat,
It was a horse
Such as you never see,
Head of a steed
Blanket of frenzy,
A wind neighing
And spending itself.
I continued to ride
And made signals:
"Follow my tracks,
You can come,
My best friends,
The road is open
The sky is clear.
But who is saying this?
I lose sight of myself
In this altitude,
Can you make me out,
I am the man who
Was speaking a minute ago,
Am I still the man
Who is speaking now,
And you, my friends,
Are you the same beings?
One blots out the other
And changes on this ride."

Vous-mêmes, amis,
Etes-vous les mêmes?
L'un efface l'autre
Et change en montant."

Poèmes 1939-45

Madame

O dame de la profondeur
Que faites-vous à la surface
Attentive à ce qui se passe
Regardant la montre à mon heure?

Madame, que puis-je pour vous
Vous qui êtes-là si tacite
Ne serez-vous plus explicite
Vous qui me voulez à genoux?

Ce regard solitaire et tendre
Aimerait à se faire entendre?
Et c'est à lui que je me dois
Puisque vous n'avez pas de voix?

Grande dame des profondeurs,
O voisine de l'autre monde,
Me voulez-vous en eaux profondes
Aux régions de votre coeur?

Pourquoi me regarder avec des yeux d'otage,
Jeunesse d'au delà les âges?
Votre fixité signifie
Qu'il faut à vous que je me fie?

Pour quelle obscure délivrance
Me demandez-vous alliance?

O vous toujours prête à finir
Vous voudriez me retenir
Sur ce bord même de l'abîme
Dont vous êtes l'étrange cime.

Madame

Lady of the depths
What are you doing on the surface
Attentive to what is happening
Looking at the watch by my hour?

Lady, what can I do for you
Who are there so quiet
Won't you be more to the point
You who want me on my knees?

Would that lonely tender look
Like to be heard?
Do I owe allegiance to it
Since you have no voice?

Proud lady of the depths,
And neighbor of the other world,
Do you want me in the deep waters,
In the regions of your heart?

Why look at me with eyes of a hostage,
Youth beyond the ages?
Does your gaze mean
That I must trust you?

For what dark deliverance
Do you ask from me alliance?

You, always ready to end,
Would like to hold me back
On this very edge of the abyss
Whose strange summit is you.

Lady, who want me faithful to your image,
Are you now changing your countenance?
How can I follow you in your ways,
For I am as simple as the day.

Dame qui me voulez fidèle à votre image
Voilà que maintenant vous changez de visage?
Comment vous suivre en vos détours,
Je suis simple comme le jour.

Comment pourrais-je me fier
A ce que vous sacrifiez,
Ou pensez-vous ainsi me dire
Que changer n'est pas se trahir
Que vous vous refusez au gel
Définitif de l'éternel?

Devez-vous donc, quoi qu'il arrive,
Demeurer secrète et furtive?
Ecoutez, mon obscure reine,
Il est tard pour croire aux sirènes.

O vous dont la douceur étonne
Venez-vous de jours sans personne?

Est-ce la cendre de demain
Que vous serrez dans votre main?
Fille d'un tout proche avenir
Venez-vous m'aider à finir
Avec ce délicat sourire
Qui veut tout dire sans le dire?

O dame de mes eaux profondes
Serais-je donc si près des ombres?
Ou venez-vous m'aider à vivre
De tout votre frêle équilibre?

Que faire d'un si beau fantôme
Dans mes misérables bras d'homme?

Oh si profonde contre moi
Vous mettez toute une buée
Fragile, bien distribuée
Dessus mon plus secret miroir.

How could I trust
What you sacrifice,
Or by that, are you saying
To change is not to betray oneself
And that you refuse the permanent
Cold of the eternal?

Whatever happens, must you now
Remain secret and furtive?
But listen, my darkening queen,
It is late to believe in sirens.

Do you, whose sweetness is miracle,
Come from solitary days?

Is it the ashes of tomorrow
You hold in your hand?
Daughter of a close by future
Are you here to help me over
That tender smile
Which says everything without speaking?

Lady of my deep waters
Would I be then so near the shades?
Or are you here to help me live
With your frail steadfastness?

What can I do with so lovely a phantom
In my poor arms of a man?

So deep down against me
You place a fragile
Blur, spread out well
On my most secret mirror.

Already unrecognizable in all your changes
Why do you now veil your face?
Is it to find at last your real
Portrait after all this charming imposture?

Déjà méconnaissable à tous vos changements
Pourquoi vous voilez-vous le visage à présent
Est-ce pour retrouver enfin votre figure
Véritable après tant de touchante imposture?

Choix de Poèmes

Insomnie

Chevaliers de la nuit blanche, cavalerie
Sans mémoire qui se concentre et qui s'agite . . .
On se heurte, on chuchote, on se félicite
Avant de repartir pour massacrer un coeur.
Et comment contenir ces voraces chimères
Antagonistes, sur l'oreiller irrité?
Le sang pousse un tumulte accru dans les artères
Et le coeur s'interroge et feint de s'arrêter.
Le matin saura-t-il demain luire sur terre.
Sur toi-même morceau de nuit épouvanté
D'être à la fois de terre et de ciel et de pluies
D'un passé très lointain que le présent essuie?
Mais où est le présent dans cette obscurité
Au fond de l'insomnie où l'on nie et renie
Et qui nous cherche noise et qui nous calomnie,
Nous verse son acide en flammes dans les yeux
Et de notre bois mort fait un feu furieux.
O souffrance, ô rocher en nous inextricable,
Tu mets en sang la chair et ses tissus secrets
Ou bien tu vas t'asseoir à notre pauvre table
Suçant l'anxiété comme un os de poulet,
Tu t'installes partout où l'on trouve de l'homme
Et tu viens fureter de tes rugueux couteaux
Ce qui se fait de triste et de grand sous la peau
Jusqu'à ce que repue enfin on fasse un somme
Et qu'on vous laisse là ouvert comme un tombeau
Qui sent l'humidité suppliante de l'homme.
Qu'un sommeil justicier allège nos paupières
Et nous confie enfin à ces concaves pierres
Qui épousent les corps aux grandes profondeurs.

Insomnia

Horsemen of the sleepless night, cavalry
Without memory concentrating, moving about . . .
They knock together, whisper, congratulate
Before leaving to assassinate a heart.
Chimeras on my irritated pillow?
The blood forces a storm grown large in the arteries
And the heart wonders and pretends to stop.
Will the morning tomorrow shine on the earth,
And over you, part of the night terrified
At being of the earth, of the sky, of rain
Of a very distant past which the present endures?
But where is the present in this darkness
In the depths of insomnia where you deny and renounce
And which picks a quarrel with us and slanders us
Pours over our eyes its flaming acid
And makes of our dead wood a fierce fire.
O suffering, O unmovable rock in us,
You bleed our flesh and its secret tissues
Or you sit down at our poor table
Sucking anxiety like a chicken bone,
You settle down wherever you find man
And come to ferret with your rough knives
What is sad and noble under the skin
Until at last sated you go to sleep
And you are left there opened like a tomb
Which smells of the supplicating humidity of man.
May a just sleep lighten our eyelids
And yield us at last to those stone concaves
Which join bodies to great depths.
The flesh about to cry stifles its horror
And you, vast night opened to the steps of silence
Come to bury us in your indifference,
Guide us into the hallways of the sleeper
Who no longer hears his heart barking at the moon
And climbs aboard the dream where we become posthumous.
May this phosphor of our eyes go out

La chair au bord du cri étouffe son horreur
Et toi, nuit grande ouverte aux marches du silence
Viens nous ensevelir dans ton indifférence,
Guide-nous dans les vestibules du dormeur
Qui n'entend plus son coeur aboyer à la lune
Et monte à bord du songe où l'on devient posthume.
Que s'éteigne tout ce phosphore de nos yeux
Traçant et retraçant ses cercles soupçonneux!
Dormir! ne plus savoir ce qu'on nomme la Terre,
Ce cercle de sommeil est le frère des cieux?
J'ignore ces pays et ces à peine lieux,
Cette géographie étrange et salutaire
Où vont couler sans fin les rêves, leurs rivières,
Où la métamorphose affine ses pinceaux
Sous un ciel de passage et toujours jouvenceau
Le long de l'océan où se défait la vie
Après sa méandreuse, aveuglante insomnie.

Naissances

Ce Pur Enfant

Ce pur enfant, rose de chasteté,
Qu'a-t-il à voir avec la volupté?
Et fallait-il qu'en luxe d'innocence
Allât finir la fureur de nos sens?

Dorénavent en cette neuve chair
Se débattra notre amoureux mystère?
Après nous avoir pris le coeur d'assaut
L'amour se change en l'hôte d'un berceau,

En petits poings fermés, en courtes cuisses,
En ventre rond sans aucune malice
Et nous restons tous deux à regarder
Notre secret si mal, si bien gardé.

Naissances

Tracing and retracing its distrustful circles!
To sleep! and know no more what is called the Earth!
Is this sleep circle the brother of the skies?
I do not know those lands and those half places
That strange beneficent geography
Where dreams and rivers endlessly flow
Where metamorphosis refines its brushes
Under a passing and always youthful sky
Along the ocean where life comes apart
After its wandering blinding sleeplessness.

This Pure Child

What does this pure rose child of chastity
Have to do with the life of the senses?
Did the madness of our feelings need
To end in luxury of innocence?

Will our loving mystery henceforth
Struggle in this new flesh?
After capturing our heart in assault,
Love changes into the guest of a cradle,

Into small closed fists, and short thighs,
Into a round belly into no malice
And both of us stay to watch
Our secret kept so well and so badly.

Le Malade

Trop grand le ciel trop grand je ne sais où me mettre
Trop profond l'océan point de place pour moi
Trop confuse la ville trop claire la campagne.
Je fais ciel, je fais eau, sable de toutes parts,
Ne suis-je pas encore accoutumé à vivre
Suis-je un enfant boudeur qui ne veut plus jouer,
Oublié-je que si je tousse
Mes soixante-six ans tousseront avec moi
Et feront avec moi tousser mon univers.
Quand le matin je me réveille
Est-ce que je ne sors pas peu à peu tout entier
De l'an quatre-vingt-quatre, du siècle précédent
Où se font les vieillards?
Mais qui ose parler de vieillards alors que
Les mots les plus retors désarment sous ma plume,
Même le mot vieillard redoutable entre tous
Fait pivoter vers moi un tout neuf tournesol
Brillant comme un jeune homme.
Hache du désespoir taciturne en ma main
Tu te mets à chanter comme fait l'espérance.

Naissances

The Sick Man

Too big the sky too big I don't know where to go
Too deep the ocean no place for me
Too jumbled the city too limpid the country.
I am the sky the water the sand everywhere,
Haven't I yet grown used to living,
Am I a sulking child who will play no more,
Do I forget that if I cough
My sixty-six years will cough with me
And will make my world cough with me.
When I wake up in the morning
Doesn't my whole being gradually leave
The year 1884, of the last century
When old men are created?
But who dares speak of old men when
The craftiest words disarm under my pen,
Even the word old man most fearful of words
Makes a new sunflower turn toward me
And it glows like a young man.
Hatchet of silent despair in my hand
You begin to sing in the manner of hope.

ST.-JOHN PERSE

THE ART OF ST.-JOHN PERSE provides one of the loftiest con-
temporary lessons on the meaning of poetry and on the role of
the poet both in his own time and in all times. His poetry is
always the act of understanding, which is equivalent to the
seizure of the intimate and essential relationship existing be-
tween orders or phenomena or objects. This seizure he nar-
rates in such sumptuous language, of such dazzling spectacular
beauty, that a unity is engendered surrounding and combining
all diversity, all antinomy. The consciousness of this poet is the
principal instrument of his art: it is the rapport between man's
deepest instincts which he learns and sings. He wills to learn
and therefore to know and dominate whatever there is to see
and feel and hear in the universe. It is his will toward—eternity,
rather than immortality, in this particular case. Behind every

manifestation of mobility and fluctuation he finds a pure and constant relationship, a pure and constant truth, a sign of the immutable. The real world, in the poetry of Perse, becomes less approximate and less degraded. To man and to every aspiration of man he ascribes some eternal meaning. Everything precarious and ephemeral appears less so in the condition of his poetry, which is a relentless conquest of reality, a transcription of reality outside of time.

The present is sung of in this poetry, so flagrantly and pervasively that it becomes eternal. The oneness of the poet is lost when he sings. What in him as a human being is a state of becoming is miraculously transposed into a state of being. This is like a decisive event which explodes and marks the end of some temporary state and the beginning of an eternal one. The sorrows and joys we associate with time lose their temporal aspect in the poems of Perse, and find a new meaning, a new accomplishment. The poet discovers in them new resources and new reasons. This is perhaps vision. At least it is consciousness by which all color and form are modified. The universe is recognizable in these poems, but it is changed. It has escaped the tyranny of minutes. It is more sovereign, more real, more powerful. And the poet, too, is more than a mere individual. He reaches in his function of poet a fullness of being which leaves far behind the imperfect and limited individual he is in every other function. What elevates him must be this new sense of existence, this new energy which joins him with the cosmos. His consciousness is an act of such fullness that it recreates him so that in him the absolute is consummated.

Aléxis Léger was born in 1887, on a coral island near Guadeloupe, Saint-Léger-les-Feuilles, which belonged to his father's family. His early years were spent there and on Guadeloupe itself where his mother's family owned plantations. At the age of eleven, he went to France to complete his education. In 1914 he entered the Diplomatic Service, and was sent to China in 1917. In 1922 he attended the Disarmament Conference in Washington in his capacity as expert on the Far East, and then accompanied back to Paris Aristide Briand whom he served for the next ten years. Legend has it that while walking with the poet beside the Potomac, Briand was struck by Léger's statement that a book is the death of a tree. (*Un livre, c'est la mort d'un arbre.*) At Briand's death, in 1932, Léger became Permanent Secretary for Foreign Affairs. At the capitulation of France, in 1940, Léger, rather than submit to appeasement, left for England and arrived in Canada on July 14th. Archibald MacLeish offered Léger a post at the Library of Congress where the French poet took up an important service for the library and French letters. At this time he wrote *Exil*, which initiated a new series of poems. He still lives in Washington today.

Eloges was first published in 1910, in the Editions de la Nouvelle Revue Française, with the signature Saint Léger Léger. The new edition, of 1925, appeared with the signature St.-John Perse. The name may well have been chosen because of Léger's admiration for the ancient writer Persius. *Eloges* are poems evocative of a childhood spent in the midst of exotic vegetation, in a harbor cluttered up with Colonial merchandise. The vision of the sea dominates this childhood with its memories of cyclones, plantations, volcanoes, tidal waves. *Anabase*, first published in Paris, in 1924, preserves the memory of the five years Léger spent in China and the Gobi Desert. This work, translated by T. S. Eliot, in 1930, is one of the key poems of our age. It represents the poet as conqueror of the word, in the guise of a literal conqueror associated with arms and horses, with a willed exile in foreign places. As soon as the plans of the future city are drawn up, the conqueror leaves. Experiences and joys are enumerated, but there is always more to see and to hear: *Beaucoup de choses sur la terre à entendre et à voir, choses vivantes parmi nous!* But the literal conquest related is not so important as the actual conquest of language carried out by the poet in the writing of his poem. The primitive meaning of words is fought over and won. The history of the poet is the history of man seeking possession of the entire earth.

In March 1942, *Poetry* (of Chicago) published the original French text of Léger's new poem, *Exil*. This is much more than a poem on the war and on the exile of Perse. It is a more profound work on the same theme of *Anabase*, on the poet's exile, on the necessary "absence" which precedes every work of art: *un grand poème né de rien*. This concept, traditionally associated with Mallarmé, is explored and revitalized in *Exil*. The poet is the man who inhabits his name. His syntax is the pure language of exile. Isolated from the rest of the long poem, the final line is both the summation of the work and the announcement of the poems to come:

Et c'est l'heure, ô Poète, de décliner ton nom, ta naissance et ta race.

The sensations which come to him from the rains, the snows, the winds and the sea are each in turn to be the subject of the new poems. Only the beginning of the sea poem, *Et vous, mers*, has appeared in print, in *Les Cahiers de la Pléiade*, of spring-autumn, 1950, and in *Poetry*, of October 1951. The poem on the winds, *Vents* (Gallimard, 1946) is to date the longest poem of Perse, and his most remarkable in scope and poetic achievement.

Claudel, in the essay he has devoted to this poem (*Revue de Paris*, Nov. 1949, and reproduced in *Les Cahiers de la Pléiade*, 1950), calls it an epic. Part I contains an invocation to all dead and dried things which have to be dispersed by the wind. Everything has to be seized again. Everything, for the poet, has to be spoken again. The west is the source of the wind and the source of the extraordinary accidents which the wind will resuscitate. Part II contains allusions to America and to the coming of evening in a new age of the earth. Part III revives the theme of conquerors and viceroys, and always throughout the conquests the problem of man and of the poet in his particular site of the century. Part IV is the conclusion. It is on the voyager's return, on the poet's gift of the horizons he has seen. The wind has both dispersed and founded. The poem is both chronicle of the past and song of the present. Denis de Rougemont sees the poem essentially as the epic of America, as one of the tonic poems of the century and one of the rare works representing a refusal of despair.

The form of these poems is non-traditional. Léger has perfected a broad stanza containing its own beat and pulsation.

He observes the world and spells it out in his verse, as it comes to him in his meditation. His speech is breath and concrete words. He enumerates all parts of the familiar world surrounding man: animals and plants and the elements, and he doesn't hesitate to use precise technical terms. The poem is a ceremonial, involving all the diverse activities of man, and stating them in successive gestures. The world of his poetry has the freshness of a new creation. It is total and totally present. Whatever legendary elements remain are actualized in this poetry which is always praise, as the title of the first volume, *Eloges*, revealed.

It is impossible to separate the scansion, or the articulation, from the words of the line in Perse's poetry. One supports the other, one authorizes the other, and to such a degree that sound and meaning are dilated far beyond their usual limits. The poem seems to form and grow before one's eyes. Language creates the work of art, and the work of art grows out of the language. Almost every critic who has written on Perse has been struck by the opulence of his work, by its solemnity, by the persistent use of *grand* and *grandeur*, of *haut* and *hauteur*, of *vaste*, and other such words which provide the work with cosmic dimensions. The figure of the Prince is associated with the themes of power and exile and language. The prince in his world is the prototype of the poet in his poem. Each has to undergo a similar paradox and learn to live in accordance with two seemingly opposed regimens. The prince: in power and impoverishment, in adornment and nudity; the poet: in silence and language, in magic and mysticism.

St.-John Perse is heir to one of the richest poetic traditions. The form of his poetry as well as the metaphysical use he puts it to, recall the examples of Rimbaud in *Les Illuminations*, of Lautréamont in *Les Chants de Maldoror*, and Claudel in *Cinq Grandes Odes*. He is the contemporary poet who comes perhaps closest to considering himself the instrument of a superior revelation. When he speaks as a poet, something is affirmed in him and in itself. He knows that the most simple object or the most trite event is capable of giving birth to a poem. In this sense, his being is the restoration of eternity, the actualizing of eternity. This doesn't mean that he always knows the full significance of what he says and does. On the contrary! His poetry is the yielding to something that cannot be defined with the research and the precision that are found in the actual stanzas. Yet the poetry reveals the desire to reach this inaccessible source. It is constantly striving to make present what is for all time. This will, by definition, is never without a struggle against death. The poet has to accomplish simultaneously two acts which appear contradictory. He has to represent himself outside of his normal state of becoming and mortal man, and at the same time he must not abolish any part of his personality, any part of his uniqueness. To become possessed by such a will is equivalent to being its martyr. Perse is obsessed and martyred by his vision, as Mallarmé and Rimbaud were by theirs. The poet's vocation is his drama. To transcend one's existence by participating in it more profoundly is the poet's honor and suffering. Whether it be Besançon or Aden or Washington, the poet's exile is his solitude and his ethics.

Selected Bibliography of Perse

1911 *Eloges,* Gallimard (new edition, 1925).
    1944 *Eloges and other poems,* translated by Louise Várèse, Norton.
1924 *Anabase,* Gallimard.
    1930 *Anabasis,* translation and preface by T. S. Eliot, Faber & Faber.
    1949 definitive edition, Harcourt.
1942 *Exil, Poetry,* Chicago. March.
1943 *Poème à l'Etrangère, Hémisphères,* New York. Summer.
1943 *Pluies, Lettres Françaises,* Argentina, October.
1944 *Neiges, Lettres Françaises,* Argentina, July.
1949 *Exile and Other Poems,* translated by Denis Devlin, Pantheon Books.
1946 *Vents,* Gallimard.

on Perse

Les Cahiers de la Pléiade, été-automne, 1950. Articles by Gide, Eliot, Fargue, Steiner, Char, Larbaud, Jouve, Claudel, Breton, Picon, Rénéville, Béguin, Ungaretti, Devlin, Zalamea, Caillois, Bournoure, Lefebvre, MacLeish, Spender, Poggioli, Raymond, Kemp, Rougemont, Fouchet, Tate.

Et Vous, Mers . . .
(début de poème)

I

Et vous, Mers, qui lisiez dans de plus vastes songes, nous laissiez-vous un soir aux rostres de la Ville, parmi la pierre publique et les pampres de bronze?

Plus large, ô foule, notre audience sur ce versant d'un âge sans déclin: la Mer, immense et verte comme une aube à l'orient des hommes,

La Mer en fête sur ses marches comme une ode de pierre: vigile et fête à nos frontières, murmure et fête à hauteur d'hommes —la Mer elle-même notre veille, comme une promulgation divine. . . .

L'odeur funèbre de la rose n'assiégera plus les grilles du tombeau; l'heure vivante dans les palmes ne taira plus son âme d'étrangère. . . . Amères, nos lèvres de vivants le furent-elles jamais?

J'ai vu sourire aux feux du large la grande chose fériée: la Mer en fête de nos songes, comme une Pâque d'herbe verte et comme fête que l'on fête,

Toute la Mer en fête des confins, sous sa fauconnerie de nuées blanches, comme domaine de franchise et comme terre de mainmorte, comme province d'herbe folle et qui fut jouée aux dés. . . .

Inonde, ô brise, ma naissance! Et ma faveur s'en aille au cirque de plus vastes pupilles! . . . Les sagaies de Midi vibrent aux portes de la joie. Les tambours du néant cèdent aux fifres de lumière. Et l'Océan de toute part, foulant son poids de roses mortes,

Sur nos terrasses de calcium lève sa tête de Tétrarque!

2

". . . Je vous ferai pleurer, c'est trop de grâce parmi nous.

"Pleurer de grâce, non de peine, dit le Chanteur du plus beau
    chant;

"Et de ce pur émoi du coeur dont j'ignore la source,

"Comme de ce pur instant de mer qui précède la brise. . . ."

And You, Seas

(The beginning of a poem)

I

And you, Seas, who once read into vaster dreams, did you
leave us one evening at the rostrums of the City, in the center
of the public stone and the bronze vinebranches?

O people, our meeting more crowded on this slope of an age
without decline: the Sea, tremendous and green like a dawn
rising to the east of men,

The Sea in celebration on her steps, like an ode of stone: vigil
and feast day at our borders, noise and festivity to the height
of men—the Sea herself our vigil, like a promulgation by the
gods. . . .

The death smell of the rose will no longer besiege the fence
around the tomb; the life hour in the palms will silence no more
its soul of a stranger. . . . Bitter? were our lips of living men
ever bitter?

I have seen the great festive thing smile at the fires of the
swell: the Sea in celebration of our dreams, like an Easter of
green grass and like a holy day we celebrate,

All the Sea celebrating her extent, under her falconry of
white clouds, like a territory of exemption, a land untaxed, a
province of wild grass which was thrown into a wager. . . .

O wind, drown my birth! And let my favor go to the circus
of vaster pupils! Let the javelins of the South vibrate at the
doors of joy. Let the drums of the void give way to the fifes of
light. And may the Ocean, on all sides, trampling its heaviness
of dead roses,

Raise over our calcium terraces its head of a Tetrarch!

2

". . . I will make you cry, there is too much grace with us.

". . . Cry from grace, not from pain, said the Singer of the most
    beautiful song;

"And from that pure feeling of the heart whose source I don't
    know,

"And from that pure moment of the sea which comes before
    the breeze. . . ."

Parlait ainsi homme de mer, tenant propos d'homme de mer.
Louait ainsi, louait l'amour et le désir de mer
Et vers la Mer, de toute part, ce ruissellement encore des sources
du plaisir.

"C'est une histoire que je dirai, c'est une histoire qu'on entendra.
"C'est une histoire que je dirai comme il convient qu'elle soit
dite,
"Et de telle grâce sera-t-elle dite qu'il faudra bien qu'on s'en
réjouisse.
"Certes, une histoire qu'on veuille entendre, dans l'insouciance
encore de la mort,
"Et telle et telle, en sa fraîcheur, au coeur de l'homme sans
mémoire,
"Qu'elle nous soit faveur nouvelle et comme brise d'estuaire
en vue des lampes de la terre.
"Et de ceux-là qui l'entendront, assis sous le grand arbre du
chagrin,
"Il en est peu qui ne se lèvent, qui ne se lèvent avec nous et
n'aillent, souriant,
"Dans les fougères encore de l'enfance et le déroulement des
crosses de la mort."

3

Poésie pour accompagner la marche d'une récitation en l'honneur de la Mer.

Poésie pour assister le chant d'une marche au pourtour de la Mer.

Comme l'entreprise du tour d'autel et la gravitation du choeur au circuit de la strophe.

Et c'est un chant de mer comme il n'en fut jamais chanté, et c'est la Mer en nous qui le chantera:

La Mer, en nous portée, jusqu'à la satiété du souffle et la péroraison du souffle,

La Mer, en nous, portant son bruit soyeux du large et toute sa grande fraîcheur d'aubaine par le monde.

Poésie pour apaiser la fièvre d'une veille au périple de mer.
Poésie pour mieux vivre notre veille au délice de mer.

Thus spoke the man of the sea, saying words of a man of the sea.
Thus did he love praise and the desire of the sea
And toward the sea, from all sides, this flowing again of the springs of pleasure.

"It's a story I will tell, it's a story you will hear.
"It's a story I will tell as it should be told,
"And with such grace will it be told, that you will be made happy by it.
"Surely, a story you will wish to hear, in an unconcern over death,
"And such a one, in its freshness, in the heart of man without memory.
"That it will be for us a new favor, like the wind from the estuary in sight of the lights from the land.

"And of those who will hear it, seated under the great tree of woe,
"There are few who will not rise, who will not rise up with us and go back, smiling,
"Into the ferns of childhood and the unrolling of the fronds of death."

3

Poetry to accompany the progress of a recital in honor of the Sea.

Poetry to assist the song of a march in the circuit of the Sea.
Like the movement around the altar and gravitating of the chorus in the circuit of the strophe.

It's a sea song as was never sung, and it's the Sea in us who will sing it:
The Sea, borne in us, until the satiety of our breath and the peroration of our breath,
The Sea, in us, bearing her silken noise of the brine and all her great coolness of fortune through the world.

Poetry to appease the fever of a vigil in the voyage around the sea. Poetry to live better our vigil in the delight of the sea.

Et c'est un songe en mer comme il n'en fut jamais songé, et c'est la Mer en nous qui le songera:

La Mer, en nous tissée, jusqu'à ses ronceraies d'abîme, la Mer, en nous, tissant ses grandes heures de lumière et ses grandes pistes de ténèbres—

Toute licence, toute naissance et toute résipiscence, la Mer! la Mer! à son afflux de mer,

Dans l'affluence de ses bulles et la sagesse infuse de son lait, ah! dans l'ébullition sacrée de ses voyelles—les saintes filles! les saintes filles!—

La Mer elle-même tout écume, comme Sibylle en fleurs sur sa chaise de fer. . . .

4

Ainsi louée, serez-vous ceinte, ô Mer, d'une louange sans offense.

Ainsi conviée serez-vous l'hôte dont il convient de taire le mérite.

Et de la Mer elle-même il ne sera question, mais de son règne au coeur de l'homme:

Comme il est bien, dans la requête au Prince, d'interposer l'ivoire ou bien le jade

Entre la face suzeraine et la louange courtisane.

Moi, m'inclinant en votre honneur d'une inclinaison sans bassesse, j'épuiserai la révérence et le balancement du corps.

Et la fumée encore du plaisir enfumera la tête du fervent,

Et le délice encore du mieux dire engendrera la grâce du sou- rire. . . .

Et de salutation telle serez-vous saluée, ô Mer, qu'on s'en souvi- enne pour longtemps comme d'une récréation du coeur.

5

. . . Or il y avait un si long temps que j'avais goût de ce poème, mêlant à mes propos du jour toute cette alliance, au loin, d'un grand éclat de mer—comme en bordure de forêt, entre les feuilles de laque noire, le gisement soudain d'azur et de ciel gemme: écaille vive, entre les mailles, d'un grand poisson pris par les ouïes!

Et qui donc m'eût surpris dans mon propos secret? gardé

And it's a dream at sea as was never dreamed, and it's the Sea in us which will dream it.

The Sea, woven in us, to the last weaving of its tangled night, the Sea, in us, weaving her great hours of light and her great trails of darkness—

All freedom, all birth and all resipiscence, the Sea! the Sea! in her rushing up of a sea,

In the abundance of her bubbles and the infused wisdom of her milk, in the sacred ferment of her vowels—the holy women! the holy women!

The Sea herself all foam, like a Sibylla bursting in flowers on her iron chair. . . .

4

Thus praised, O Sea, you will be girded with blameless praise.

Thus invited, you will be the hostess whose merit we must not speak.

And of the Sea herself it will not be a question, but of her reign in the heart of man:

As it is well, in the request to the Prince, to interpose ivory or jade

Between the suzerain face and the courtesan praise.

And I, bowing in your honor with a bow not too low, shall exhaust reverence and balance of the body.

And the smoke of pleasure still will encircle the head of the fervent one,

And still the delight of the fine speech will engender the grace of a smile.

And with such greeting will you be greeted, O Sea, that it will be remembered for a long time like a relaxation of the heart.

5

. . . For so long a time I had felt the savor of this poem in me, joining with my day-words all that alliance, in the distance, of a great shaft of sea—as on the edge of the forest, between the leaves of black lacquer, the sudden layer of blue and gem sky: living scale, between the meshes, of a great fish caught by the gills!

par le sourire et par la courtoisie; parlant, parlant langue d'aubain parmi les hommes de mon sang—à l'angle peut-être d'un Jardin Public, ou bien aux grilles effilées d'or de quelque Chancellerie; la face peut-être de profil et le regard au loin, entre mes phrases, à tel oiseau chantant son lai sur la Capitainerie du Port.

Car il y avait un si long temps que j'avais goût de ce poème, et ce fut tel sourire en moi de lui garder ma prévenance: tout envahi, tout investi, tout menacé du grand poème, comme d'un lait de madrépores; à son afflux, docile, comme à la quête de minuit, dans un soulèvement très lent des grandes eaux du songe, quand les pulsations du large tirent avec douceur sur nos aussières et sur nos câbles.

Et comment il nous vint à l'esprit d'engager ce poème, c'est ce qu'il faudrait dire. Mais n'est-ce pas assez d'y trouver son plaisir? Et bien fût-il, ô dieux! que j'en prisse soin, avant qu'il ne nous fût repris. . . . Va voir, enfant, au tournant de la rue, comme les Filles de Halley, les belles visiteuses célestes en habit de Vestales, engagées dans la nuit à l'hameçon d'ivoire, sont promptes à se reprendre au tournant de l'ellipse.

Morganatique au loin l'Epouse, et l'alliance, clandestine! . . . Chant d'épousailles, ô Mer, sera pour vous le chant: "Mon dernier chant! mon dernier chant! et qui sera d'homme de mer. . . ." Et si ce n'est ce chant, je vous le demande, qu'est-ce qui témoignerait en faveur de la Mer—la Mer sans stèles ni portiques, sans Alyscamps ni Propylées; la Mer sans dignitaires de pierre à ses terrasses circulaires, ni rang de bêtes bâtées d'ailes à l'aplomb des chaussées?

Moi j'ai pris charge de l'écrit, j'honorerai l'écrit. Comme à la fondation d'une grande oeuvre votive, celui qui s'est offert à rédiger le texte et la notice; et fut prié par l'Assemblé des Donateurs, y ayant seul vocation. Et nul n'a su comment il s'est mis à l'ouvrage: dans un quartier, vous dira-t-on, d'équarrisseurs ou de fondeurs—par temps d'émeute populaire—entre les cloches du couvre-feu et les tambours d'une aube militaire. . . .

And who then would have come upon me in my secret word? protected by my smile and courtesy; speaking the tongue of an alien with men of my blood—at the corner perhaps of a Public Garden, or at the gold-spiked iron fence of some Chancellery; my face perhaps in profile and looking far off, between my sentences, to some bird singing its lay over the roof of the Harbor Master.

For I had felt the savor of this poem in me for so long a time, and such a smile in me kept my preference for it: I was invaded, invested and threatened by the great poem, as by the milk of madrepores: at its flooding, I obeyed, as at the turn of midnight, at a very slow rising of the great waters of one's dream, when the swell of the open sea pulls gently on our ropes and cables.

And how it came to us to induce this poem is what we will have to tell. But isn't it enough to take pleasure in it? And how good it was, O gods, that I took care of it before it was taken away from us. . . . Go and see, child, where the street turns, how the daughters of Halley, the beautiful heavenly visitors dressed like Vestal Virgins, caught in the night on the ivory hook, are eager to escape at the turn of the ellipse.

Morganatic the Bride far off, and the alliance, clandestine! . . . The marriage song, O Sea, will be for you the song: "My last song! my last song! and which will be of a man of the sea. . . . And if it is not this song, I ask you, what would testify in favor of the Sea—the Sea without steles and porticoes, with no Alyscamps and no Propylaea, the Sea without stone dignitaries on her circular terraces, nor a row of animals saddled with wings upright to the highways?

I have taken charge of the writing and I shall honor the writing. Like the man who at the beginning of a great work of thanks, has offered to draw up the statement and the announcement; and was asked by the Assembly of Donors, he alone having a vocation for this. And no one learned how he set about the work: in one district, they will tell you, of horse slaughterers or smelters—at the time of a people's riot—between the curfew bells and the drums of a martial dawn. . . .

Et au matin déjà la Mer cérémonielle et neuve lui sourit au-dessus des corniches. Et voici qu'en sa page se mire l'Etrangère. ... Car il y avait un si long temps qu'il avait goût de ce poème; y ayant telle vocation. . . . Et ce fut telle douceur un soir de lui marquer sa prévenance; et d'y céder, telle impatience. Et le sourire aussi fut tel de lui prêter alliance. . . . "Mon dernier chant! mon dernier chant! . . . et qui sera d'homme de mer. . . ."

6

Et c'est la Mer qui vint à nous sur les degrés de pierre du drame:

Avec ses Princes, ses Régents, ses Messagers vêtus d'emphase et de métal, ses grands Acteurs aux yeux crevés et ses Prophètes à la chaîne, ses Magiciennes trépignant sur leurs socques de bois, la bouche pleine de caillots noirs, et ses tributs de Vierges chemi-nant dans les labours de l'hymne,

Avec ses Pâtres, ses Pirates et ses Nourrices d'enfants-rois, ses vieux Nomades en exil et ses Princesses d'élégie, ses grandes Veuves silencieuses sous des cendres illustres, ses grands Usurpa-teurs de trônes et Fondateurs de colonies lointaines, ses Pré-bendiers et ses Marchands, ses grands Concessionnaires de pro-vinces d'étain, et ses grands Sages voyageurs à dos de buffles de rizières,

Avec tout son cheptel de monstres et d'humains, ah! tout son croît de fables immortelles, nouant à ses ruées d'esclaves et d'ilotes ses grands Bâtards divins et ses grandes filles d'étalons—une foule en hâte se levant aux travées de l'Histoire et se por-tant en masse vers l'arène, dans le premier frisson du soir au parfum de fucus,

Récitation en marche vers l'Auteur et vers la bouche peinte de son masque.

—o—

Ainsi la Mer vint-elle à nous dans son grand âge et dans ses grands plissements hercyniens—toute la mer à son affront de mer, d'un seul tenant et d'une seule tranche!

Et comme un peuple jusqu'à nous dont la langue est nouvelle, et comme une langue jusqu'à nous dont la phrase est nouvelle, menant à ses tables d'airain ses commandements suprêmes,

Par grands soulèvements d'humeur et grandes intumescences

And already in the morning the ceremonious and new Sea smiled at him above the cornices. And She, such an Alien, was reflected in his page. . . . For he had felt the savor of this poem in him for so long a time; having such a strong vocation for it. . . . And it was such joy one evening to show it his attention; and such an impatience it was to surrender to it. And with such a smile also we joined allegiance with it. . . . "My last song! my last song! and which will be of a man of the sea. . . ."

6

And the Sea came to us on the stone steps of the drama:

With her Princes, her Regents, her Messengers clothed in pomp and metal, her great Actors with their eyes gouged out and her Prophets on a chain, her women Magicians stamping with their wooden clogs, their mouths full of black clots, and her tributes of Virgins walking in the furrows of the hymn,

With her Shepherds, her Pirates and Nurses of childkings, her old Nomad Chiefs in exile and her elegiac Princesses, her tall silent Widows under their illustrious ashes, her great Usurpers of thrones and Founders of distant colonies, her Prebendaries and Merchants, her great Grantees of provinces rich in tin, and her great travelling Sages on the backs of rice-field buffaloes,

With all her lease of monsters and men, and all her increase of immortal fables, joining with her masses of slaves and helots her tall Bastards of the gods and her large daughters of stallions—a crowd in haste rising up on the tiers of History and all moving together toward the arena, in the first cool of evening with the smell of fucus,

Recital moving toward the Author and toward the painted mouth of his mask.

—o—

Thus the Sea came to us in her great age and in her great Hercynian folds—the whole sea with her sea facing, in one part and one flank!

And like a people reaching to us whose language is new, and like a language reaching to us whose sentence is new, carrying to its bronze tablets its highest commandments.

With great rising of humors and great tumors of language,

du langage, par grands reliefs d'images et versants d'ombres lumineuses, courant à ses splendeurs massives d'un très beau style périodique, et telle, en ses grands feux d'écailles et d'éclairs, qu'au sein des meutes héroïques,

La Mer mouvante et qui chemine au glissement de ses grands muscles errants, la Mer gluante au glissement de plèvre, et toute à son afflux de mer, s'en vint à nous sur ses anneaux de python noir,

Très grande chose en marche vers le soir et la transgression divine. . . .

—o—

Et ce fut au couchant, dans les premiers frissons du soir encombré de viscères, quand sur les temples frettés d'or et dans les Colisées de vieille fonte ébréchés de lumière, l'esprit sacré s'éveille aux nids d'effraies, parmi l'animation soudaine de l'ample flore pariétale.

Et comme nous courions à la promesse de nos songes, sur un très haut versant de terre rouge chargé d'offrandes et d'aumaille, et comme nous foulions la terre rouge du sacrifice, parée de pampres et d'épices, comme un front de bélier sous les crépines d'or et sous les ganses, nous avons vu monter au loin cette autre face de nos songes: la chose sainte à son étiage, la Mer, étrange, là, et qui veillait sa veille d'Etrangère—inconciliable, et singulière, et à jamais inappariée—la Mer errante prise au piège de son aberration.

Elevant l'anse de nos bras à l'appui de notre "Aââh . . . ," nous avons eu ce cri de l'homme à la limite de l'humain; nous avons eu, sur notre face, cette charge royale de l'offrande: toute la Mer fumante de nos voeux comme une cuve de fiel noir, comme un grand bac d'entrailles et d'abats aux cours pavées du Sacrificateur!

Nous avons eu, nous avons eu. . . . Ah! dites-le encore, était-ce bien ainsi? . . . Nous avons eu—et ce fut telle splendeur de fiels et de vins noirs!—la Mer plus haut que notre face, à hauteur de notre âme; et dans sa crudité sans nom à hauteur de notre âme, toute sa dépouille à vif sur le tambour du ciel, comme aux grands murs d'argile désertés,

with great reliefs of images and slopes of shining shadows, hastening to her massive splendors of a very handsome period style, and such, among her great flaming scales, as in the midst of heroic animal packs,

The moving Sea who progresses in the gliding of her great wandering muscles, the viscous Sea gliding as a pleura, and all in her affluence of sea, came up to us on her coils of a black python,

A very great thing moving toward the night and divine transgression. . . .

—o—

And it was at sunset, in the early cool of evening encumbered with viscera, when on the temples fretted with gold and in the Coliseums of old casting notched with light, the sacred spirit awakens in nests of screech owls, in the midst of the sudden coming to life of the rich wall flora.

And as we were running to the promise of our dreams, on a very high slope of red earth heavy with offerings and horned beasts, and as we were trampling the red earth of sacrifice, adorned with vinebranches and spices, like the brow of a ram under gold fringes and cords, we saw mounting in the distance that other face of our dreams: the holy thing at its water mark, the Sea, so strange over there keeping her Stranger's watch—irreconcilable and singular and forever unmatched—the wandering Sea caught in the trap of her aberration.

Raising the arch of our arms to sustain our "Aaah . . ." we gave that cry of a man at the human limit; we carried, on our head, that royal charge of an offering: all the Sea steaming with our wishes like a tank of black gall, like a great vat of entrails and viscera in the paved courtyards of the Sacrificer!

We had, we had. . . . Oh! say it again, was it really like that? . . . We had—and it was such splendor of gall and dark wines!—the Sea higher than our face, on a level with our soul; and in her nameless crudity on a level with our soul, all her raw skin on the drum of heaven, as on the great deserted walls of clay,

On four wooden stakes, stretched out, a buffalo skin on a cross!

Sur quatre pieux de bois, tendue! une peau de buffle mise en croix.

—o—

. . . Et de plus haut, et de plus haut déjà, n'avions-nous vu la Mer plus haute à notre escient,

Face lavée d'oubli dans l'effacement des signes, pierre affranchie pour nous de son relief et de son grain?—et de plus haut encore et de plus loin, la Mer plus haute et plus lointaine encore . . . inallusive et pure de tout chiffre, la tendre page lumineuse contre la nuit sans tain des choses? . . .

Ah! quel grand arbre de lumière prenait ici la source de son lait! . . . Nous n'avons pas été nourris de ce lait-là! Nous n'avons pas été nommés pour ce rang-là! Et filles de mortelles furent nos compagnes éphémères, menacées dans leur chair. . . . Rêve, ô rêve tout haut ton rêve d'homme et d'immortel! . . . "Ah! qu'un Scribe s'approche et je lui dicterai. . . ."

Nul Asiarque chargé d'un ordre de fêtes et de jeux eût-il jamais rêvé pareille rêverie d'espace et de loisir? Et qu'il y eût en nous un tel désir de vivre à cet accès, n'est-ce point là, ô dieux! ce qui nous qualifiait? . . . Ne vous refermez point, paupière, que vous n'ayez saisi l'instant d'une telle équité! "Ah! qu'un autre s'approche et je lui dicterai. . . ."

Le Ciel qui vire au bleu de mouette nous restitue déjà notre présence, et sur les golfes assaillis vont nos millions de lampes d'offrande, s'égarant—comme quand le cinabre est jeté dans la flamme pour exalter la vision.

—o—

Car tu nous reviendras, présence! au premier vent du soir,

Dans ta substance et dans ta chair et dans ton poids de mer, ô glaise! dans ta couleur de pierre d'étable et de dolmen, ô Mer! —parmi les hommes engendrés et leurs contrées de chênes rouvres, toi Mer de force et de labour, Mer au parfum d'entrailles femelles et de phosphore, dans les grands fouets claquants du rapt! Mer saisissable au feu des plus beaux actes de l'esprit! . . . (Quand les Barbares sont à la Cour pour un très bref séjour, l'union avec les filles de serfs rehausse-t-elle d'un si haut ton le tumulte du sang? . . .)

"Guide-moi, plaisir, sur les chemins de toute mer; au frémis-

. . . And from higher, and higher up, hadn't we seen the Sea higher in our intimacy,

Face of forgetfulness washed in the effacing of signs, stone emancipated for us from its relief and its grain?—and from still higher up and from farther off, the higher and more distant Sea . . . without allusion and pure of all number, the tender luminous page raised against the night of things without silvering? . . .

Oh! what great tree of light found here the source of its milk? We have not fed on that milk! We have not been nominated for that rank! Daughters of mortal women were our ephemeral companions, threatened in their flesh. . . . Dream, O dream out loud your dream of man and immortal! "Ah! let a Scribe come near and I will dictate to him."

Would no Asiarch, charged with an order for festivities and games, ever have dreamed such a dream of space and leisure? And that there were in us such a desire to live at that height, isn't that, O heavens, what gave us title to it? . . . Do not close again, eyelid, until you have seized the moment of such fairness! "Ah! let some one else come near and I will dictate to him. . . ."

The sky, turning to a sea-gull's blue, already is giving us back our presence, and over the assaulted bays, go our millions of votive lamps, losing their way—as when cinnabar is thrown into the fire to exalt man's vision.

For you will return to us, presence! with the first wing of evening,

In your substance and in your flesh and in your sea weight, O clay! in your color of stable stone and dolmen, O Sea!—among men begotten and their lands of oaktrees, you open again, Sea of power and furrows, Sea of smells of female entrails and phosphor, in the great snapping whips of abduction! Sea seizable in the fire of the noblest acts of the spirit! . . . (When the Barbarians are at Court for a very brief visit, does union with the daughters of serfs enhance the blood's wildness with so high a fever? . . .)

"Pleasure, guide me over the ways of the whole sea; at the

sement de toute brise où s'alerte l'instant, comme l'oiseau vêtu de son vêtement d'ailes. . . . Je vais, je vais un chemin d'ailes, où la tristesse elle-même n'est plus qu'aile. . . . Le beau pays natal est à reconquérir, le beau pays du Roi qu'il n'a revu depuis l'enfance, et sa défense est dans mon chant. Commande, ô fifre, l'action, et cette grâce encore d'un amour qui ne nous mette en mains que les glaives de joie! . . ."

Et vous, qu'êtes-vous donc, ô Sages? pour nous réprimander, ô Sages! Si la fortune de mer nourrit encore, en sa saison, un grand poème hors de raison, m'en refuserez-vous l'accès? Terre de ma seigneurie, et que j'y entre, moi! N'ayant nulle honte à mon plaisir. . . . "Ah! qu'un Scribe s'approche et je lui dicterai. . . ." Et qui donc, né de l'homme, se tiendrait sans offense aux côtés de ma joie?

—Ceux-là qui, de naissance, tiennent leur connaissance au-dessus du savoir.

trembling of each wind when the instant turns alert, like the bird clothed in the clothing of wings. . . . I go, I go down a road of wings where sadness itself is only a wing. The fine native land has to be reconquered, the beautiful land of the king he has not seen since childhood, and its defense is in my song. Fifer, command action, and again that grace of a love which will put in our hands only the swords of joy! . . ."

And who are you, then, O Sages, to reprove us, O Sages? If the sea fortune still provides, in its season, a great poem beyond reason, will you refuse to let me go to it? Land of my Seigniory, let me enter it, me! With no shame in my pleasure. . . . "Ah! let a Scribe come near, and I will dictate to him. . . ." And who, then, born of man, without offending, would stand by my joy?

—Those who, from birth, place their knowing above knowledge.

JEAN COCTEAU

THE LESSON OF EQUILIBRIUM which Cocteau refers to so constantly in *Le Rappel à l'Ordre* he learned at the Cirque Médrano with Picasso, Apollinaire and Max Jacob. It seemed first to be a lesson of simplicity in formal structure. But more than that, it appears now to have been a lesson of simplicity in a spiritual sense: the meaning of the creative process, the value of a work of art as contrasted with the value of man, the whole psychological and religious problem of "man the artist," which has become for our age the most tenacious of literary themes. The acrobats of Picasso epitomize the frailty of our age and the spiritual hope in something as yet unrealized. They represent both the period and its legend. They have lived through two wars telling us uninterruptedly that no war is ever ended. And the deep sea divers of Cocteau's poetry and his angels repeat on their white pages that this age is enacted in a dream, that both its order and its disorder spring from dilemmas.

Poetry Cocteau has called the secular mystery (*Le mystère laïc*), because the poet, like the alchemist and the astrologer, has his fetishes and his miraculous tricks. The ultimate mystery to be achieved by a poem is its self-sufficiency. Words lose their usual meanings and connotations by cutting themselves off from their native world, by severing all the bonds which hold them back. The poem finally exists alone, as a trick does, as a house of cards, without any of the usual props. Words of a poem bear the minimum of their daily alliances. This research in magic might also be called the search of preciosity where a word will exist in a new and unpredictable meaning.

Cocteau belongs natively not to Bohemian Montmartre or Montparnasse, but to the section of the Champs-Elysées. His Paris is the elegance of the Madeleine, or, in his wonder world, the flora and fauna of the deep ocean. His legend of scandal and surprise has been eagerly promulgated by the Paris public, but behind the legend is a man guided by his sense of proportion and purity and labor. His début was like the eruption of a ballet russe. He was ushered into the world of art as a brilliant fêted genius. His first real teacher was Picasso through whom avowedly he learned the low depths of his bad taste and the universe of beauty which up until his meeting with Picasso he had not known.

Cocteau's earliest poems were publicly read when he was sixteen years old by the celebrated actor, Edouard de Max. It was a dangerous triumph for so young a poet. As a result of a criticism of this poetry, written by Gide and Ghéon and published in *La Nouvelle Revue Française*, Cocteau repudiated his first three books and started afresh. His first important poetry was published after the war, in 1919, *Cap de bonne espérance*, dedicated to Roland Garros, an air-pilot friend. Garros, who had escaped from Germany, inspired Cocteau with a new sense of lyricism, comparable to the pilot's evasion from the earth. At the same time Cocteau published his first important critical tract, *Le Coq et L'Arlequin* (1918), in which he states his anti-Wagner position and his theory that the poet is an inhabited man, a man sheltering an angel whom he is constantly shocking. (*Nous abritons un ange que nous choquons sans cesse.*) A few years later, in *Le Secret Professionnel* (1922), he will define angelism as "disinterestedness, egoism, tender gaiety, cruelty, purity in debauchery." His poem of 1925, *L'Ange Heurtebise*, was written under the stimulation of this theory. An angel bearing the same name occurs in the play *Orphée* of 1927, and in the film, of the same title, of 1950.

Cocteau is a creator on many different levels. He is a creator of poems, novels, plays, movies, criticism, ballets, and it is impossible to speak of any one alone without reference to the others. They are all joined by the dominance of what he himself calls "poetry" in his work. He is constantly re-writing and re-working the myth of Orpheus, the poet's myth. In the film version, Death is a princess riding about in a Rolls-Royce. Heurtebise is her chauffeur and assistant. Cégeste is her doomed protégé. When Orpheus hears the radio signals in this auto, he divines in them the essence of poetic power. He writes out the radio's hieratic message, "L'oiseau chante avec ses doigts." This particular phrase had been sent to Cocteau by Apollinaire in 1917, as an emblem at the end of a poem. Cocteau uses it in his film of 1950 as the poet's secret message. In his poems, plays and films, Cocteau is unable to control Death and so he makes her into a familiar companion.

During the thirty-five years of his poet's career, Jean Cocteau has perfected a method which is very much his own and which he has explained in his critical writings and exemplified in his poems. It is a method of swiftness, hardness, economy. When once a poet realizes that he possesses the gift of poetry in himself, he must set about to dominate and submerge the gift. The first duty incumbent on the poet is to forget he is a poet and to allow the phenomenon to come into being without willing or forcing it. Cocteau was fortunate enough to have two exceptional guides: Raymond Radiguet at the age of 15, whom Cocteau used to call his "examiner," and Eric Satie at the age of 60, whom Cocteau called his "schoolmaster." In referring to the poets who preceded him, Cocteau used to say that they hid the object under poetry and that his role was to hide poetry under the object.

Jean Cocteau has become an enigmatical figure in our day, a sphinx whose influence is probably more far-reaching than is realized. In the *Entre-Deux*, the period between the two world wars, when the surrealists were studying their so-called "disorder" of the human spirit, and Gide and Claudel were continuing with their particular forms of humanism, Cocteau turned inwardly to that study of self which other men will call wearing a mask. He became one of the solitary men of his age, who had neither the faith of a Claudel nor the animation of a literary movement which guided Breton and Eluard. And yet Cocteau always maintained some faint allegiance to the two beliefs in order and disorder, to catholicism and to surrealism.

When the five years of the second war were ended, it became apparent that Cocteau had been adding steadily to his work which has now reached the proportions of one of the major works of the period. Since 1945, a collection of his poetry has appeared with the first major critical essay on Cocteau by Lannes, and a new poem, *La Crucifixion*. He has done two new ballets (*Le Jeune Homme et la Mort* and *Phèdre*), a new play (*L'Aigle à deux têtes*), six new films of which *Les Parents Terribles* (1948) and *Orphée* (1950) are perhaps the most remarkable, and a new book of personal criticism, *La Difficulté d'Etre* (1947), one of the most illuminating books he has yet produced, a summation of his wisdom and perceptive genius which may one day place Cocteau in the unpredicted category of French moralists.

A. POETRY

1919 *Le Cap de Bonne-Espérance.*
      L'Ode à Picasso.
1922 *Vocabulaire.*
1923 *Plain-Chant.*
1925 *L'Ange Heurtebise.*
1927 *Opéra.*
1946 *Crucifixion.*
1948 *Jean Cocteau: Poètes d'Aujourd'hui,* No. 4, Seghers.

B. CRITICISM

1918 *Le Coq et l'Arlequin.*
1920 *Carte Blanche.*
1922 *Le Secret Professionnel.*
1926 *Lettre à Jacques Maritain.*
1928 *Le Mystère Laïc.*
1932 *Essai de Critique Indirecte.*
1947 *La Difficulté d'Etre.*
1949 *Lettre aux Américains.*

on Cocteau

Fergusson, Francis, *The Idea of a Theatre,* Princeton Univ. Press.
Fowlie, Wallace, *Age of Surrealism,* Morrow.
Lannes, Roger, Intro. to *Poètes d'Aujourd'hui,* Seghers.
Mauriac, Claude, *Jean Cocteau ou la Vérité du Mensonge,* 1945.

Poetry is often represented by a langorous veiled lady, reclining on a cloud. This lady has a musical voice and speaks only lines.

Do you know the surprise of finding yourself suddenly facing your own name as if it belonged to someone else, seeing its form and hearing the sound of its syllables without the blind and deaf habit which a long intimacy provides?

The same phenomenon can take place for an object or an animal. In a flash we *see* a dog, a cab, a house *for the first time.* What is special, mad, ridiculous, beautiful in them is overwhelming. But immediately afterwards, habit rubs out this powerful image with its eraser. We pat the dog, hail the cab, inhabit the house. We don't see them any more.

That is the role of poetry. It unveils, in the full meaning of the term. It strips bare, under a light which shatters our indifference, the surprising things around us which our senses register automatically.

It is useless to look far afield for strange objects and sentiments, with which to startle the day dreamer. That is the method of the bad poet, and it gives exoticism.

He should be shown what his heart and his eyes touch on each day, but so viewed and with such speed that he see it and be moved by it for the first time.

That is the only kind of creation permitted a man.

For if it is true that the great number of eyes cover statues with patina,—commonplaces, those eternal masterpieces, are covered over with a thick patina which makes them invisible and hides their beauty.

Put a commonplace in place, clean it, rub it, light it so that it will give forth with its youth and freshness the same purity it had at the beginning, and you will be doing the work of a poet.

The rest is literature.

I have few words in my pen. I turn them over and over. The idea rushes ahead and when it stops and looks back, it sees me dragging along. It grows impatient and goes off. I can't find it again.

I leave the paper, take up something else, open my door. I'm free. That's easily said. The idea comes back at top speed and sets me to work.

Du travail et de la légende

. . . This natural inclination to live by the Gospels separates me from dogma. Joan of Arc is my great writer. No one expresses himself better than she, in form and substance. Doubtless if she had adopted a style, she would have lost her penetration. As she is, she is style itself and I never tire reading her trial. Antigone is my other saint. These two anarchists represent the seriousness I love, which Gide claims I don't have, a seriousness which belongs to me and which doesn't jibe with the kind usually meant. It is the seriousness of poets which Encyclopedists of all periods disdain.

De mon physique

The profound and atmospheric lightness of dreams favors meetings, surprises, knowledge and a naturalness which our folded world (I mean, a world on the surface of a fold) can only ascribe to the supernatural. I say "naturalness," because one of the characteristics of the dream is that nothing surprises us in it. With no regret, we agree to live in it with strangers, completely cut off from our habits and friends. That is what frightens us when we look at a face of someone we love and who is sleeping. Where is the figure moving to, who wears that mask? Where is it expending itself and with whom? The spectacle of sleep has always terrified me more than a dream. From it I made the stanzas of *Plain-Chant*.

After sleep the dream fades. It is a marine plant which dies out of water. It dies on my sheets. Its reign fascinates me. I admire its fables, and I profit from them by leading a double life. But I never use my dreams.

What they teach is the hard fact of our limitations. Since Nerval, Ducasse and Rimbaud, the study of their mechanism has often given the poet the means of conquering them, of adjusting our world with something else than common sense, of confusing the order of factors to which reason condemns us, and in a word, of making out of poetry a lighter, swifter, newer vehicle.

Du rêve

. . . A work is to such a degree the expression of our solitude that you can wonder what strange need for contacts urges the artist to release the work to the public.

The work of art with whose undertaking a man exposes himself heroically or with an extreme unawareness (another form of heroism) will take root in someone else by means of subterfuges comparable to those nature uses to perpetuate itself. Does the work of art practice an indispensable priestcraft, or hasn't man, by mimicry, submitted, in the long run, to the universal methods of creation?

De la beauté

To write is an act of love. If it is not, it is only scribbling. It means obeying the mechanism of plants and trees and projecting the sperm far off around us. The luxury of the world is in this waste. Some fecundates, some falls by the wayside. It is the same with sex. The center of pleasure is very vague although it is very strong. It invites the race to perpetuate itself, but that doesn't prevent its functioning blindly. . . .

Des moeurs

You take this book out of your pocket. You read, And if you succeed in reading it without anything distracting you from my words, gradually you will feel that I inhabit you and you will resuscitate me. You may even acquire surreptitiously one of my gestures, one of my glances. I am speaking now to the youth of a period when I won't exist in the flesh and when my blood will not be joined with my work.

De la responsabilité

1

J'ai, pour tromper du temps la mal-sonnante horloge,
　　Chanté de vingt façons.
Ainsi de l'habitude évitai-je l'éloge,
　　Et les nobles glaçons.

C'est peu que l'habitude une gloire couronne
　　Lorsqu'elle a vieux le chef;
Il faut qu'un long amour souvent le coeur étonne
　　A force d'être bref.

Alors, jeune toujours, libre de récompenses,
　　Et son livre à la main,
On devine les jeux, les manoeuvres, les danses,
　　Qui formeront demain.

Voilà pourquoi la mort également m'effraye,
　　Et me fait les yeux doux;
C'est qu'une grande voix murmure à mon oreille:
　　Pense à mon rendez-vous;

Laisse partir des gens, laisse fermer la porte,
　　Laisse perdre le vin,
Laisse mettre au sépulcre une dépouille morte;
　　Je suis ton nom divin.

2

Chaque fois que je m'amuse
Ou ne souffre pas par lui
Mon ange, espèce de muse,
Me replonge dans la nuit.

Chaque fois que je dégaîne,
Comme un bouquet de muguet,
Mon coeur fatigué de haine,
L'ange cruel fait le guet.

Cet ange, ce monstre informe,
Ne dort jamais un moment,

Plain Song

1

I have sung, to deceive the evil-sounding clock of time,
    In twenty ways.
And thus have I avoided the praise of habit
    And the noble coldness.

It is little if habit crowns a glory
    When its head is old;
A long love must often amaze the heart
    By being brief.

Then, always young, free of rewards
    And carrying some book,
You half see the games, the drills, the dances
    Which will form tomorrow.

That is why death terrifies me just as much,
    And makes eyes at me;
It's a great voice murmuring in my ear:
    Think of my rendez-vous;

Let the people go home, let the door close,
    Let the wine turn;
Let a dead body be placed in the tomb;
    I am your divine name.

2

Each time I play
Or do not suffer through him
My angel, a kind of muse,
Pushes me back into my night.

Each time I leave cover
Like a bunch of lilies of the valley,
My heart tired with hate,
The cruel angel sets up watch.

This angel, this formless monster,
Never sleeps a moment,

Et non plus il ne m'informe
De quoi je suis l'instrument.

3

Mon ange, vois, je te loue,
Après t'avoir oublié.
Par le bas je suis lié
A mes chaussures de boue.

Notre boue a des douceurs,
Notre humaine, tendre boue,
Mais tu me couches en joue,
Ange, soldat des neuf soeurs.

Tu sais quel est sur la carte
Mon mystérieux chemin,
Et dès que je m'en écarte,
Tu m'empoignes par la main.

Ange de glace, de menthe,
De neige, de feu, d'éther,
Lourd et léger comme l'air,
Ton gantelet me tourmente.

4

Je peux regarder le soleil en face,
    Ton oeil ne le peut.
Voilà bien mon tour, c'est la seule place
    Où je gagne au jeu.

Lorsque nous devrons aux enfers descendre,
    S'il est des enfers,
Nous n'habiterons le même scaphandre,
    Ni la même mer.

Tu sauras trouver d'autre compagnie
    Au séjour des morts.
Ah! comment guérir ta folle manie
    De quitter ton corps.

5

J'ai peine à soutenir le poids d'or des musées,
    Cet immense vaisseau.

And he doesn't tell me
Of what I am the instrument.

3
My angel, see, I praise you,
After forgetting you.
I am tied to the earth below
To my shoes of mud.

Our mud has tenderness,
Our human sweet mud,
But you aim at me,
Angel, soldier of the nine sisters.

You know what on the map
Is my road of mystery,
And when I lose my way,
You seize me by the hand.

Angel of ice, of mint,
Of snow and fire and ether,
Heavy and light as air,
Your glove torments me.

4
I can look squarely into the sun,
    But your eye cannot.
It is my turn now, it is the one place
    Where I win at gambling.

When we will have to go down to hell,
    If there is a hell,
We will not inhabit the same diving suit
    Nor the same sea.

You will be able to find someone else
    In the land of the dead.
But how can I cure your mad will
    To leave your body?

5
I have trouble in supporting the gold weight of museums.
    Such a large vessel!

Combien me parle plus que leurs bouches usées
    L'oeuvre de Picasso.

Là, j'ai vu les objets qui flottent dans nos chambres,
    Trop grands ou trop petits,
Enfin, comme l'amour mêle bouches et membres,
    Profondément bâtis!

Les muses ont tenu ce peintre dans leur ronde,
    Et dirigé sa main,
Pour qu'il puisse, au désordre adorable du monde,
    Imposer l'ordre humain.

6

Si ma façon de chant n'est pas ici la même,
    Hélas, je n'y peux rien.
Je suis toujours en mal d'attendre le poème,
    Et prends ce qui me vient.

Je ne connais, lecteur, la volonté des muses,
    Plus que celle de Dieu.
Je n'ai rien deviné de leurs profondes ruses,
    Dont me voici le lieu.

Je les laisse nouer et dénouer leurs danses,
    Ou les casser en moi,
Ne pouvant me livrer à d'autres imprudences
    Que de suivre leur loi.

7

Muses qui ne songez à plaire ou à déplaire,
Je sens que vous partez sans même dire adieu.
Voici votre matin et son coq de colère.
De votre rendez-vous je ne suis plus le lieu.

Je n'ose pas me plaindre, ô maîtresses ingrates;
Vous êtes sans oreille et je perdrais mon cri.
L'une à l'autre nouant la corde de vos nattes,
Vous partirez, laissant quelque chose d'écrit.

C'est ce que vous voulez. Allez, je me résigne,
Et si je dois mourir, reparaissez avant.

To me, more than their wasted mouths
    The work of Picasso speaks.

There I have seen objects moving in our rooms,
    Too big or too small,
Well, like love mingling lips and limbs
    Deeply built!

The muses kept that painter in their dance,
    And guided his hand,
So that he, on the lovable disorder of the world
    Might impose man's order.

6

If my manner of song is not the same here,
    I cannot be blamed, alas.
I am in the throes of waiting for the poem,
    And take what comes my way.

I do not know, reader, the will of the muses,
    Any more than the will of God.
I have discovered nothing in the obscure ruses
    They have made in me.

I let them form and unform their dances
    Or break them in me,
Since I can embark on no other boldness
    Save observing their law.

7

Muses who have no thought of pleasing or displeasing,
I feel you go without even saying goodby.
Here is your morning with its angry cock.
I am no longer the site of your meeting place.

I dare not complain, ungrateful mistresses;
You have no ears, my cry would be wasted.
As the cord of your hair joins you together,
You will go, leaving something in words.

That is your will. Go, I am resigned,
And if I should die, come back before that.

L'encre dont je me sers est le sang bleu d'un cygne,
Qui meurt quand il le faut pour être plus vivant.

Du sommeil hivernal, enchantement étrange,
Muses, je dormirai, fidèle à vos décrets.
Votre travail fini, c'est fini. J'entends l'ange
La porte refermer sur vos grands corps distraits.

Que me laissez-vous donc? Amour, tu me pardonnes,
Ce qui reste, c'est toi: l'agnelet du troupeau.
Viens vite, embrasse-moi, broute-moi ces couronnes,
Arrache ce laurier qui me coupe la peau.

L'Ange Heurtebise

II

L'ange Heurtebise, d'une brutalité
Incroyable, saute sur moi. De grâce
Ne saute pas si fort,
Garçon bestial, fleur de haute
Stature.
Je m'en suis alité. En voilà
Des façons. J'ai l'as; constate.
L'as-tu?

III

L'ange Heurtebise me pousse;
Et vous roi Jésus, miséricorde,
Me hissez, m'attirez jusqu'à l'angle
De vos genoux pointus;
Plaisir sans mélange. Pouce! dénoue
La corde, je meurs.

IV

L'ange Heurtebise et l'ange
Cégeste tué à la guerre—quel nom
Inouï—jouent
Le rôle des épouvantails
Dont le geste *non* effraye

The ink I use is the blue blood of a swan
Who dies when he must to be more alive.

With the winter sleep, strange bewitchment,
I shall sleep, Muses, faithful to your decrees.
Your work over, all is over. I hear the angel
Close the door behind your large distracted bodies.

What do you leave me then? Pardon me, Love,
What remains is you, the lamb of the flock.
Here quickly! Your kiss! and graze in these crowns of mine,
Pull off this laurel which cuts into my skin.

Angel Heurtebise

II
Angel Heurtebise, with unbelievable
Brutality, falls on me. For pity sake,
Don't fall so hard,
Strong fellow, flower of high
Stature.
I'm in bed because of it. What
Manners are these? I hold the ace, see for yourself.
Do you have it?

III
Angel Heurtebise shoves me;
And you, Lord Jesus, mercy,
Hoist me, pull me into the angle
Of your pointed knees;
Pleasure without defect. Thumb! untie
The rope, I die.

IV
Angel Heurtebise and angel
Cégeste killed in war—what an unusual
Name—play
The role of scarecrows
Whose gesture *no* frightens

Les cerises du cerisier céleste,
Sous le vantail de l'église
Habituée au geste *oui*.

VI

Ange Heurtebise, en robe d'eau,
Mon ange aimé, la grâce
Me fait mal. J'ai mal
A Dieu, il me torture.
En moi le démon est tortue, animal
Jadis mélodieux. Arrive,
Sors de l'agate
Dure fumée, ô vitesse qui tue;
Sur tes patins de diamant raye
Le miroir des malades.
Les murs
Les murs
Ont des oreilles
Et les miroirs
Des yeux d'amant.

VIII

L'ange Heurtebise, aux pieds d'animal
Bleu de ciel, est venu. Je suis seul
Tout nu sans Eve, sans moustaches,
Sans carte.
Les abeilles de Salomon
S'écartent, car je mange très mal mon miel
De thym amer, mon miel des Andes.
En bas, la mer ce matin recopie
Cent fois le verbe aimer. Des anges d'ouate,
Les indécents, les sales,
Sur l'herbe traient les pis des grandes
Vaches géographiques.

XII

La mort de l'ange Heurtebise
Fut la mort de l'ange, la mort
Heurtebise fut une mort d'ange,

The cherries of the heavenly cherry-tree,
Under the door of the church
Accustomed to the gesture *yes*.

VI

Angel Heurtebise, in a robe of water,
Beloved angel, grace
Hurts me. God
Hurts me, he tortures me.
In me the demon is a tortoise, animal
Once melodious. Come,
Leave the agate
Hard smoke, O speed that kills;
On your diamond skates, scratch
The mirror of the sick.
The walls
The walls
Have ears
And mirrors
Eyes of a lover.

VIII

Angel Heurtebise, with feet of a heaven-blue
Animal, came. I am alone
All naked without Eve, without moustache,
Without a card.
The bees of Solomon
Withdraw because I eat badly my honey
Of bitter thyme, my honey of the Andes.
Down below, the sea this morning copies out
A hundred times the verb love. Angels of cotton-wool,
Indecent and dirty,
On the grass milk the udders of big
Geographical cows.

XII

The death of angel Heurtebise
Was the death of the angel, death
Heurtebise was a death of an angel,

Une mort d'ange Heurtebise,
Un mystère du change, un as
Qui manque au jeu, un crime
Que le pampre enlace, un cep
De lune, un chant de cygne qui mord.
Un autre ange le remplace dont je
ne savais pas le nom hier;
En dernière heure: Cégeste.

PROCES-VERBAL

Dans la nuit du . . . Quai . . . Les Anges:
Heurtebise, Elzévir, Dimanche, Cégeste,
Après avoir . . . ont . . . du sexe féminin . . .
Il paraîtrait . . . malgré l'heure . . .
Elles virent . . . lumière diffuse . . . l'âne . . .
Fit mine de . . . une aile . . . par le manche
En fer . . . sur la bouche . . . l'atrocité
Du geste.

Menés au poste, ils refusèrent
De s'expliquer; bien entendu.

La Crucifixion

17
Un accident est si vite
arrivé. L'autre
épouvantail trop attentif
à sa métamorphose en branches
d'arbre en noeuds d'arbre en os
d'arbre toute une écorce
de peau de pin tordu qui saigne
et craque enfermé dans un rêve presque
mythologique effrayait
les anges criant: *Vite! Vite!*
Il n'y a pas une minute

A death of angel Heurtebise,
A mystery of exchange, an ace
Missing from the pack, a crime
Which the vinebranch entwines, a moon
Vineplant, a song of a biting swan.
Another angel replaces him whose name
I didn't know yesterday;
The last to be posted: Cégeste.

OFFICIAL REPORT

The night of . . . Quai . . . Angels
Heurtebise, Elzévir, Dimanche, Cégeste,
After . . . have . . . of female sex . . .
It would seem . . . despite the hour . . .
They saw . . . diffused light . . . the ass . . .
Pretended to . . . a wing . . . by the sleeve
Of iron . . . on the mouth . . . the atrocity
Of the gesture.

Taken to the station, they refused
To explain; naturally.

The Crucifixion

17
An accident happens
so fast. The other
scarecrow too attentive
to its metamorphosis into branches
of a tree into knots of trees into bones
of a tree a whole bark
of skin of a twisted pine which bleeds
and cracks closed within a dream almost
mythological terrified
the angels crying: *Quick! Quick!*
There's not a minute

à perdre. Ces naïfs
tournoyant autour
criant à tue-tête et perdant des plumes
qui l'aveuglaient et se
collaient à ses blessures.

18

Sérénissime. L'écusson
des meurtres.
Les animaux
agenouillés qui pleurent. Les clefs au nombre
de sept. La roue
triangulaire des miracles.
La main
qui n'en est pas une. L'oeil
qui n'en est pas un.
L'écoeurement mortel
du rêve. La simple
difficulté d'être. La bohémienne
endormie. La tour
du jeu d'échecs. Son fou
libre.

19

Sur un pupitre noir d'école
où elle élève
ses hannetons la mort
mord ses ongles mord son porte-plume
lèche le scarabée d'or de l'encre
violette mord règle et réglisse
rature tire des lignes
mord le papier buvard pie
tire des lignes tire la langue
louche lèche le scarabée
sous les yeux de l'abbé quelle audace!
Mais comment ne voit-il
pas qu'elle
copie.

to lose. Those innocent fellows
circling around
crying at the top of their lungs and losing feathers
which blinded him and
stuck fast to his wounds.

18

Most Serene. The escutcheon
of murders.
Animals
kneeling and in tears. Keys to the number
of seven. The triangular
wheel of miracles.
The hand
which is not one. The eye
which is not one.
The mortal nausea
of the dream. The simple
difficulty of being. The bohemian girl
asleep. The castle
of the chess game. Its free
bishop.

19

On a black school desk
where she raises
her June bugs death
bites her nails bites her penholder
licks the gold beetle of the purple
ink bites rule and licorice
crosses out draws lines
bites the piebald blotter
draws lines sticks out her tongue
squints licks the beetle
under the eyes of the priest what boldness!
But why doesn't he see
that she's copying.

20

Tout l'organisme stupéfait expulse
à l'extérieur son liquide
pour fuir les chemins boueux
devenus impraticables.
Cela commence
sous les bras fait des détours
se perd se regroupe et forme un réseau
fluvial d'anatomie.
La débacle venait des clous rouillés broyant
les mécanisme très fragiles d'une usine
habituée à travailler la nuit sans lumières.
C'est pourquoi tout le dedans
fuyait dehors
cherchant quelque issue.
Cette eau d'angoisse accrochait à l'angle
des corniches un peu vivantes
ses gouttes folles de peur qui sautent
désespérément dans le vide.

21

Ce qui ne peut se dire (et cependant
que ne puis-je dire avec
ma façon de forcer les mots
à se taire) ce qui ne peut
se dire c'est le miel
des abeilles de l'agonie. Il
coule de la ruche il ligote
d'une infecte résille vertigineuse
des profils perdus à la base
d'une caducée. On devine
fait de quoi.

22

Et voici qu'un profil
de face à la renverse relié au cep
des jambes par
une draperie d'un bleu pareil au rouge

20

The entire stupefied organism expels
outside its liquid
to avoid the muddy roads
becoming impassable.
It begins under the arms makes detours
loses its way regroups itself and forms a river
net of anatomy.
The rout came from rusty nails crushing
the very delicate mechanisms of a factory
accustomed to working at night without lights.
That is why the whole inside
rushed out
looking for some exit.
That water of anguish hooked on to the angle
of the still living cornices
its drops mad with fear which leap
into the void with desperation.

21

What cannot be said (and yet
what can't I say with
my way of forcing words
to be silent) what can't
be said is the honey
of the bees of the agony. It
flows from the hive it binds
with a filthy vertiginous net
the lost profiles at the foot
of a caduceus. You guess
what it's made of.

22

And here, a profile
of a face thrown backwards linked to the vinestock
of the legs by
a cloth of a blue similar to the red

porte
en équilibre sur le front une colonne
de sel. Et cette autre face
de profil informe à cause
de la loupe des larmes
colle sa joue contre la résine
épouvantable.

23
Un tonnerre de chars à bancs enrubannés
un tonnere de grappes d'acacia un
tonnere de lits de noces
qu'on traîne à l'étage au-dessus
un tonnerre de barricades
un tonnerre de canonnade
un tonnerre de gens criant: *Par là!*
Par là! Un tonnerre
d'immeubles pavoisés acclame
au ciel un jet
de sang devenu vin. L'ange Cégeste
sonna de la trompette. Et l'ombre
de l'objet se redressant devint
l'objet.

24
Cela déchira d'est en ouest
l'étoffe du silence. On entendit
le silence crier de telle
sorte que ce fut insupportable
aux oreilles du coeur. Une
gerbe d'encre à coup sûr
pleine de chefs-d'oeuvre
éclaboussant un vol noir
de papiers compromettants brûlés en hâte.
Tandis qu'une pluie torrentielle
de baïonnettes
achevait sauvagement les victimes.

bears
evenly balanced on the brow a pillar
of salt. And that other face
in profile shapeless because
of the wen of tears
glues its cheek against the terrible
resine.

23

A thunder of bedecked wagons with benches
a thunder of clusters of acacia a
thunder of marriage beds
dragged to the floor above
a thunder of barricades
a thunder of cannonade
a thunder of men crying: *Over here!*
Over here! A thunder
of houses decked with flags acclaims
to heaven a spurt
of blood turned wine. Angel Cégeste
blew the trumpet. And the shadow
of the object rising up became
the object.

24

It tore from east to west
the cloth of silence. You heard
silence cry out in such
a way that it was unbearable
to the ears of the heart. A
spray of ink most certainly
full of masterpieces
splashing a black flight
of compromising papers burned in haste.
While a torrential rain
of bayonets
savagely finished off the victims.

25

A genoux à droite
et à gauche. Seul hélas
de mon espèce (il n'y a pas de quoi
être fier) sous une cotte
de maille faite en chiffres sous
une armure de vacarme
seul à genoux à gauche
à droite—la neige aux mains d'aveugle
mettant la nappe—je ferme
à genoux seul de mon espèce
hélas dans cette chambre où le crime
eut lieu la bouche
jaune de ma savante
blessure capable
de prononcer quelques mots.

25

On my knees to the right
and to the left. Alone alas
of my species (no reason
to be proud) under a coat
of mail made in figures under
an armor of noise
alone on my knees on the left
on the right—the snow with hands of a blind woman
putting on the table cloth—I close
on my knees alone of my species
alas in this room whose crime
took place the yellow
mouth of my learned
wound capable
of saying a few words.

ANDRE BRETON

SURREALISM WAS FOUNDED in the years which immediately followed World War I, when the young intellectuals, returning from the front, discovered in the older thinkers and artists an inadequacy and an unrelatedness to their own thought and state of mind. Those who like Breton were to become surrealists turned against Barrès, Claudel, and even Bergson, to some degree. The death of Apollinaire, at the precise moment of the Armistice, had upset them. His had been the intellectual adventure they had followed the most confidently and joyously, as they had literally followed the large figure of the man in his pale blue uniform of first lieutenant to the Café de Flore on the Boulevard St.-Germain during the war years. They were tired and disgusted with the literary eloquence and verboseness of the 20th century. Their age had become a verbal nightmare for them. The radio, with its perpetual flow of words, was converting the world into a delirious cacophony. The language of man was being prostituted and degraded as it had never been before.

In his first manifesto of 1924, André Breton emphasized the meaning of the word *liberty* as being the basis for surrealism (*le seul mot de liberté est tout ce qui m'exalte encore*). Liberty for the artist means first a liberation from the rules of art. The artist expresses his liberty iconoclastically. In poetry, the leading examples would be Lautréamont, Rimbaud, Mallarmé in his final poem, *Un coup de dés*, Apollinaire—especially in his "poèmes-conversations" of *Calligrammes*. In painting, the examples would be Van Gogh, Seurat, Rousseau, Matisse, Picasso, Duchamp. These lists vary from year to year with Breton. His life is a series of fervent friendships and violent denunciations of former friends.

The few dates in Breton's biography which might be recalled here mark not only the stages of evolution of surrealism but designate some of the important artistic and intellectual efforts of the past three decades. His early medical studies during the war led Breton to the reading of Siegmund Freud, whom he was to meet later in Vienna, in 1921. His first poems, *Mont de Piété*, were published in 1919, the year he founded the magazine, *Littérature*, with Philippe Soupault and Louis Aragon. A text published in this magazine, *Les Champs Magnétiques*, written by Soupault and Breton, is usually considered the first authentic surrealist writing. "Dada" as a movement preceded surrealism, and Breton took part in Dadaism between 1919 and 1920. The first Manifesto of Surrealism was published by Breton in 1924, in which he defined the purpose of psychic automatism as the effort to express the real functioning of thought, the dictation of thought in the absence of any control practiced by reason, outside of any moral or aesthetic preoccupation. The second manifesto, equally important, appeared in 1930. In it Breton analyzed especially the philosophical implication of surrealism.

Two years later the magazine *Minotaure* was founded, with

which Breton was closely associated. In 1935 Breton broke off relations with the Communist Party. The International Exposition of Surrealism was held in Paris in 1938, after which Breton went to Mexico where he met Diego Rivera and Leon Trotsky. He came to New York in 1941 where he founded the magazine VVV in collaboration with Marcel Duchamp, Max Ernst and David Hare. In 1942 he gave at Yale University an important lecture on "Situation du surréalisme entre les deux guerres." Before leaving America, he published *Arcane 17*. On his return to Paris, he organized a new International Exposition of Surrealism in 1947. Two years later he was member of the committee in Paris interested in the American Garry Davis. He was among the first to sense forgery in the publication of Rimbaud's *Chasse Spirituelle* and published his accusation in *Flagrant Délit*.

If the realist is concerned with establishing contact between a man and his life (the physical objects and forces which touch his life), the surrealist is concerned with establishing the contact between a poet and his destiny (the physical objects and the supernatural forces which form his destiny.) This latter, the coming together of an artist and his destiny is always the mark of a great work of art. One has to break with the things that are, in order to unite with the things that may be. Breton, in his first manifesto defined man as that "definitive dreamer" (*l'homme ce rêveur définitif*). Poetry, if there is to be poetry, has to be conquered in the midst of great danger. It is comparable to the chance meeting of a man and woman on a Paris sidewalk, comparable to the danger for the man in the mystery and the unknowable in the woman's past. This is the subject matter of *Nadja*, in which Breton reaches a philosophical and even a mystical attitude. Poetry is the domain of the marvellous (*le merveilleux*) which becomes so familiar that it becomes real. The surrealists refrain from analyzing this experience of the marvellous in order to safeguard and preserve the power of the imagination, and thereby belong to the tradition of the visionaries (of the voyants) who see without explaining.

The example and the writings of André Breton have had an unusually profound effect on those who followed him. They were made over by him, converted to a new life, reinvigorated by the ideas which had first changed him. Those outside of surrealism, the non-believers and the opponents, easily forget both the extent of the transformation of the world and of man it claims, and the subtle power of dialectitian possessed by its leader. The final objective of surrealism Breton has defined in his book, *Les Vases Communicants*, as "the knowledge of the eternal destiny of man, of man in general, whom alone the Revolution will return to this destiny." His disciples have often claimed that from him they derived the best reasons they could find for living. Breton has constantly intervened in the gravest problems of his age and has often commented on them with the authority of a leader.

The power of critic and spokesman which Breton has exercised for many years has falsely obscured his role of poet. In his case especially it is impossible to dissociate the poet from the prose writer. Throughout all of his writing he remains the artist fanatically bent upon dissolving the age-long divorce between action and dream which has characterized Western art and thought. To terminate this dualism was perhaps the basic hope of surrealism. More than any other single artist, Breton has striven to unite the natural with the supernatural, or to reach that epoch in civilization when surreality will be contained within what is commonly called reality.

Selected Bibliography of Breton

1924 *Manifeste du Surréalisme*, Kra.
1928 *Nadja*, Gallimard.
1930 *Second Manifeste du Surréalisme*, Kra.
1932 *Les Vases Communicants*, Ed. des Cahiers Libres.
1945 *Arcane 17*, Brentano's, New York.
1948 *Poèmes: 1919-1948*, Gallimard.
1950 *André Breton: Poètes d'Aujourd'hui*, No. 18, Seghers.

on Breton

Bédouin, Jean-Louis, intro. in *Poètes d'Aujourd'hui*.
Eigeldinger, Marc, *André Breton: essais et témoignages*, A la Baconnière, Neuchatel, 1949.
Fowlie, Wallace, *Age of Surrealism*, 1950.
Gracq, Julien, *André Breton*, 1948.

In the noise of walls collapsing, in the songs of jubilation mounting from cities already rebuilt, at the top of the torrent which shouts the perpetual return of forms ceaselessly taken by change, on the beating wing of affections, of passions alternately raising and lowering men and things, above straw fires in which civilizations are shrivelled up, beyond the confusion of languages and customs, I see man, and what remains of him forever immobile in the center of the whirlwind. Detached from the contingencies of time and place, he appears really as the pivot of this very whirlwind, as the supreme mediator. And how would I reconcile myself to him if I didn't restore him essentially to that fundamental faculty which is sleep, namely sinking each time it is necessary into the depths of that superabundantly peopled night in which all, men and objects, are himself, participate by force in his eternal being, falling with the stone, flying with the bird? I see in the center of the public square that motionless man in whom, far from annihilating themselves, are combined and marvellously limited the adverse wills of all things for the sole glory of life, of that man who is, I repeat, near and who is all men. However theoretically separated I want him to be from the social mêlés, withdrawn from the sting of a limitless ambition and always unworthy, I am sure that the entire world is being recomposed, in its essential principle, with him as its center. Let him free himself then, and to begin with, let him undo, if need be, the other man, the one in whom all interiority is forbidden, the hurried traveller in the fog! This fog is. Contrary to current view, it is made of the thickness of things immediately sensible when I open my eyes. These things I love. Why shouldn't I hate them also for hiding derisively from me all the other things? It has seemed to me and it still seems to me, that by closely examining the contents of the most irresponsible activity of the mind, if you go beyond the extraordinary and only slightly reassuring foment on the surface, it is possible to reveal a capillary tissue in ignorance of which you would strive in vain to imagine the mental circuits. The purpose of this tissue is to assure the constant exchange which should take place in thought between the outer and the inner worlds, an exchange necessitating the continuous inter-penetration of conscious activity and sleep activity. My whole ambition has been to give here a picture of its structure. What-ever be the common pretention to full consciousness and the slight necessary delirium, it cannot be denied that this tissue covers a vast region. Therein takes place for man the perma-nent exchange of his satisfied and dissatisfied needs, therein his spiritual thirst is exalted which from birth to death it is indis-pensable that he placate and not cure.

From *Devant le Rideau* (1947)

We intend to leave to the specialists of the occult the respon-sibility of deciding whether a certain number of poetic works, those on which attention today has been concentrated, were conceived in close relationship with what the adepts consider "the first religious, moral and political doctrine of humanity," or whether they derived in a more or less conscious manner, or whether they tend—intuitively—to recreate this doctrine by other means. It is for these specialists to establish whether works like *Théorie des quatre mouvements*, *Les Chimères*, *Les Chants de Maldoror*, *La Science de Dieu* of Brisset, *La Dragonne* of Jarry proceed from traditional esoteric knowledge or whether they endow the spirit with new keys, invest it with a new power of comprehension and action. "I am an end or a beginning," said Kafka. Such a judgment, which will entail a whole series of contradictory references, is certainly not ready to be pro-nounced. For a long time critics will discuss the more or less figurative meaning which Rimbaud (nourished—this can not be exaggerated—on occult readings) wished attributed to the words "Alchemy of the word," and they will wonder whether the secret of the impassioned interest aroused in the midst of sur-realism by the "puns" of Marcel Duchamp, of Robert Desnos, the discovery of the entire work of Jean-Pierre Brisset and the last book of Raymond Roussel, *Comment j'ai écrit certains de mes livres* does not derive from the remarkable fortune we have seen today enhance the activity called "phonetic Kabbala." "It is traditionally Kabalistic," writes Ambelain, "to insist that in the 'world of sounds' two words or two sounds whose resonance is alike (and not merely assonance) have in the 'world of images' an unquestionable closeness."

This is not the place to speak of the difficult question of whether the "absence of a myth" is another myth and should be considered today's myth. Despite rationalistic protests, everything transpires today as if the relatively new poetic and plastic works exercise over the minds of men a power far exceeding the power of a work of art. These works, for those who consider them when young, and it is noteworthy that their numbers are constantly growing, determine a devoted movement and provoke such a total offering of self that everything which previously had conditioned these people is now questioned. "He spoke to friends about revelations, trials ended." It is as if these words were marked with the seal of revelation. And the fact that they give opportunity to interpretations always increasing in number like the wake of a stone thrown into a bottomless pool, substantiates this conviction. The *leavening* character of these works, as well as their questions, the always ardent solicitation they call up, the resistance they oppose to the means of understanding which human reason confers in its present state —and which would order it alone to "redo" this reason, at the same time as the extreme ease, pre-ecstatic ease, with which it overcomes us—take, for example, *Dévotion* of Rimbaud—are reasons to credit the idea of a myth beginning in them, which we have only to define and coordinate. . . .

Ma Femme à la Chevelure de Feu de Bois

Ma femme à la chevelure de feu de bois
Aux pensées d'éclairs de chaleur
A la taille de sablier
Ma femme à la taille de loutre entre les dents du tigre
Ma femme à la bouche de cocarde et de bouquet d'étoiles de
    dernière grandeur
Aux dents d'empreintes de souris blanche sur la terre blanche
A la langue d'ambre et de verre frottés
Ma femme à la langue d'hostie poignardée
A la langue de poupée qui ouvre et ferme les yeux
A la langue de pierre incroyable
Ma femme aux cils de bâtons d'écriture d'enfant
Aux sourcils de bord de nid d'hirondelle
Ma femme aux tempes d'ardoise de toit de serre
Et de buée aux vitres
Ma femme aux épaules de champagne
Et de fontaine à têtes de dauphins sous la glace
Ma femme aux poignets d'allumettes
Ma femme aux doigts de hasard et d'as de coeur
Aux doigts de foin coupé
Ma femme aux aisselles de martre et de fênes
De nuit de la Saint-Jean
De troène et de nid de scalares
Aux bras d'écume de mer et d'écluse
Et de mélange du blé et du moulin
Ma femme aux jambes de fusée
Aux mouvements d'horlogerie et de désespoir
Ma femme aux mollets de moelle de sureau
Ma femme aux pieds d'initiales
Aux pieds de trousseaux de clés aux pieds de calfats qui boivent
Ma femme au cou d'orge imperlé
Ma femme à la gorge de Val d'or
De rendez-vous dans le lit même du torrent
Aux seins de nuit
Ma femme aux seins de taupinière marine
Ma femme aux seins de creuset du rubis

My wife with her wood-fire hair
With her thoughts of heatsparks
With her shape of an hour-glass
My wife with her shape of an otter between the tiger's teeth
My wife with her cockade mouth and bouquet of stars of the
    last greatness
With her teeth of imprints of a white mouse on the white earth
With her tongue of rubbed amber and glass
My wife with her tongue of a pierced host
With the tongue of a doll opening and closing its eyes
With the tongue of an unbelievable stone
My wife with lashes of a child's writing stick
With eyebrows like the edge of a swallow's nest
My wife with temples of slate of a garden roof
And with moisture on the panes
My wife with champagne shoulders
And of a fountain with heads of dolphins under the ice
My wife with her match wrists
My wife with her fingers of chance and the ace of hearts
With her fingers of cut hay
My wife with armpits of marten and beechnut
Of Saint-John's night
Of privet and eventletrap's nest
With arms of sea and mill-dam foam
And with mixture of wheat and mill
My wife with her rocket legs
With movements of clockwork and despair
My wife with her calves of elder-tree marrow
My wife with her feet of initials
With her feet of bunches of keys with feet of caulkers who drink
My wife with her pearled neck of barley
My wife with her throat of golden Valley
Of the rendez-vous in the very bed of the torrent
With its night breasts
My wife with her breasts of a marine molehill
My wife with her breasts of a ruby crucible

Aux seins de spectre de la rose sous la rosée
Ma femme au ventre de dépliement d'éventail des jours
Au ventre de griffe géante
Ma femme au dos d'oiseau qui fuit vertical
Au dos de vif-argent
Au dos de lumière
A la nuque de pierre roulée et de craie mouillée
Et de chute d'un verre dans lequel on vient de boire
Ma femme aux hanches de nacelle
Aux hanches de lustre et de pennes de flèche
Et de tiges de plumes de paon blanc
De balance insensible
Ma femme aux fesses de grès et d'amiante
Ma femme aux fesses de dos de cygne
Ma femme aux fesses de printemps
Au sexe de glaïeul
Ma femme au sexe de placer et d'ornithorynque
Ma femme au sexe d'algue et de bonbons anciens
Ma femme au sexe de miroir
Ma femme aux yeux pleins de larmes
Aux yeux de panoplie violette et d'aiguille aimantée
Ma femme aux yeux de savane
Ma femme aux yeux d'eau pour boire en prison
Ma femme aux yeux de bois toujours sous la hache
Aux yeux de niveau d'eau de niveau d'air de terre et de feu

Hôtel des Etincelles

Le papillon philosophique
Se pose sur l'étoile rose
Et cela fait une fenêtre de l'enfer
L'homme masqué est toujours debout devant la femme nue
Dont les cheveux glissent comme au matin la lumière sur un
        réverbère qu'on a oublié d'éteindre
Les meubles savants entraînent la pièce qui jongle
Avec ses rosaces
Ses rayons de soleil circulaires
Ses moulages de verre

With her breasts of a rose spectre under the dew
My wife with her stomach like the unfolding of a day fan
With her stomach of a giant tendril
My wife with a bird's back in vertical flight
With her back of quick-silver
With her back of light
With her nape of rolled stone and wet chalk
And of a glass's fall from which you have just drunk
My wife with hips of a small boat
With hips of lustre and arrow feathers
And with stalks of white peacock plumes
Of insensible balance
My wife with buttocks of sandstone and amianthus
My wife with buttocks of a swan's back
My wife with springtime buttocks
With a gladiolus sex
My wife with her placer sex and duckbill
My wife with her sex of seaweed and old candy
My wife with her mirror sex
My wife with her eyes full of tears
With her eyes of violet panoply and magnetic needle
My wife with her savanna eyes
My wife with water eyes to drink in prison
My wife with wood eyes always under the axe
With eyes on the level of water on the level of air of earth and
        of fire

Hotel of Sparks

The philosophic butterfly
Rests on the rose star
And that makes a window of hell
The masked man is always standing in front of the nude woman
Whose hair glides as light does in the morning on a street lamp
        they have forgotten to put out
The learned furniture stimulates the room which juggles
With its rose windows

A l'intérieur desquels bleuit un ciel au compas
En souvenir de la poitrine inimitable
Maintenant le nuage d'un jardin passe par-dessus la tête de
    l'homme qui vient de s'asseoir
Il coupe en deux la femme au buste de magie aux yeux de Parme
C'est l'heure où l'ours boréal au grand air d'intelligence
S'étire et compte un jour
De l'autre côté la pluie se cabre sur les boulevards d'une grande
    ville
La pluie dans le brouillard avec des traînées de soleil sur des
    fleurs rouges
La pluie et le diabolo des temps anciens
Les jambes sous le nuage fruitier font le tour de la serre
On n'aperçoit plus qu'une main très blanche le pouls est figuré
    par deux minuscules ailes
Le balancier de l'absence oscille entre les quatre murs
Fendant les têtes
D'où s'échappent des bandes de rois qui se font aussitôt la guerre
Jusqu'à ce que l'éclipse orientale
Turquoise au fond des tasses
Découvre le lit équilatéral aux draps couleur de ces fleurs dites
    boules de neige
Les guéridons charmants les rideaux lacérés
A portée d'un petit livre griffé de ces mots *Pas de lendemain*
Dont l'auteur porte un nom bizarre
Dans l'obscure signalisation terrestre

                 Le Revolver à Cheveux Blancs

Rideau Rideau

Les théâtres vagabonds des saisons qui auront joué ma vie
Sous mes sifflets
L'avant-scène avait été aménagée en cachot d'où je pouvais
    siffler
Les mains aux barreaux je voyais sur fond de verdure noire
L'héroïne nue jusqu'à la ceinture
Qui se suicidait au début du premier acte

Its circular rays of sun
The glass mouldings
Inside which a sky turns blue by rule
In memory of the inimitable breast
Now the cloud of a garden passes over the head of the man who
    has just sat down
It cuts in two the woman with the magic bust with eyes of
    Parma
It's the time when the boreal bear with his imposing air of
    intelligence,
Stretches and counts a day
On the other side the rain rears up on the boulevards of a big
    city
The rain in the fog with trails of sunlight on red flowers
The rain and the devil of ancient times
Legs under the fruit cloud walked around the conservatory
You can see only a very white hand the pulse is indicated by
    two tiny wings
The pendulum of absence swings between the four walls
Splitting open the heads
Whence escape bands of kings who immediately wage war on
    one another
Until the eastern turquoise
Eclipse in the bottom of the cups
Reveals the equilateral bed with sheets of the color of those
    flowers you call snow balls
The charming pedestal tables the torn curtains
Beside a small book written over with the words *No tomorrow*
Whose author bears a strange name
In the dark signalling of the earth

Curtain Curtain

The wandering theatres of the seasons which have played my
    life
Under my catcalls
Down stage had been arranged in a cell from where I could hiss
My hands on the bars I saw on a background of dark green

La pièce se poursuivait inexplicablement dans le lustre
La scène se couvrant peu à peu de brouillard
Et je criais parfois
Je brisais la cruche qu'on m'avait donnée et de laquelle s'échap-
    paient des papillons
Qui montaient follement vers le lustre
Sous prétexte d'intermède encore de ballet qu'on tenait à me
    donner de mes pensées
J'essayais alors de m'ouvrir le poignet avec les morceaux de terre
    brune
Mais c'étaient des pays dans lesquels je m'étais perdu
Impossible de retrouver le fil de ces voyages
J'étais séparé de tout par le pain du soleil
Un personnage circulait dans la salle seul personnage agile
Qui s'était fait un masque de mes traits
Il prenait odieusement parti pour l'ingénue et pour le traître
Le bruit courait que c'était arrangé comme mai juin juillet août
Soudain la caverne se faisait plus profonde
Dans les couloirs interminables des bouquets tenus à hauteur
    de main
Erraient seuls c'est à peine si j'osais entr'ouvrir ma porte
Trop de liberté m'était accordée à la fois
Liberté de m'enfuir en traîneau de mon lit
Liberté de faire revivre les êtres qui me manquent
Les chaises d'aluminium se resserraient autour d'un kiosque de
    glaces
Sur lequel se levait un rideau de rosée frangé de sang devenu vert
Liberté de chasser devant moi les apparences réelles
Le sous-sol était merveilleux sur un mur blanc apparaissait en
    pointillé de feu ma silhouette percée au coeur d'une balle

Vigilance

A Paris la tour Saint-Jacques chancelante
Pareille à un tournesol
Du front vient quelquefois heurter la Seine et son ombre glisse
    imperceptiblement parmi les remorqueurs

The heroine nude to her waist
Who killed herself at the beginning of the first act
The play continued inexplicably in the chandelier light
The set being gradually covered with fog
And I called out at times
I broke the pitcher they had given me and from which butter-
    flies escaped
Which madly flew up to the chandelier
Under the pretext of another ballet interlude of my thoughts
    they wanted to give me
I tried then to open my wrist with pieces of brown earth
But they were countries in which I had lost my way
Impossible to rediscover the thread of those voyages
I was separated from everything by the bread of the sun
A character walked about in the room the only agile character
Who had made a mask for himself of my features
Vilely he took the side of the ingenue and the villain
The rumor spread that it was arranged like May June July
    August
Suddenly the pit became deeper
In the endless corridors bouquets held up by hands
Wandered alone I scarcely dared open my door
Too much freedom was granted me at the same time
Freedom to flee in the sled of my bed
Freedom to call back to life those whom I miss
Aluminum chairs were crowded around a kiosk of ice-cream
Over which rose a curtain of dew fringed with blood turned
    green
Freedom to chase ahead of me real forms
The basement was delightful on a white wall appeared dotted
    with fire my silhouette pierced to the heart with a bullet

Vigilance

In Paris the tottering tower of St. James
Like to a sunflower
With its brow comes at times to strike the Seine and its shadow
    glides imperceptibly among the tugboats

A ce moment sur la pointe des pieds dans mon sommeil
Je me dirige vers la chambre où je suis étendu
Et j'y mets le feu
Pour que rien ne subsiste de ce consentement qu'on m'a arraché
Les meubles font alors place à des animaux de même taille qui
    me regardent fraternellement
Lions dans les crinières desquels achèvent de se consumer les
    chaises
Squales dont le ventre blanc s'incorpore le dernier frisson des
    draps
A l'heure de l'amour et des paupières bleues
Je me vois brûler à mon tour je vois cette cachette solennelle de
    riens
Qui fut mon corps
Fouillée par les becs patients des ibis du feu
Lorsque tout est fini j'entre invisible dans l'arche
Sans prendre garde aux passants de la vie qui font sonner très
    loin leur pas traînants
Je vois les arêtes du soleil
A travers l'aubépine de la pluie
J'entends se déchirer le linge humain comme une grande feuille
Sous l'ongle de l'absence et de la présence qui sont de connivence
Tous les métiers se fanent il ne reste d'eux qu'une dentelle par-
    fumée
Une coquille de dentelle qui a la forme parfaite d'un sein
Je ne touche plus que le coeur des choses je tiens le fil
             Le Revolver à Cheveux Blancs

Le Marquis de Sade

Le marquis de Sade a regagné l'intérieur du volcan en éruption
D'où il était venu
Avec ses belles mains encore frangées
Ses yeux de jeune fille
Et cette raison à fleur de sauve-qui-peut qui ne fut
Qu'à lui
Mais du salon phosphorescent à lampes de viscères

At that moment on the top of my toes in my sleep
I move toward the room where I am lying
And I set it on fire
So that nothing will remain of that consent taken from me
The furniture then gives way to animals of the same size who
    look on me as a brother
Lions in whose manes chairs are finally consumed
Dog-fish whose white bellies join with the last rustle of the
    sheets
At the moment of love and blue eyelids
I see myself in turn burning I see that solemn hiding place of
    nothings
Which was my body
Dug into by the patient beaks of fire ibises
When everything is over I enter the ark invisibly
Without paying attention to the passers-by of life whose drag-
    ging footsteps resound far off
I see a skeleton of the sun
Through the rain hawthorn
I hear the human linen tear like a great leaf
Under the nail of absence and presence which are in connivance
All trades fade out and of them there remains only a perfumed
    lace
A shell of lace having the perfect form of a breast
I touch nothing but the heart of things I hold the thread.

The Marquis de Sade

The marquis de Sade reached the inside of the erupting volcano
Whence he had come
With his beautiful hands still fringed
His eyes of a girl
And that reason on a level with the head-long flight which was
Only his
But from the phosphorescent room of visceral lamps
He has not stopped issuing mysterious orders

Il n'a cessé de jeter les ordres mystérieux
Qui ouvrent une brèche dans la nuit morale
C'est par cette brèche que je vois
Les grandes ombres craquantes la vieille écorce minée
Se dissoudre
Pour me permettre de t'aimer
Comme le premier homme aima la première femme
En toute liberté
Cette liberté
Pour laquelle le feu même s'est fait homme
Pour laquelle le marquis de Sade défia les siècles de ses grands
    arbres abstraits
D'acrobates tragiques
Cramponnés au fil de la Vierge du désir

L'Air de L'Eau

Au Beau Demi-Jour

Au beau demi-jour de 1934
L'air était une splendide rose couleur de rouget
Et la forêt quand je me préparais à y entrer
Commençait par un arbre à feuilles de papier à cigarettes
Parce que je t'attendais
Et que si tu te promènes avec moi
N'importe où
Ta bouche est volontiers la nielle
D'où repart sans cesse la roue bleue diffuse et brisée qui monte
Blêmir dans l'ornière
Tous les prestiges se hâtaient à ma rencontre
Un écureuil était venu appliquer son ventre blanc sur mon coeur
Je ne sais comment il se tenait
Mais la terre était pleine de reflets plus profonds que ceux de
    l'eau
Comme si le métal eût enfin secoué sa coque
Et toi couchée sur l'effroyable mer de pierreries
Tu tournais
Nue

Which make an opening in the moral night
It is through that opening I see
The great cracking shadows the old wasted away bark
Dissolve
To permit me to love you
As the first man loved the first woman
In full freedom
That freedom
For which fire itself became man
For which the marquis de Sade defied the centuries of his great
    trees abstracted
From tragic acrobats
Clinging to the gossamer thread of desire

In the Lovely Half-Daylight

In the lovely half-daylight of 1934
The air was a fine rose color of red mullet
And the forest when I prepared to go into it
Began by a tree with leaves of cigarette paper
Because I was waiting for you
And if you walk with me
Anywhere at all
Your mouth is easily the niello
Whence ceaselessly goes out the blue diffused and broken wheel
    which climbs
To grow white in the rut
All the illusions hasten to meet me
A squirrel had come to press his white belly against my heart
I don't know how he stayed there
But the earth was full of deeper reflections than those of water
As if the metal at last had shaken off its husk
And you lying on the terrible sea of shining stones
Turned
Naked
In a great sun of fireworks
I saw you slowly taking down from the radiolarians

Dans un grand soleil de feu d'artifice
Je te voyais descendre lentement des radiolaires
Les coquilles même de l'oursin j'y étais
Pardon je n'y étais déjà plus
J'avais levé la tête car le vivant écrin de velours blanc m'avait
　　quitté
Et j'étais triste
Le ciel entre les feuilles luisait hagard et dur comme une libellule
J'allais fermer les yeux
Quand les deux pans du bois qui s'étaient brusquement écartés
　　s'abattirent
Sans bruit
Comme les deux feuilles centrales d'un muguet immense
D'une fleur capable de contenir toute la nuit
J'étais où tu me vois
Dans le parfum sonné à toute volée
Avant qu'elles ne revinssent comme chaque jour à la vie chan-
　　geante
J'eus le temps de poser mes lèvres
Sur tes cuisses de verre

L'Air de l'eau

Toujours pour la Première Fois

Toujours pour la première fois
C'est à peine si je te connais de vue
Tu rentres à telle heure de la nuit dans une maison oblique à
　　ma fenêtre
Maison tout imaginaire
C'est là que d'une seconde à l'autre
Dans le noir intact
Je m'attends à ce que se produise une fois de plus la déchirure
　　fascinante
La déchirure unique
De la façade et de mon coeur
Plus je m'approche de toi
En réalité

The very shells of the sea-urchin I was
Excuse me I wasn't there any more
I had raised my head because the living casket of white velvet
      had left me
And I was sad
The sky between the leaves shone wild and hard like a dragonfly
I was about to close my eyes
When two panels of wood which had abruptly separated fell
      down
Noiselessly
Like the two central leaves of a huge May lily
Of a flower able to hold the entire night
I was where you see me
In the perfume ringing in full peals
Before they returned as each day to changing life
I had the time to place my lips
On your thighs of glass.

Always for the First Time

Always for the first time
I scarcely know you by sight
You come home at some hour of the night into a house oblique
      to my window
An imaginary house
It is there that from one moment to the next
In the complete dark
I wait until once more the fascinating ripping takes place
The one ripping
Of the façade of my heart
The closer I come to you
In reality
The more does the key sing in the door of the unknown room
Where you appear to me alone
You are first completely melted into the glittering
The fugitive angle of a curtain
Is a field of jasmine I looked at at dawn on a road near Grasse

Plus la clé chante à la porte de la chambre inconnue
Où tu m'apparais seule
Tu es d'abord tout entière fondue dans le brillant
L'angle fugitif d'un rideau
C'est un champ de jasmin que j'ai contemplé à l'aube sur une
    route des environs de Grasse
Avec ses cueilleuses en diagonale
Derrière elles l'aile sombre tombante des plants dégarnis
Devant elles l'équerre de l'éblouissant
Le rideau invisiblement soulevé
Rentrent en tumulte toutes les fleurs
C'est toi aux prises avec cette heure trop longue jamais assez
    trouble jusqu'au sommeil
Toi comme si tu pouvais être
La même à cela près que je ne te rencontrerai peut-être jamais
Tu fais semblant de ne pas savoir que je t'observe
Merveilleusement je ne suis plus sûr que tu le sais
Ton désoeuvrement m'emplit les yeux de larmes
Une nuée d'interprétations entoure chacun de tes gestes
C'est une chasse à la miellée
Il y a des rocking-chairs sur un pont il y a des branchages qui
    risquent de t'égratigner dans la forêt
Il y a dans une vitrine rue Notre-Dame-de-Lorette
Deux belles jambes croisées prises dans de hauts bas
Qui s'évasent au centre d'un grand trèfle blanc
Il y a une échelle de soie déroulée sur le lierre
Il y a
Qu'à me pencher sur le précipice
De la fusion sans espoir de ta présence et de ton absence
J'ai trouvé le secret
De t'aimer
Toujours pour la première fois

With its women fruit pickers diagonally
Behind them the dark falling wing of untrimmed seedlings
In front of them the square of the dazzling light
The invisibly raised curtain
In an uproar all the flowers come back
It is you at grips with the too long hour never troubled enough
        with sleep
You as if you could be
The same so close that I will perhaps never meet you
You pretend not to know I see you
Miraculously I am no longer sure you know it
Your idleness fills my eyes with tears
A cloud of interpretations surrounds each of your gestures
It is a honeyed-sweetened chase
There are rocking chairs on a bridge there are branches which
        might scratch you in the forest
In a shop window on rue Notre-Dame-de-Lorette there are
Two beautiful legs crossed wearing high stockings
Which open out in the center of a large white clock
There is a silk ladder unrolled over the ivy
There is
Hopeless fusion of your presence and your absence
I have found the secret
Of loving you
Always for the first time

Tiki

Je t'aime à la face des mers
Rouge comme l'oeuf quand il est vert
Tu me transportes dans une clairière
Douce aux mains comme une caille
Tu m'appuies sur le ventre de la femme
Comme contre un olivier de nacre
Tu me donnes l'équilibre
Tu me couches
Par rapport au fait d'avoir vécu
Avant et après
Sous mes paupières de caoutchouc

Rano Raraku

Que c'est beau le monde
La Grèce n'a jamais existé
Ils ne passeront pas
Mon cheval trouve son picotin dans le cratère
Des hommes-oiseaux des nageurs courbes
Volètent autour de ma tête car
C'est moi aussi
Qui suis là
Aux trois quarts enlisé
Plaisantant des ethnologues
Dans l'amicale nuit du Sud
Ils ne passeront pas
La plaine est immense
Ceux qui s'avancent sont ridicules
Les hautes images sont tombées
                    Xénophiles

Tiki

I love you opposite the seas
Red as the egg when it's green
You move me into a clearing
Gentle with hands like a quail
You lean me against the belly of the woman
As against a mother-of-pearl olive tree
You give me balance
You put me to bed
By the fact of having lived
Before and after
Under my rubber eyelids

Rano Raraku

How beautiful is the world
Greece never existed
They will not pass
My horse finds its feed in the crater
Bird-men curved swimmers
Fly around my head for
I too
Am there
Three quarters sunk
Joking with ethnologists
In the friendly night of the South
They will not pass
The plain is vast
Those who advance are ridiculous
The high images have fallen

PAUL ELUARD

ELUARD WAS BORN in the outskirts of Paris, at Saint-Denis. He studied in Paris from twelve to sixteen, and then spent two years in Switzerland, in recovering from an illness. He returned from Switzerland just in time to leave for the front in 1914. The first poems he published in 1917 had been written on a Swiss mountain or in a trench. The permanent themes of his poetry were apparent in his earliest verse: an awareness of the poverty and suffering of the masses, as well as the humble sources of his happiness derived from street scenes, from animals, the play of light on objects in the world. Patiently the poet Eluard learned to look at the world and to reveal what he saw in a new delicate light: the face of a passer-by, a pebble on the road, the color of rain or fire. The general effect of Eluard's poetry is one of a disarming simplicity.

In 1918 he met Jean Paulhan who had already by then begun his remarkable career of impressario of poets, and he met also those who were to become the leading surrealists: Breton (this meeting is related by Breton's *Nadja*), Aragon, Philippe Soupault, Tzara. The scandals of the Dada movement united these young men and prepared them for what they considered were to be the conquests of surrealism.

The surrealist revolution, when it first broke out in its eloquent statements and histrionic behavior, called for total liberty in all human activities. At the beginning, this freedom of love, in the surrealistic sense, seemed to be synonymous with the freedom for licence or licentiousness. Love was an experiment with unusual sensations. But this initial intoxication with freedom in love never developed to any degree within the ranks of the surrealists.

The two leaders especially, Breton and Eluard, due perhaps to the very freedom they felt about such problems, discovered in the experience and the meaning of love a lesson of purity quite opposed to the purity of love's absence. They discovered the pure love of woman and have sung of this love as ecstatically and vibrantly as any Ronsard. It would not be exaggerated to say that the surrealists have contributed to a rehabilitation in literature of the role of woman as the fleshly and spiritual partner of man. Love is at the same time, paradoxically, our surest way of escaping from the world and our profoundest way of knowing the world. Paul Eluard is perhaps the most eminent among the surrealists to maintain a lofty awareness of this truth. He knows that despite the delirious profusions of love, it is the one force in man capable of breaking through the iron gates of language and reason: the two obstacles to love which have been inherited from man's age-old fear of love and its falsely named debilitating power.

In such a poem as *Première du Monde*, it is quite possible to see what surrealist inspiration, largely under the influence of Rimbaud, whose methodology in *Les Illuminations* is here appropriated, has been successful in creating. What once was epic drama and historical recital, is now cerebral and psychic. The drama of love is played in the mind. It is lyricism of one moment, a flash of time, that is never over, that is anonymous and universal and hence mythical. The mind appears before itself, filled with the image of woman so resplendent in her nudity that she is all degrees of light: angelic and demonic, carnal and spiritual, unique and universal.

The last eight lines of the poem, *Celle de toujours, toute,* provide a definition of the poet. He is the singer, the one who sings the joy of singing about woman, whether she is present or absent. This would seem to be the key to the new erotology of Eluard. Woman, by her very existence, suppresses the concept of absence. The mystery of the poet's song is that mystery in which love created him and liberated itself. Creation is freedom. By the fact of his existing, he knows that woman exists and surrounds him at all moments. His principle is defined by his freedom to move within woman.

Capitale de la Douleur is the collection of Eluard's poetry written between 1919 and 1926. Even in this work, composed when Eluard was closest to the doctrine of Breton, there are very few traces of surrealist exaggerations. The freedom with which he uses words may have been encouraged by surrealist teaching, however. In *La Vie Immédiate* of 1932 there is a deepening of Eluard's idealism and mythology. The beloved in his poetry has now gone beyond the limitations of a single individual. She penetrates all beings and finally the poet identifies her with the universe itself. This is the theme of predilection for Eluard. He has never come to its end. Each poem is a new reflection of a central secret radiation. Only the words themselves cast shadows over this light.

During the four years of German Occupation, Paul Eluard courageously participated in the Resistance. The poet showed himself to be a clear-sighted man of action, constantly changing his address in order to avoid the Gestapo, walking through Paris to distribute tracts and articles and poems which contributed so much to the spiritual health of the nation. His poems during this period are of Paris, a city unable to resign itself to the enemy's regime, of the masses and the poet's faith in the masses unwilling to accept injustice, of the faces of the condemned. His writing became the poetic chronicle of the new terrorism. It was used as propaganda throughout the maquis. But for Eluard these poems were not purely propagandistic or circumstantial. They are on themes he has sung since his earliest poetry of 1918.

The miracle of Eluard's work is the extremes it contains and the ease with which he moves from one extreme to the other, from the poet's solitude, from his deep and secret intimacy, to his sense of communion with everyone, to his civic hope. His solitude is his generosity. His sense of the collective comes from what is most individual in him. He is the poet of love, in one of its highest forms, love which will not allow a man to remain within himself.

Selected Bibliography of Eluard

1926 *Capitale de la Douleur*, Gallimard.
1929 *L'Amour la Poésie*, Gallimard.
1932 *La Vie Immédiate*, Ed. des Cahiers Libres.
1934 *La Rose Publique*, Gallimard.
1935 *Facile*, Ed. G.L.M.
1936 *Les Yeux Fertiles*, Ed. G.L.M.
1938 *Cours Naturel*, Ed. du Sagittaire.
1939 *Chanson Complète*, Gallimard.
1941 *Choix de Poèmes 1914-1941*, Gallimard.
1944 *Au Rendez-vous allemand*, Ed. de minuit.
1946 *Le dur désir de durer*, Ed. Arnold Bordas.
1948 *Corps Mémorable*, Seghers.
1948 *Paul Eluard: Poètes d'Aujourd'hui*, No. 1, Seghers.

on Eluard

Bogan, Louise, *Partisan Review*, Feb. 1939.
Carrouges, Michel, *Eluard et Claudel*, Du Seuil, 1945.
Fowlie, Wallace, *Age of Surrealism*, 1950.
Parrot, Louis, intro. to *Poètes d'Aujourd'hui*.
Renéville, Rolland de, *Univers de la Parole*, 1944 (p. 115-126).

1924: A Fragment from *Un Cadavre*, the first Collective Surrealist
Text, Published at the Death of Anatole France.

. . . Life, which I can no longer imagine without tears in my
eyes, still appears today in small insignificant things, from which
tenderness alone now serves as support. What is scepticism,
irony, cowardice, Anatole France, the French spirit? A great
wave of oblivion separates me from all that. Perhaps I have never
read or seen anything of what dishonors life.

1936: Two Fragments from a Lecture Given at the
Surrealist Exhibition in London.

. . . Everything, in present day society, crosses our path to
humble us and to make us turn back. But we do not forget that
it is because we are evil itself, evil in the sense of Engels, because
with men like ourselves we contribute to the destruction of the
bourgeoisie, to the destruction of its wealth and its understand-
ing of beauty.

It is that wealth and that beauty enslaved to the ideas of prop-
erty, family, religion, nation that we are fighting together. Poets,
worthy of their name, refuse, as the proletariat does, to be ex-
ploited. Real poetry is included in all that does not conform
to that morality which, in order to maintain its order and its
prestige, builds only banks, barracks, prisons, churches, brothels.
Real poetry is included in everything that delivers man from
that terrible wealth which has the appearance of death. . . . For
more than a hundred years, poets have come down from the
summits where they thought they lived. They have gone into
the streets, insulted their masters, given up their gods, embraced
beauty and love, learned the revolutionary songs of the unhappy
masses, and without discouragement, are trying to teach them
their songs.

I don't invent words. But I invent objects, creatures, events,
and our senses are able to perceive them. I create sentiments in
myself. I suffer from them or am happy with them. Indifference
may surround them. I remember them. I even foresee them. If
I had to doubt this reality, nothing would be sure for me: life,

nor love, nor death. Everything would seem foreign to me. My reason refuses to deny the testimonial of my senses. The object of my desires is always real and sensible.

You don't take the story of a dream for a poem. Both are living reality, but the first is a memory, immediately altered and transformed, an adventure, and of the second nothing is lost, nothing is changed. The poem desensitizes the universe to the advantage of human faculties, permits man to see differently other things. His former vision is dead, or false. He discovers a new world, he becomes a new man.

People have thought that automatic writing made poems useless. On the contrary! It increases or develops the domain of examination of poetic awareness, by enriching it. If awareness is perfect, the elements which automatic writing draws from the inner world and the elements of the outer world are balanced. Thus made equal, they mingle and merge in order to form poetic unity.

Première du Monde
(à Pablo Picasso)

Captive de la plaine, agonisante folle,
La lumière sur toi se cache, vois le ciel:
Il a fermé les yeux pour s'en prendre à ton rêve,
Il a fermé ta robe pour briser tes chaînes.

Devant les roues toutes nouées
Un éventail rit aux éclats.
Dans les traîtres filets de l'herbe
Les routes perdent leur reflet.

Ne peux-tu donc prendre les vagues
Dont les barques sont les amandes
Dans ta paume chaude et câline
Ou dans les boucles de ta tête?

Ne peux-tu prendre les étoiles?
Ecartelée tu leur ressembles,
Dans leur nid de feu tu demeures
Et ton éclat s'en multiplie.

De l'aube bâillonnée un seul cri veut jaillir,
Un soleil tournoyant ruisselle sous l'écorce,
Il ira se fixer sur tes paupières closes.
O douce, quand tu dors, la nuit se mêle au jour.

Capitale de la Douleur

Celle de Toujours, Toute

Si je vous dis: "J'ai tout abandonné"
C'est qu'elle n'est pas celle de mon corps,
Je ne m'en suis jamais vanté,
Ce n'est pas vrai
Et la brume de fond où je me meus
Ne sait jamais si j'ai passé.
L'éventail de sa bouche, le reflet de ses yeux,
Je suis le seul à en parler,
Je suis le seul qui soit cerné

MODERN FRENCH POETS / ELUARD

First in the World

Prisoner of the field, frenzied in agony,
The light hides on you, see the sky:
It closed its eyes to attack your dream,
It closed your dress to break your chains.

Before the tied wheels
A fan laughs out loud.
In the treacherous nets of the grass
The roads lose their reflexion.

Can't you take the waves
Whose barges are almonds
In your warm coaxing palm
Or in the ringlets of your head?

Can't you seize the stars?
Stretched on the rack you resemble them,
In their nest of fire you dwell
And your light multiplies from them.

From the gagged dawn only one cry wants to rush out,
A turning sun streams under the bark,
It will be imprinted on your closed eyelids.
Sweet one, when you sleep, night mingles with day.

The One for All Time

If I say to you: "I have given up everything"
It means she is not the one of my body,
I never boasted of that,
It is not true
And the low fog where I move
Doesn't know whether I passed through.

The fan of her mouth, the reflection of her eyes,
I am the only one to speak of them,
I am the only one to be encircled
By this empty mirror where the air flows through me

Par ce miroir si nul où l'air circule à travers moi
Et l'air a un visage, un visage aimé,
Un visage aimant, ton visage,
A toi qui n'as pas de nom et que les autres ignorent,
La mer te dit: sur moi, le ciel te dit: sur moi,
Les astres te devinent, les nuages t'imaginent
Et le sang répandu aux meilleurs moments,
Le sang de la générosité,
Te porte avec délices.

Je chante la grande joie de te chanter,
La grande joie de t'avoir ou de ne pas t'avoir,
La candeur de t'attendre, l'innocence de te connaître,
O toi qui supprimes l'oubli, l'espoir et l'ignorance,
Qui supprimes l'absence et qui me mets au monde,
Je chante pour chanter, je t'aime pour chanter
Le mystère où l'amour me crée et se délivre.
Tu es pure, tu es encore plus pure que moi-même.

Capitale de la Douleur

Ce que Dit l'Homme de Peine Est Toujours Hors de Propos

Un hiver tout en branches et dur comme un cadavre
Un homme sur un banc dans une rue qui fuit la foule
Et que la solitude comble
Place à l'appareil banal du désespoir
A ses miroirs de plomb
A ses bains de cailloux
A ses statues croupissantes
Place à l'oubli du bien
Aux souvenirs en loques de la vérité
Lumière noire vieil incendie
Aux cheveux perdus dans un labyrinthe
Un homme qui s'est trompé d'étage de porte de clé
Pour mieux connaître pour mieux aimer

Où commence le paysage
A quelle heure

And the air has a face, a beloved face,
A loving face, your face,
To you who have no name and whom other men do not know,
The sea says: on me, the sky says: on me,
The stars sense your presence, the clouds imagine you
And the blood spilled at the best moments,
The blood of generosity
Bears you with delight.

I sing the great joy of singing you,
The great joy of having you or not having you,
The candor of waiting for you, the innocence of knowing you,
You who efface forgetting, hope, ignorance,
Who efface absence and put me in the world,
I sing to sing, I love you for singing
The mystery where love creates me and frees itself.

You are pure, you are purer than I am.

What the Laborer Says Is Always Beside the Point

A winter all in branches and hard as a corpse
A man on a bench in a street who avoids the crowd
And whom solitude gratifies
Make way for the banal apparatus of despair
For its lead mirrors
For its pebble baths
For its stagnating statues
Make way for the forgetting of fortune
For the torn memories of truth
Black light old fire
For the lost hair in a labyrinth
A man who was mistaken over the floor the door the key
In order to know better to love better

Where the landscape begins
At what time

Où donc se termine la femme
Le soir se pose sur la ville
Le soir rejoint le promeneur dans son lit
Le promeneur nu
Moins gourmand d'un sein vierge
Que de l'étoile informe qui nourrit la nuit

Il y a des démolitions plus tristes qu'un sou
Indescriptibles et pourtant le soleil s'en évade en chantant
Pendant que le ciel danse et fait son miel
Il y a des murs déserts où l'idylle fleurit
Où le plâtre qui se découd
Berce des ombres confondues
Un feu rebelle un feu de veines
Sous la vague unique des lèvres
Prenez les mains voyez les yeux
Prenez d'assaut la vue
Derrière les palais derrière les décombres
Derrière les cheminées et les citernes
Devant l'homme
Sur l'esplanade qui déroule un manteau de poussière
Traîne de fièvre
C'est l'invasion des beaux jours
Une plantation d'épées bleues
Sous des paupières écloses dans la foule des feuilles
C'est la récolte grave du plaisir
La fleur de lin brise les masques
Les visages sont lavés
Par la couleur qui connaît l'étendue

Les jours clairs du passé
Leurs lions en barre et leurs aigles d'eau pure
Leur tonnerre d'orgueil gonflant les heures
Du sang des aubes enchaînées
Tout au travers du ciel
Leur diadème crispé sur la masse d'un seul miroir
D'un seul coeur

Mais plus bas maintenant profondément parmi les routes abolies

Where woman ends
The evening rests over the city
The evening rejoins the walker in his bed
The naked walker
Less greedy for a virgin breast
Than for the formless star nourishing the night

There are demolitions sadder than a penny
Indescribable and yet the sun moves away from them singing
While the sky dances and makes its honey
There are deserted walls where the idyl flowers
Where the plaster which is loosened
Rocks mingled shadows
A rebellious fire a fire of veins
Under the one wave of the lips
Take your hands see your eyes
Take by assault the sight
Behind the palaces behind the ruins
Behind the chimneys and cisterns
Before the man
On the esplanade unfolding a cloak of dust
Trail of fever
It's the coming of fine days
A plantation of blue swords
Under hatched lids in the maze of leaves
It's the grave harvest of pleasure
The linseed flower breaks the masks
The faces are washed
By the color which knows the land

The clear days of the past
Their lions in bars and their eagles of pure water
Their thunder of pride swelling the hours
Blood of enchained dawns
Across the sky
Their diadem bent over the mass of a single mirror
Of a single heart

But lower now deeply amid the abolished roads

Ce chant qui tient la nuit
Ce chant qui fait le sourd l'aveugle
Qui donne le bras à des fantômes
Cet amour négateur
Qui se débat dans les soucis
Avec des larmes bien trempées
Ce rêve déchiré désemparé tordu ridicule
Cette harmonie en friche
Cette peuplade qui mendie

Parce qu'elle n'a voulu que de l'or
Toute sa vie intacte
Et la perfection de l'amour.

La Rose Publique

Tu Te Lèves

Tu te lèves l'eau se déplie
Tu te couches l'eau s'épanouit

Tu es l'eau détournée de ses abîmes
Tu es la terre qui prend racine
Et sur laquelle tout s'établit

Tu fais des bulles de silence dans le désert des bruits
Tu chantes des hymnes nocturnes sur les cordes de l'arc-en-ciel
Tu es partout tu abolis toutes les routes

Tu sacrifies le temps
A l'éternelle jeunesse de la flamme exacte
Qui voile la nature en la reproduisant

Femme tu mets au monde un corps toujours pareil
Le tien

Tu es la ressemblance

Facile

This song which holds night
This song pretending to be deaf and blind
Which offers its arm to ghosts
This negating love
Which struggles in worries
With very wet tears
This dream torn bewildered twisted ridiculous
This uncultivated harmony
This begging tribe

Because it wanted only gold
All its life intact
And perfection of love.

You Rise Up

You rise up the water unfolds
You lie down the water opens

You are the water turned aside from its depths
You are the earth taking root
And on which everything is built

You make bubbles of silence in the desert of noises
You sing night hymns on the strings of the rainbow
You are everywhere you abolish all roads

You sacrifice time
To the eternal youth of the exact flame
Which veils nature in reproducing it

Woman you put into the world a body always the same
Yours

You are resemblance.

A Pablo Picasso

I

Bonne journée j'ai revu qui je n'oublie pas
Qui je n'oublierai jamais
Et des femmes fugaces dont les yeux
Me faisaient une haie d'honneur
Elles s'enveloppèrent dans leurs sourires
Bonne journée j'ai vu mes amis sans soucis
Les hommes ne pesaient pas lourd
Un qui passait
Son ombre changée en souris
Fuyait le ruisseau

J'ai vu le ciel très grand
Le beau regard des gens privés de tout
Plage distante où personne n'aborde

Bonne journée journée qui commença mélancolique
Noire sous les arbres verts
Mais qui soudain trempée d'aurore
M'entra dans le coeur par surprise.

II

Montrez-moi cet homme de toujours si doux
Qui disait les doigts font monter la terre
L'arc-en-ciel qui se noue le serpent qui roule
Le miroir de chair où perle un enfant
Et ces mains tranquilles qui vont leur chemin
Nues obéissantes réduisant l'espace
Chargées de désirs et d'images
L'une suivant l'autre aiguilles de la même horloge

Montrez-moi le ciel chargé de nuages
Répétant le monde enfoui sous mes paupières
Montrez-moi le ciel dans une seule étoile
Je vois bien la terre sans être ébloui
Les pierres obscures les herbes fantômes
Ces grands verres d'eau ces grands blocs d'ambre des paysages

I

It's a good day I saw again those I will not forget
Whom I will never forget
And fleeting women whose eyes
Made for me a path of honor
They were wrapped in their smiles
It's a good day my friends were carefree
Men weren't weighted down
One who went by
His shadow, changed into a mouse,
Was running into the river.

I saw the tremendous sky
The beautiful look of people deprived of everything
A distant beach where no one gets off

It's a good good day which began sad
Black under the green trees
But which suddenly, dipped in dawn,
Entered my heart by surprise.

II

Show me that man always so gentle
Who said fingers make the earth rise up
The rainbow which is tied the snake which rolls
The flesh mirror where a child sparkles
And those calm hands going their way
Obedient clouds reducing space
Weighted with desires and images
One following the other hands of the same clock

Show me the sky heavy with clouds
Show me the sky in a single star
I clearly see the earth without being dazzled
The dark stones the phantom grasses
Great glasses of water great amber blocks of land
Games of fire and ash
Solemn geographies of human limits

Les jeux du feu et de la cendre
Les géographies solennelles des limites humaines

Montrez-moi aussi le corsage noir
Les cheveux tirés les yeux perdus
De ces filles noires et pures qui sont d'ici de passage et d'ailleurs
    à mon gré
Qui sont de fières portes dans les murs de cet été
D'étranges jarres sans liquide toutes en vertus
Inutilement faites pour des rapports simples
Montrez-moi ces secrets qui unissent leurs tempes
A ces palais absents qui font monter la terre.

           Les Yeux Fertiles

La Victoire de Guernica

1

Beau monde des masures
De la mine et des champs

2

Visages bons au feu visages bons au froid
Aux refus à la nuit aux injures aux coups

3

Visages bons à tout
Voici le vide qui vous fixe
Votre mort va servir d'exemple

4

La mort coeur renversé

5

Ils vous ont fait payer le pain
Le ciel la terre l'eau le sommeil
Et la misère
De votre vie

6

Ils disaient désirer la bonne intelligence
Ils rationnaient les forts jugeaient les fous

Show me also the black corsage
The tightly drawn hair the lost eyes
Of those dark pure girls who are travellers here and elsewhere
    at my will
Who are proud gates in walls of this summer
Strange jars with no liquid all in powers
Uselessly made for simple blendings
Show me those secrets which unite their temples
With those absent palaces which make the earth rise up.

Victory of Guernica

1

Beautiful world of huts
Of mines and fields

2

Good faces in the fire good faces in the cold
In refusals in nights in name calling in blows

3

Faces good for everything
Here is the void looking at you
Your death will be an example

4

Death a heart thrown backwards

5

They made you pay for the bread
The sky earth water sleep
And the misery
Of your life.

6

They claimed they wanted good minds
They rationed the strong and judged the imbeciles

Faisaient l'aumône partageaient un sou en deux
Ils saluaient les cadavres
Ils s'accablaient de politesses

7

Ils persévèrent ils exagèrent ils ne sont pas de notre monde

8

Les femmes les enfants ont le même trésor
De feuilles vertes de printemps et de lait pur
Et de durée
Dans leurs yeux purs

9

Les femmes les enfants ont le même trésor
Dans les yeux
Les hommes le défendent comme ils peuvent

10

Les femmes les enfants ont les mêmes roses rouges
Dans les yeux
Chacun montre son sang

11

La peur et le courage de vivre et de mourir
La mort si difficile et si facile

12

Hommes pour qui ce trésor fut chanté
Hommes pour qui ce trésor fut gâché

13

Hommes réels pour qui le désespoir
Alimente le feu dévorant de l'espoir
Ouvrons ensemble le dernier bourgeon de l'avenir

14

Parias la mort la terre et la hideur
De nos ennemis ont la couleur
Monotone de notre nuit
Nous en aurons raison.

Cours Naturel

Gave alms divided a penny in halves
They bowed before corpses
They vied in politeness

7

They persevere they exaggerate they are not of our world

8

Women and children have the same treasure
Of green leaves of spring and pure milk
And time
In their pure eyes

9

Women and children have the same treasure
In their eyes
Men defend it as best they can

10

Women and children have the same red roses
In their eyes
Each one shows his blood

11

The fear and courage of living and dying
Death so hard and so easy

12

Men for whom this treasure was sung
Men for whom this treasure was wasted

13

Real men for whom despair
Feeds the devouring fire of hope
Let us open together the last bud of the future

14

Pariahs death earth and hideousness
Of our enemies have the monotonous
Color of our night
We will triumph over them.

Nous Sommes

Tu vois le feu du soir qui sort de sa coquille
Et tu vois la forêt enfouie dans la fraîcheur

Tu vois la plaine nue aux flancs du ciel traînard
La neige haute comme la mer
Et la mer haute dans l'azur

Pierres parfaites et bois doux secours voilés
Tu vois des villes teintes de mélancolie
Dorée des trottoirs pleins d'excuses
Une place où la solitude a sa statue
Souriante et l'amour une seule maison

Tu vois les animaux
Sosies malins sacrifiés l'un à l'autre
Frères immaculés aux ombres confondues
Dans un désert de sang

Tu vois un bel enfant quand il joue quand il rit
Il est bien plus petit
Que le petit oiseau du bout des branches

Tu vois un paysage aux saveurs d'huile et d'eau
D'où la roche est exclue où la terre abandonne
Sa verdure à l'été qui la couvre de fruits

Des femmes descendant de leur miroir ancien
T'apportent leur jeunesse et leur foi en la tienne
Et l'une sa clarté la voile qui t'entraîne
Te fait secrètement voir le monde sans toi.

—o—

C'est avec nous que tout vivra

Bêtes mes vrais étendards d'or
Plaines mes bonnes aventures
Verdure utile villes sensibles
A votre tête viendront des hommes

Des hommes de dessous les sueurs les coups les larmes
Mais qui vont cueillir tous leurs songes

We Are

You see the evening fire coming out from its shell
And you see the buried forest in its coolness

You see the bare plain on the side of the dragging sky
The snow high as the sea
And the sea high in the blue

Perfect stones and sweet wood veiled help
You see cities colored with sadness
Gilded with sidewalks full of excuses
A square where solitude has its smiling
Statue and love a single house

You see animals
Clever twins sacrificed one to the other
Immaculate brothers in mingled darkness
In a desert of blood

You see a beautiful child when he plays and laughs
He is much smaller
Than the small bird on the end of the branches

You see a landscape with the smell of oil and water
Whence rock is excluded where the earth yields
Its verdure to the summer covering it with fruit

Women coming down from their ancient mirror
Bring you their youth and their faith in yours
And one her light the sail which leads you off
Makes you secretly see the world without you.

—o—

It is with us that everything will live

Foolish my true gold standards
Plains my good adventures
Useful verdure delicate cities
To your head men will come

Men under sweat blows tears
But who are going to gather all their dreams

Je vois des hommes vrais sensibles bons utiles
Rejeter un fardeau plus mince que la mort
Et dormir de joie au bruit du soleil.

Chanson Complète

Notre Mouvement

Nous vivons dans l'oubli de nos métamorphoses
Le jour est paresseux mais la nuit est active
Un bol d'air à midi le filtre et l'use
La nuit ne laisse pas de poussière sur nous

Mais cet écho qui roule tout le long du jour
Cet écho hors du temps d'angoisse ou de caresses
Cet enchaînement brut des mondes insipides
Et des mondes sensibles son soleil est double

Sommes-nous près ou loin de notre conscience
Où sont nos bornes nos racines notre but

Le long plaisir pourtant de nos métamorphoses
Squelettes s'animant dans les murs pourrissants
Les rendez-vous donnés aux formes insensées
A la chair ingénieuse aux aveugles voyants

Les rendez-vous donnés par la face au profil
Par la souffrance à la santé par la lumière
A la forêt par la montagne à la vallée
Par la mine à la fleur par la perle au soleil

Nous sommes corps à corps nous sommes terre à terre
Nous naissons de partout nous sommes sans limites.

Le dur désir de durer

A l'Infini

Elle surgissait de ses ressemblances
Et de ses contraires

On la voyait mieux parfois plus publique

I see men true sensitive good useful
Throw away a burden slighter than death
And sleep joyfully in the noise of the sun.

Movement

We live in the oblivion of our changes
The day is lazy but night is active
A bowl of air at noon is filtered and used by day
Night leaves no trace on us

But that echo which rolls all the day long
That echo outside the time of anguish or love
That gross series of insipid worlds
And sensitive worlds its sun is double

Are we far from or near to our conscience
Where are our bounds our roots our goal

And yet the long pleasure of our changes
Skeletons coming to life in rotting walls
Rendez-vous given to mad forms
To ingenious flesh to blind visionaries

Rendez-vous given by the face to the profile
By suffering to health by light
To the forest by the mountain to the valley
By the mine to the flower by the pearl to the sun

We are body to body we are earth to earth
We are born everywhere we are without limitations.

To the Infinite

She rose up from her resemblances
And from her opposites

At times you saw her better more public

Que cachant ses seins sous un coeur de mère

Peut-elle inspirer de l'indifférence
Celle qui est moi-même

—o—

Elle exalte mon frère
Mon frère la première image

—o—

Le soleil brille à travers lui il est né d'elle
Et c'est ainsi que je suis sûr que chacun l'aime

—o—

Elle surgissait de l'homme
Et l'homme surgissait d'elle

Elle surgissait du désir de l'homme
D'un homme
De moi
Et d'un autre homme
Et peut-être aussi d'une femme
De plusieurs femmes désirables idéales
Et de plusieurs femmes sans charmes
Surgissait des enfances vagues
Des plus beaux rêves en spirales colorées
Et des réalités rigides
Bossues cassées blanches et noires

Rêve et réalité la rose et le rosier
La douleur et ses murs le long d'une rue calme
La douleur acceptable et le plaisir possible

—o—

Sèche
Des pied à la tête
Elle allait sur les marais
Et s'enlisait dans les dunes

Moi frais ou chaud
De temps en temps j'étais son lit
Ses draps blancs ses draps sales
Et son plaisir intime

Than hiding her breasts under a mother's heart

Can she inspire indifference
She who is myself

—o—

She exalts my brother
My brother the first image

The sun shines through him he was born from her
And that is how I am sure each one loves her

She rose up from man
And man rose up from her
She rose up from the desire of man
From a man
From me
And from another man
And perhaps also from a woman
From several desirable ideal women
And from several women with no charms
Rose up from vague childhoods
From the most beautiful dreams in colored spirals
And from rigid realities
Hunchbacked broken white and black

Dream and reality the rose and the rose bush
Sorrow and its walls along a calm street
Acceptable sorrow and possible pleasure

—o—

Dry
From head to foot
She went over the swamps
And sank into the dunes

Cool or warm
From time to time I was her bed
Her white sheets or her dirty sheets
And her intimate pleasure

Son sang naviguait à la rame
Autour de l'île de son coeur
Nous chassions à deux le sommeil
Deux soleils se levaient en nous.

Corps Mémorable

Her blood navigated with oars
Around her heart's island
The two of us hunted sleep
Two suns arose in us.

ROBERT DESNOS

In THE SPRING OF 1945, Robert Desnos was moved to the German Concentration Camp in Terezine, Czechoslovakia. Several weeks after the liberation, in June, a Czech student, Josef Stuna, who had read the surrealists and had seen a photograph of Desnos in *Nadja,* identified the French poet. Stuna and a nurse did all they could to save him, but his fever did not go down and he died on June 8. On his person, the student found a poem: *J'ai rêvé tellement fort à toi,* which is a revision of the poem published nineteen years earlier, *J'ai tant rêvé de toi.* The manuscript is a curious recreation of the same theme on the same love of Desnos.

The poet was born near the Bastille, on July 4, 1900, in a section called Saint-Merri, on the rue Saint Martin. This part of Paris, which is not far from Les Halles (the central market), is very much associated with the Middle Ages and an alchemist, Nicolas Flamel of the 14th century, chosen by the friends of Desnos as his real ancestor. He bears a resemblance also with the 19th century alchemist, Rimbaud. The volumes of Fantômas had the same effect on the imagination of Desnos as the illustrated travel magazines had on Rimbaud. The domain of the "marvellous" or the exotic had for both poets its source in popular poetry. The romanticism of Desnos was not so much the Paris of Nicolas Flamel as it was the Chicago of the 20th century seen by a boy growing up in the Quartier Saint Martin.

Before meeting Breton, Desnos had published his first poems and written down his first dreams. In a sense, he was addicted to much of the surrealist aesthetics before it was defined. After the war, in 1919, he became secretary of Jean de Bonnefon and a manager of the Bonnefon publishing house. This was the year of Dada, directed by Breton, Tzara, Picabia, Aragon, Desnos and Benjamin Péret. His 20th year was given over to military service in Morocco, and when he returned to Paris, the movement of surrealism was engaged in its first activities. The official magazine, *Littérature*, published, for example, in 1922, the famous article, *Lâchez tout!* On one of his leaves from the army, Desnos met Breton who was to claim in his first *Manifeste* (1924) that Robert Desnos had come closest to the surrealist truth, that he justified the hope which men were placing in surrealism. Breton noted in particular that Desnos was able to speak surrealistically at will (*Desnos parle surréaliste à volonté*), that he read in himself as in an open book. . . . With Breton, Eluard and Artaud, it might well be advanced that Desnos is one of the four authentic surrealist poets.

With total honesty and passion and with more naturalness than the other surrealists, Desnos practiced automatic writing. He seemed to live within poetry, guided throughout his life by an authentic poetic inspiration. There were tragic premonitions in his life, but no pessimism. When, on September 25, 1922, the first sleep seance was held at the house of Breton, Crevel and Péret first tried the experiment. Desnos was the third to experiment, and he turned out to be the most gifted medium of all. As soon as he was asleep, his power of speech was released and flowed abundantly. His improvisations were the most highly charged with poetry. In the second *Manifeste* Breton acknowledged the poet: "Desnos played in surrealism a necessary, unforgettable role." He was one of the most animated and most loved in the surrealist gatherings: at noon at the Deux Magots, at the Cyrano for the apéritif hour, at the dinners at Breton's address, 42, rue Fontaine. For Breton, Desnos had discovered the way of translating himself into poetry without the help of books, without the need of writing. Eluard, also, acknowledged this remarkable freedom of Desnos, his state of constant inspiration, his power of speaking as few poets can write.

At the time of writing his poem, *The Night of Loveless Nights* (1928), Desnos was living on the rue Blomet in a studio next to those of André Masson and Joan Miró. It was a center of surrealism, comparable to the rue Fontaine of Breton and the rue du Château of Prévert and Aragon. At that time, Youki had come into his life, the woman who was to remain his companion and inspiration until the end. The poem is a kind of modern epic, a study of despair which takes its place after *La Chanson du Mal-Aimé* of Apollinaire. Despite its classical form, the poem may well be the result of automatism.

From Havana, where Desnos had attended a convention of journalists, he brought back to Paris the first records of Cuban music and the rumba. The dance hall (bal nègre) next to Desnos' apartment on the rue Blomet began its period of fame with its Martinique and Guadaloupe dances.

In 1930, André Breton was publicly opposed in a tract, *Un Cadavre*, by the surrealists Desnos, Georges Bataille, Prévert, Artaud, Soupault, Masson, Delteil. Soon after this, Desnos published a text he called *Troisième Manifeste du Surréalisme*, directed against Breton. A major text of satire and polemics. From this time on, Desnos continued alone, separated from any strong alliance wtih surrealism.

In 1932, Paul Deharme, one of the leading radio experts in Paris, offered a position to Desnos, who worked on the radio until the mobilization in 1939. During most of this period he lived at 15, rue Mazarine. He continued his work with the unusual and the *merveilleux*. His closest friends were Jean-Louis Barrault, Madeleine Renaud, Georges Hugnet, Eluard, Lise Deharme, Masson, Artaud, Salacrou, Picasso, Hemingway, Dos Passos. Desnos wrote many original scenarios for the movies, some of which were published in ephemeral magazines.

Eroticism is one of the important aspects of Desnos' poetry, as it is with Breton's and Eluard's. He perpetuates the myth of Don Juan in *Night of Loveless Nights* and in *La Ville de Don Juan*, and yet the world which this Don Juan sees is the semblance of a void, of failure. During 1936, Desnos wrote a poem each day of the year, as an experiment recalling the earlier surrealist experiments with automatic writing. To celebrate his thirty-sixth birthday he wrote a poem about his childhood neighborhood, *Quartier Saint-Merri*.

At the beginning of the war, Desnos was more active than ever. He held a literary chronicle in *Aujourd'hui* where he ably defended Gide, who was being severely attacked at the moment. He participated in the Resistance Movement and joined the group directing the underground publications, Les Editions de Minuit. He was taken by the Gestapo in February 1944, on the very day when his new film, *Bonsoir Mesdames, bonsoir Messieurs*, was advertised on the Paris bulletin boards. In April he was transported to Buchenwald.

Selected Bibliography of Desnos

1924   *Deuil pour Deuil*, Kra.
1930   *The Night of Loveless Nights*, Gallimard.
        Corps et Biens (poèmes 1919-1929), Gallimard.
1942   *Fortunes*, Gallimard.
1946   *Choix de Poèmes*, Ed. de Minuit (préface de Georges Hugnet).
1949   *Robert Desnos: Poètes d'Aujourd'hui*, No. 16, Seghers.

on Desnos

Berger, Pierre, Intro. à *Poètes d'Aujourd'hui*.
Signes du Temps, No. 5: Vous avez le bonjours de Robert Desnos, Paris, 1951.

These ruins are situated on the banks of a winding river. The town must have been important at an older period. There are still monumental buildings, an underground network, towers of a strange confused architecture. On the deserted sunny squares we were overcome with fear. Despite our anxiousness, no one, no one at all, came to us. The ruins are uninhabited. To the south-west rises a metallic open-work construction, very high, whose use we couldn't determine. It looks about to collapse because it tilts and leans way over the river:

Strange sicknesses, curious customs, bell-tolling love, where have you led me? In these stones I find no trace of what I seek. The impassive and always new mirror shows only myself. Is it in a deserted village, a sahara where the wondrous meeting should logically take place? From afar I saw coming toward me the beautiful millionairesses with their caravans of bedecked camels bearers of gold. I waited for them impassive and tormented. Before reaching me they turned into little old dust covered women and the camel drivers into blockheads. I developed the habit of laughing out loud at funerals which serve me as landscapes. I lived endless existences in dark corridors, in the heart of mines. I fought white marble vampires but, despite my clever speeches, I was always alone in reality in the padded cell where I strove to create fire from the impact of my hard head against the walls so delightfully soft to make me miss the imagined thighs.

What I didn't know I invented better than an eighteen carat America, or the cross or the wheelbarrow. Love! love! to describe you I won't use any more roaring epithets of airplane motors. I will speak of you with banality because the banal will perhaps provide me with that extraordinary adventure I have been preparing since the age of tenderness and whose sex I don't know. I taught old men to respect my black hair, and women to worship my limbs; but from these latter I have always preserved my great yellow domain where, ceaselessly, I strike against the metallic remains of the tall inexplicable construction of a distant pyramid form. Love do you condemn me to make of these ruins a ball of clay where I will sculpture my image, or must I have it come out from my eyes as a weapon? In this case, what eye must I use, and isn't it to my interest to use both for the re-creation of a pair of lovers whom I will violate blindly, a new Homer on the pont des Arts whose sinister piers I will have to mine gropingly, at the risk of being abandoned without being able to guide my steps in those vast yellow sunny lands where guns keep guard over the dead sentries. Love do you condemn me to become the guardian demon of those ruins and shall I live henceforth an eternal youth in what the white heaps will let me see of the moon?

They appeared at that very moment. The planes without pilots encircled with rounds of smoke the large immobile air beacons, perched on reefs of changing forms in an unfolding of apotheosis. They appeared at that very moment:

The first woman wore an open hat, black suit and white vest, the second puffed sleeves and a Medici collar, and the third a black silk shirt low cut which, continually sliding from left to right and from right to left, revealed in turn as far as the breasts her two shoulders of a white a bit sunburned.

I possess to the highest degree the pride of my sex. The humilia-ation of a man before a woman either makes me speechless and sick for several days, or gives me a raging anger which I abandon by deliberate cruelty on certain animals, on certain objects, and yet I seek out those irritating spectacles which sometimes force me to stop my ears and close my eyes.

I do not believe in God, but I have the sense of the infinite No one has a more religious spirit than I. I am always coming up against insoluable questions. The questions I want to admit are all insoluble. The others would be asked only by men lack-ing in imagination and do not interest me.

These ruins are situated on the banks of a winding river. The climate is only of air. On the southwest rises an openworked metallic construction, very high, whose use we haven't been able to determine.

Déshabille-toi

Déshabille-toi
Baigne-toi dans cette eau noire
Tu n'as rien à craindre
Tu l'as déjà fait
Le corps humain imperméable ne se mouille pas comme une
       éponge
Le soleil séchera la boue
Elle tombera en poussière
Baigne-toi
Vas-y
La terre est vaste et ton coeur aussi
qui, tous comptes faits et bien faits
ne contient pas encore d'erreur
et n'a jamais contenu de boue.
(Inédit)

Tu Prends la Première Rue

Tu prends la première rue à droite
Tu suis le quai
Tu passes le pont
Tu frappes à la porte de la maison

Le soleil rayonne
La rivière coule
A une fenêtre frémit un pot de géranium
Une voiture passe sur l'autre rive.

Tu te retournes sur le gai paysage
Sans t'apercevoir que la porte s'est ouverte derrière toi
L'hôtesse se tient sur le seuil
La maison est pleine d'ombre.

Mais sur la table on aperçoit le reflet
Le reflet du jour sur un fruit et une bouteille
Sur une assiette de faïence et sur un meuble
Et tu restes-là sur le seuil entre le

Undress

Undress
Bathe in this black water
You have nothing to fear
You have already done it
The waterproof human body doesn't wet like a sponge
The sun will dry the mud
It will fall into dust
Wash
Go to it
The earth is vast and your heart too
Which, when all is well accounted for
doesn't yet contain any error
and has never contained mud.

You Take the First Street

You take the first street on the right
You go along the quai
You cross the bridge
You knock at the door of the house.

The sun shines
The river flows
At a window a geranium pot trembles
An auto goes by on the other bank.

You turn around to the cheerful landscape
Without seeing that the door has opened behind you
The woman stands on the threshold
The house is full of darkness.

But on the table you see the reflection
The reflection of daylight on a piece of fruit and a bottle
On an earthen-ware plate and on some furniture
And you stay there on the threshold between the

Monde plein de semblables à toi-même
Et ta solitude bourdonnante
Du monde entier.

(*Inédit*)

Rencontre

Passez votre chemin.
Le soir lève son bâton blanc devant les piétons.
Cornes des boeufs les soirs d'abondance vous semez l'épouvante
    sur le boulevard.
Passez votre chemin.
C'est la volute lumineuse et contournée de l'heure.
Lutte pour la mort. L'arbitre compte jusqu'au 70.
Le mathématicien se réveille et dit
"J'ai eu bien chaud!"
Les enfants surnaturels s'habillent comme vous et moi.
Minuit ajoute une perle de fraise au collier de Madeleine
et puis on ferme à deux battants les portes de la gare.
Madeleine, Madeleine, ne me regarde pas ainsi;
un paon sort de chacun de tes yeux.
La cendre de la vie sèche mon poème.
Sur la place déserte l'invisible folie imprime son pied dans le
    sable humide.
Le second boxeur se réveille et dit
"J'ai eu bien froid."
Midi l'heure de l'amour torture délicatement
nos oreilles malades.
Un docteur très savant coud les mains de la prieuse
en assurant qu'elle va dormir.
Un cuisinier très habile mélange des poisons dans mon assiette
en assurant que je vais rire.
Je vais bien rire en effet.
Le soleil pointu, les cheveux s'appellent romance dans la langue
    que je parle avec Madeleine.
Un dictionnaire donne la signification des noms propres:
Louis veut dire coup de dés,

World full of people like you
And your droning solitude
Of the entire world.

Meeting

Go on your way.
The evening raises his white club before the pedestrians.
Horns of cattle in evenings of fullness you spread fear over the
    boulevard.
Go on your way.
Now is the shining twisted volute of the hour.
A death struggle. The referee counts to 70.
The mathematician wakes up and says
"I was very hot!"
Supernatural children dress like you and me.
Midnight adds a red pearl to Madeleine's necklace
and then closes the folding doors of the station.
Madeleine, Madeleine, don't look at me that way;
a peacock comes out from each of your eyes.
The ashes of life dry my poem.
On the deserted square invisible madness leaves its footstep on
    the wet sand.
The second boxer awakens and says
"I was very cold."
Noon the love hour deftly tortures
our sick ears.
A very learned doctor sews the hands of the praying woman
assuring her she will sleep.
A very skilful cook mixes poisons in my plate
and assures me I will laugh.
It's true I'm going to laugh.
With the pointed sun, hair is called romance in the language I
    speak with Madeleine.
A dictionary gives the meaning of proper names:
Louis means a throw of dice,

André veut dire récif,
Paul veut dire etc. . . .
mais votre nom est sale:
>   Passez votre chemin!
>>   (C'est les bottes de sept lieues
>>   cette phrase: "Je me vois.")

Poème à la Mystérieuse

J'ai tant rêvé de toi
que tu perds ta réalité
Est-il encore temps d'atteindre ce corps vivant
    et de baiser sur cette bouche la naissance
    de la voix qui m'est chère.
J'ai tant rêvé de toi
que mes bras habitués en étreignant ton ombre
    à se croiser sur ma poitrine ne se plieraient pas
    au contour de ton corps peut-être.
Et que, devant l'apparence réelle de ce qui me hante
    et me gouverne depuis des jours et des années
Je deviendrais une ombre sans doute,
O balances sentimentales.
J'ai tant rêvé de toi qu'il n'est plus temps sans doute que
    je m'éveille. Je dors debout le corps exposé à toutes
    les apparences de la vie et de l'amour et que toi, la seule
    qui compte aujourd'hui pour moi, je pourrais moins toucher
    ton front et les lèvres,
que les premières lèvres et le premier front venu.
J'ai tant rêvé de toi
tant marché, parlé, couché avec ton fantôme qu'il ne me reste
    plus peut-être, et pourtant, qu'à être
    fantôme parmi les fantômes et plus ombre cent fois
    que l'ombre qui se promène et se promènera
    allégrement sur le cadran solaire de ta vie.

Corps et Biens

André means reef,
Paul means etc. . . .
but your name is filthy:
      Go on your way!
            (It's the seven league boots
            this sentence: "I see myself.")

Poem to the Mysterious Woman

I have dreamed so much of you
that you lose your reality
Is there still time to reach that living body
    and kiss on that mouth the birth
    of the voice which is dear to me.
I have dreamed so much of you
that my arms accustomed while embracing your shadow
    to folding over my breast would not bend
    to the shape of your body perhaps.
And that, before the real appearance of what has haunted me
    and ruled me for days and years
I should become doubtless a shade,
O sentimental scales.
I have dreamed of you so much that it is no longer right
    for me to awaken. I sleep standing my body exposed to
    all the appearances of life and love, and you, the only
    one who counts today for me, I could touch your brow
    and your lips less
than the lips and brow of the first person who came.
I have dreamed so much of you
walked so much, spoken, lain with your phantom that all
    I have to do now perhaps is to be a phantom among
    phantoms and a ghost a hundred times more than the
    ghost who walks and will walk gaily over the sun-dial
    of your life.

1

Ecoutez. . . . Faites silence
La triste énumération
De tous les forfaits sans nom,
Des tortures, des violences
Toujours impunis, hélas!
Du criminel Fantômas.

2

Lady Beltham, sa maîtresse,
Le vit tuer son mari
Car il les avait surpris
Au milieu de leurs caresses.
Il coula le paquebot
Lancaster au fond des flots.

3

Cent personnes il assassine
Mais Juve aidé de Fandor
Va lui faire subir son sort
Enfin sur la guillotine. . . .
Mais un acteur très bien grimé,
A sa place est exécuté.

4

Un phare dans la tempête
Croule, et les pauvres bateaux
Font naufrage au fond de l'eau.
Mais surgissent quatre têtes:
Lady Beltham aux yeux d'or,
Fantômas, Juve et Fandor.

5

Le monstre avait une fille
Aussi jolie qu'une fleur.
La douce Hélène au grand coeur
Ne tenait pas de sa famille,

Complaint of Fantomas

with music by Kurt Weill, this poem was broadcast on the 3 Nov. 1933, by Radio-Paris, Radio-Luxembourg, Radio-Toulouse, Radio-Normandie, Radio-Agen, Radio-Lyon and Nice—Juan-les-Pins.

1

Silence. . . . Listen to
The sad list
Of the nameless crimes
Tortures, violences,
Always unpunished, alas,
Of the criminal Fantomas.

2

Lady Beltham, his mistress,
Saw him kill her husband
For he had found them
In an ardent embrace.
He sank the steamship
Lancaster to the bottom of the sea.

3

He has killed one hundred persons
But Juve helped by Fandor
Is going to have him meet his fate
At last on the guillotine. . . .
But a cleverly made-up actor
Is executed in place of him.

4

A lighthouse in the storm
Collapses, and the poor boats
Are shipwrecked in the sea.
But four heads rise up:
Lady Beltham with her golden eyes,
Fantomas, Juve and Fandor.

5

The monster had a daughter
As pretty as a flower.

Car elle sauva Fandor
Qu'était condamné à mort.

6

En consigne d'une gare
Un colis ensanglanté!
Un escroc est arrêté!
Qu'est devenu le cadavre?
Le cadavre est bien vivant
C'est Fantômas, mes enfants!

9

Certain secret d'importance
Allait être dit au tzar.
Fantômas, lui, le reçut car
Ayant pris sa ressemblance
Il remplaçait l'empereur
Quand Juv' l'arrêta sans peur.

10

Il fit tuer par la Toulouche,
Vieillarde aux yeux dégoûtants
Un Anglais à grands coups de dents
Et le sang remplit sa bouche.
Puis il cacha un trésor
Dans les entrailles du mort.

11

Cette grande catastrophe
De l'autobus qui rentra
Dans la banque qu'on pilla
Dont on éventra les coffres . . .
Vous vous souvenez de ça . . .
Ce fut lui qui l'agença.

12

La peste en épidémie
Ravage un grand paquebot
Tout seul au milieu des flots.

Sweet Helen with her generous ways
Didn't resemble her family
For she saved Fandor
Condemned to die.

6

In the baggage room of a station
A bloody bag!
A swindler is arrested!
What has happened to the corpse?
The corpse is alive
It's Fantomas, my children!

9

A certain important secret
Was to be said to the czar.
Fantomas received it, for,
Taking on his looks
He replaced the emperor
When Juve fearlessly arrested him.

10

He had La Toulouche
An old woman with filthy eyes
Kill an Englishman with her teeth
And the blood filled her mouth.
Then he hid a treasure
In the entrails of the dead man.

11

That great catastrophe
Of the bus which crashed
Into the bank they robbed
And split open the coffers . . .
You remember it. . . .
He arranged it all.

12

The plague in epidemic
Lays waste a great boat

Quel spectacle de folie!
Agonies et morts hélas!
Qui a fait ça? Fantômas.

13
Il tua un cocher de fiacre.
Au siège il le ficela
Et roulant cahin-caha,
Malgré les clients qui sacrent,
Il ne s'arrêtait jamais
L'fiacre qu'un mort conduisait.

14
Méfiez-vous des roses noires,
Il en sort une langueur
Epuisante et l'on en meurt.
C'est une bien sombre histoire
Encore un triste forfait
De Fantômas en effet!

15
Il assassina la mère
De l'héroïque Fandor.
Quelle injustice du sort
Douleur poignante et amère . . .
Il n'avait donc pas de coeur,
Cet infâme malfaiteur!

16
Du Dôme des Invalides
On volait l'or chaque nuit,
Qui c'était? Mais c'était lui,
L'auteur de ce plan cupide.
User aussi mal son temps
Quand on est intelligent!

17
A la Reine de Hollande
Même, il osa s'attaquer.
Juve le fit prisonnier

Alone in the midst of the sea.
What a spectacle of terror!
The dying and the dead, alas!
Who did it? Why, Fantomas!

13

He killed a cabby.
Tied him to the seat,
And rolling slowly
With the clients swearing
The coach a dead man drove
Never stopped.

14

Beware of black roses
A heavy languor comes
From them and you die.
It's a gruesome story
Another terrible crime
Of Fantomas himself!

15

He assassinated the mother
Of heroic Fandor.
O injustice of fate
Heartrending grief. . . .
He had no heart,
That wretched criminal!

16

From the dome of the Invalides
Each night gold was stolen.
Who did it? It was he,
The author of this greedy plan.
For an intelligent man
To spend his time so ill!

17

He even dared attack
The queen of Holland.

Ainsi que toute sa bande.
Mais il échappa pourtant
A un juste châtiment.

18

Pour effacer sa trace
Il se fit tailler des gants
Dans la peau d'un trophée sanglant,
Dans d'la peau de mains d'cadavre
Et c'était ce mort qu'accusaient
Les empreintes qu'on trouvait.

19

A Valmondois un fantôme
Sur la rivière marchait.
En vain Juve le cherchait.
Effrayant vieillards et mômes,
C'était Fantômas qui fuyait
Après l'coup qu'il avait fait.

20

La police d'Angleterre
Par lui fut mystifiée.
Mais, à la fin, arrêté,
Fut pendu et mis en terre.
Devinez ce qui arriva:
Le bandit en réchappa.

21

Dans la nuit, sinistre et sombre
A travers la Tour Eiffel,
Juv' poursuit le criminel.
En vain guette-t-il son ombre.
Faisant un suprême effort
Fantômas échappe encor.

23

Dans la mer un bateau sombre
Avec Fantômas à bord,
Hélène, Juve et Fandor

Juve made him prisoner
And all his men.
But yet he escaped
A just punishment.

18

To disguise his marks
He had gloves made for himself
From the skin of a bloody trophy,
From the skin of the hands of a corpse
And they accused the dead man
Whose finger prints they found.

19

In Valmondois a ghost
Walked on the river.
In vain Juve searched for him.
Scaring old men and children,
It was Fantomas in flight
After the deed he had done.

20

The English police
Was mystified by him.
But at last arrested,
He was hung and buried in the earth.
Guess what happened:
The bandit escaped once more.

21

Through the night dark and sinister
Up the Eiffel Tower
Juve pursued the criminal.
He watched for his shadow in vain.
Making a supreme effort
Fantomas again escaped.

23

In the sea a dark boat
With Fantomas on board,

Et des passagers sans nombre.
On ne sait s'ils sont tous morts,
Nul n'a retrouvé leurs corps.

25

Pour ceux du peuple et du monde,
J'ai écrit cette chanson
Sur Fantômas, dont le nom
Fait tout trembler à la ronde.
Maintenant vivez longtemps
Je le souhaite en partant.

Final

Allongeant son ombre immense
Sur le monde et sur Paris,
Quel est ce spectre aux yeux gris
Qui surgit dans le silence?
Fantômas, serait-ce toi
Qui te dresses sur les toits?

Quartier Saint-Merri

Au coin de la rue de la Verrerie
Et de la rue Saint-Martin
Il y a un marchand de mélasse.

Un jour d'avril, sur le trottoir
Un cardeur de matelas
Glissa, tomba, éventra l'oreiller qu'il portait.

Cela fit voler des plumes
Plus haut que le clocher de Saint-Merri.
Quelques-unes se collèrent aux barils de mélasse.

Je suis repassé un soir par là,
Un soir d'avril,
Un ivrogne dormait dans le ruisseau.

La même fenêtre était éclairée.
Du côté de la rue des Juges-Consuls
Chantaient des gamins.

Helen, Juve and Fandor
And many passengers.
We don't know if they're all dead,
For their bodies have not been found.

25
For the humble and the proud
I have written this song
Of Fantomas whose name
Strikes terror far and wide.
A long life to you now
Is my parting wish.

                              Finale
Stretching his tremendous shadow
Over the world and over Paris,
Who is this gray-eyed spectre
Rising up in silence?
Is it you, Fantomas,
Standing up over the roofs?

The Neighborhood of Saint-Merri

At the corner of the rue de la Verrerie
And the rue Saint-Martin
There is a molasses vendor.

One April day, on the sidewalk
A mattress carder
Slipped, fell and split open the pillow he carried.

That made the feathers fly
Higher than the steeple of Saint-Merri.
Some stuck to the kegs of molasses.

I went back there one evening,
An April night,
A drunk was asleep in the gutter.

The same window was lighted.
On the side of the rue des Juges-Consuls
Some youngsters were singing.

Là, devant cette porte, je m'arrête.
C'est de là qu'elle partit.
Sa mère échevelée hurlait à la fenêtre.

Treize ans, à peine vêtue,
Des yeux flambant sous des cils noirs,
Les membres grêles.

En vain le père se leva-t-il
Et vint à pas pesants,
Traînant ses savates,

Attester de son malheur
Le ciel pluvieux.
En vain, elle courait à travers les rues.

Elle s'arrêta un instant rue des Lombards
A l'endroit exact où, par la suite,
Passa le joueur de flûte d'Apollinaire.

Du cloître Saint-Merri naissaient des rumeurs.
Le sang coulait dans les ruisseaux,
Prémice du printemps et des futures lunaisons.

L'horloge de la Gerbe d'or
Répondait aux autres horloges,
Au bruit des attelages roulant vers les Halles.

La fillette à demi nue
Rencontra un pharmacien
Qui baissait sa devanture de fer.

Les lueurs jaune et verte des globes
Brillaient dans ses yeux,
Les moustaches humides pendaient.

—Que fais-tu la gosse, à cette heure, dans la rue?
Il est minuit,
Va te coucher.

—Dans mon jeune temps, j'aimais traîner la nuit
J'aimais rêver sur des livres, la nuit.
Où sont les nuits de mon jeune temps?

There, in front of that door I stopped.
She came out from there.
Her mother, with hair down, shouted from the window.

Thirteen, with little on,
Her eyes flaming under black lashes,
Her legs thin.

All in vain the father rose
And came slowly
Shuffling his old shoes,

To call on the rainy sky
For his woe.
No use, she ran through the streets.

Stopped a moment rue des Lombards
At the very place where, in a later year,
The flute player Apollinaire passed.

From the cloister of Saint-Merri noises rose.
Blood flowed in the gutters,
First sign of spring and future lunations.

The clock of the Golden Sheaf
Answered other clocks,
In the noise of carts rolling toward the market.

The girl half naked
Met a pharmacist
Who was lowering his iron window shade.

The green-yellow lights of the globes
Shone in his eyes,
His wet moustaches drooped.

—What are you doing, child, at this hour, in the street?
It is midnight.
Go home to bed.

—When I was young, I made the night last
I used to dream over my books at night.
Where are the nights of my youth?

—Le travail et l'effort de vivre
M'ont rendu le sommeil délicieux,
C'est d'un autre amour que j'aime la nuit.

Un peu plus loin, au long d'un pont
Un régiment passait
Pesamment.

Mais la petite fille écoutait le pharmacien.
Liabeuf ou son fantôme maudissait les menteurs
Du côté de la rue Aubry-le-Boucher.

—Va te coucher, petite
Les horloges sonnent minuit
Ce n'est ni l'heure ni l'âge de courir les rues.

L'eau clapotait contre un ponton
Trois vieillards parlaient sous le pont
L'un disait oui et l'autre non.

—Oui le temps est court, non le temps est long. . . .
—Le temps n'existe pas dit le troisième.
Alors parut la petite fille.

En sifflotant le pharmacein
S'éloignait dans la rue Saint-Martin
Et son ombre grandissait.

—Bonjour petite dit l'un des vieux
—Bonsoir dirent les deux autres
—Vous sentez mauvais dit la petite.

Le régiment s'éloignait dans la rue Saint-Jacques,
Une femme criait sur le quai,
Sur la berge un oiseau blessé sautillait.

—Vous sentez mauvais dit la petite
—Nous sentirons tous mauvais, dit le premier vieillard
Quand nous serons morts.

—Vous êtes morts déjà dit la petite
Puisque vous sentez mauvais!
Moi seule ne mourrai jamais.

—Work and the effort of living
Have made sleep a joy for me.
Now I love night with another love.

A bit farther, along a bridge
A regiment passed
With heavy steps.

But the girl listened to the pharmacist.
Liabeuf or his ghost cursed all liars
On the side of the rue Aubry-le-Boucher.

—Go home to bed, child
The clocks are striking twelve
This is no time to be on the streets at your age.

The water splashed against the pontoon.
Three old men spoke under the bridge.
One said yes and the other no.

—Yes time is short, no time is long. . . .
—Time doesn't exist said the third.
Then the child appeared.

Whistling the pharmacist
Went off down the rue Saint-Martin
And his shadow grew big.

—Hello little girl said one of the old men
—Good evening said the other two
—You smell bad said the child.

The regiment went off down the rue Saint-Jacques,
A woman shouted on the quai,
On the bank a wounded bird hopped about.

—You smell bad said the little girl
—We'll all smell bad, said the first old man
When we're dead.

—You are dead now said the little girl
Since you smell bad!
I alone will never die.

On entendit un bruit de vitre brisée.
Presque aussitôt retentit
La trompe grave des pompiers.

Des lueurs se reflétaient dans la Seine.
On entendit courir des hommes.
Puis ce fut le bruit de la foule.

Les pompes rythmaient la nuit,
Des rires se mêlaient aux cris,
Un manège de chevaux de bois se mit à fonctionner.

Chevaux de bois ou cochons dorés
Oubliés sur le parvis
Depuis la dernière fête.

Charlemagne rougeoyait,
Impassibles les heures sonnaient,
Un malade agonisait à l'Hôtel-Dieu.

L'ombre du pharmacien
Qui s'éloignait vers Saint-Martin-des-Champs
Epaississait la nuit.

Les soldats chantaient déjà sur la route:
Des paysans pour les voir
Collaient aux fenêtres leurs faces grises.

La petite fille remontait l'escalier
Qui mène de la berge au quai.
Une péniche fantôme passait sous le pont.

Les trois vieillards se préparaient à dormir
Dans les courants d'air au bruit de l'eau.
L'incendie éventrait ses dernières barriques.

Les poissons morts au fil de l'eau,
Flèches dans la cible des ponts,
Passaient avec des reflets.

Tintamarre de voitures
Chants d'oiseaux
Son de cloche

They heard the noise of a smashed window-pane.
Almost at the same time rang out
The grave trumpet of the firemen.

Lights were reflected in the Seine.
They heard men run,
Then it was the noise of the crowd.

Pumps made rhythm with the night
Laughter mingled with shouts,
A riding-school of wooden horses began to perform.

Wooden horses or golden pigs
Left behind on the square
Since the last holiday.

Charlemagne turned red,
Impassive the hours rang out,
A sick man turned to die in the Hôtel-Dieu.

The shadow of the pharmacist
Who went off toward Saint-Martin-des-Champs
Thickened the night.

Soldiers were already singing in the street:
To see them peasants
Glued their gray faces to the windows.

The little girl climbed up the stairs
Which go from the bank to the quai.
A phantom boat passed under the bridge.

The three old men made ready to sleep
In the night wind to the sound of water.
The fire split open its last barrels.

Dead fish on the current of the water
Arrows in the target of the bridges,
Passed with reflections.

Racket of carts
Songs of birds
Sound of a bell

—Ho! petite fille
Ta robe tombe en lambeaux
On voit ta peau.

—Où vas-tu petite fille?
—C'est encore toi le pharmacien
Avec tes yeux! ronds comme des billes!

Détraqué comme une vieille montre,
Là-bas, sur le Parvis Notre-Dame
Le manège hennissait sa musique.

Des chevaux raides se cabraient aux carrefours.
Hideusement nus,
Les trois vieillards s'avançaient dans la rue.

Au coin des rues Saint-Martin et de la Verrerie
Une plume flottait à ras de trottoir
Avec de vieux papiers chassés par le vent.

Un chant d'oiseau s'éleva square des Innocents.
Un autre retentit à la Tour Saint-Jacques.
Il y eut un long cri rue Saint-Bon

Et l'étrange nuit s'effilocha sur Paris.
                    Fortunes

L'Epitaphe

J'ai vécu dans ces temps et depuis mille années
Je suis mort. Je vivais, non déchu mais traqué.
Toute noblesse humaine étant emprisonnée
J'étais libre parmi les esclaves masqués.

J'ai vécu dans ces temps et pourtant j'étais libre.
Je regardais le fleuve et la terre et le ciel
Tourner autour de moi, garder leur équilibre
Et les saisons fournir leurs oiseaux et leur miel.

Vous qui vivez qu'avez-vous fait de ces fortunes?
Regrettez-vous les temps où je me débattais?

—Oh! little girl
Your dress is falling to shreds
We can see your flesh.

—Where are you going, little girl?
—Is it you again, pharmacist,
With your eyes round like marbles!

Broken down like an old watch,
Over yonder, on the square of Notre-Dame
The carousel was neighing its music.

Stiff horses reared up at the crossroads.
Hideously naked
The three old men came down the street.

At the corner of the streets Saint-Merri and la Verrerie
A feather floated just over the sidewalk
With old papers blown by the wind.

A bird call rose up from the square des Innocents.
Another sounded at the Tour Saint-Jacques.
There was a long cry on the rue Saint-Bon.

And the strange night lost its tattered threads over Paris.

Epitaph

I have lived through these times and for a thousand years
I have been dead. I lived, not fallen but tracked.
All human nobility being imprisoned
I was free among the masked slaves.

I lived through these times and yet I was free.
I watched the river the earth and the sky
Turn around me, hold their balance
And the seasons provide their birds and their honey.

You who live, what have you done with those fortunes?
Do you miss the time when I fought?

Avez-vous cultivé pour des moissons communes?
Avez-vous enrichi la ville où j'habitais?

Vivants, ne craignez rien de moi, car je suis mort.
Rien ne survit de mon esprit ni de mon corps.

Contrée

Have you sown for common harvests?
Have you enriched the city where I lived?

Living men, do not fear me, for I am dead.
Nothing survives my spirit and my body.

HENRI MICHAUX

WHEN IN 1941 André Gide published the lecture he never delivered, *Découvrons Henri Michaux*, the poet was far from being unknown in France. It is true that he had not reached a large public, but already by that time he was one of the most highly esteemed poets, the one who has created in his work a world totally different from the real world. Maurice Blanchot calls him, in the few pages he devotes to Michaux in *Faux Pas*, "l'ange du bizarre," a most apt title for one of the really authentic poetic talents of today who is taking his place beside those writers who investigate the strange and the unusual and who therefore, more than others, transpose or even upset the literary perspective. The relationship which Michaux has established between the natural and the unbelievable has created a surreal world which has become the familiar world of his poetry. More than any other contemporary writer, far more, I would say, than the authentic surrealists, he has willed the invention of a new land, and unlike Swift, never uses it for any edifying or didactic purpose. His is a gratuitous creation, one that invites no comparison and no justification. It demands of the reader that he enter this extravagant world without any hope of discovering its meaning, that he enter it as if he were entering the void.

Until the age of twenty-one, Michaux lived principally in Brussels, where he witnessed the German occupation between 1914 and 1918. He was born in Namur, in 1899, into a family of Wallon and Ardennes ancestry. His childhood was solitary. No bond existed between him and his family. He turned inwardly, away from the world, read the mystics and books of travel. After his first voyage, at twenty-one, to England and Brazil, as a sailor, he began writing, and his first pages were published in the Belgian magazine, *Le Disque Vert*. The discovery of Lautréamont, when he was twenty-five, was important and initiated his first real acceptance of literature. About this time he met Jules Supervielle, who became a close friend and helped complete the revelation of poetry to Michaux. He met many of the surrealist writers in Paris, but preferred the companionship of painters: Ernst, Klee, Masson. Jean Paulhan was among the first to realize the great talent of Michaux and published at Gallimard's his first book in France, *Qui-je-fus*. Other poems Paulhan published in his magazines *Commerce* and *Mesures*. Michaux' next trip to South America provoked the writing of *Ecuador* which, with *Un Barbare en Asie*, are his two principal travel books. During the two years before the Second World War he was director of *Hermès*, a Belgian magazine devoted to philosophy and poetry. During the occupation years he lived in the south of France with his wife, and spent much of his time painting. Ever since 1937, Michaux has held regularly in Paris exhibitions of his paintings and drawings.

The illustrations he has made for his own poetry: drawings, gouaches, watercolors, which have been appearing in his recent volumes, at first seemed to be contributions to the poems in words. But now they appear more independent, as separate means of expression. Like the poems, they are images fearful of taking on a deliberate form, of renouncing the infinite suggestiveness of their lines and their beginnings. A certain degree of indeterminateness is his fundamental style. The poem and the gouache are the site of a change or a creation taking place, but they don't necessarily reveal the accomplished metamorphosis, the finished art. The quality as well as the subject matter of his work is indeterminate: half-tragic, half-ironic. A work that seems essentially precarious.

The character he has created, Plume, is the type of innocent who never escapes the violence and the cruelty of the world. It has been often pointed out that a refusal of the world, in some form or other, is at the basis of modern poetry. This refusal is unquestionably a major element in the art of Mallarmé, Rimbaud and Lautréamont. The character Plume, who appears on so many pages of Michaux, is one further illustration of this refusal. His place is with the contemporary innocents who have not escaped the world's cruelty. He is innocent but he is tormented by a sense of guilt. A comparison of Plume with the characters of Kafka has often been pointed out, but there is a greater struggle in the Kafka characters than in Plume who accepts whatever happens to him as part of his fate. His embarrassments and his timidity recall Chaplin and the humorous aspects of situations which are fundamentally tragic. Michaux himself has written of the "narcissism and the quietism" in his poems. Alfred Kazin, in reviewing Michaux' first book to appear in English, *A Barbarian in Asia* (translated by Sylvia Beach), spoke of the "ultimate strain of human solitude" he sensed in the writings of Michaux.

One of the volumes is significantly called *Mes Propriétés*. The poet owns the objects he uses by experimenting with them, and thus experimenting with the powers of his mind. He is the discoverer of laws controlling his own world. His poems contain a disarming series of changes and actions, of births and deaths of all kinds of objects and bodies. Michaux is a magician-creator, watching, almost terrified, the world that has come into being through his mind and his art. The objects and bodies he conjures up become obsessions and often give the impression of turning against their creator. The power to perform metamorphoses carries with it a very particular kind of panic which is the poet's. Michaux is the man who questions the universe and ends by being questioned himself. This is the poet's condition, his ambivalence, the two extremities between which he moves, where a triumph is never reached without a defeat at the same time.

Selected Bibliography of Michaux

1927 *Qui je fus*, Gallimard.
1929 *Ecuador*, Gallimard.
      Mes Propriétés, Ed. Fourcade.
1931 *La nuit remue*, Gallimard.
1932 *Un Barbare en Asie*, Gallimard.
1937 *Plume* précédé de *Lointain Intérieur*, Gallimard.
1939 *Peintures*, Ed. G.L.M.
1948 *Ailleurs*, Gallimard.
1949 *Henri Michaux: Poètes d'Aujourd'hui*, No. 5, Seghers.
1950 *Passages*, Gallimard.

on Michaux

Bertelé, René, Intro. to *Poètes d'Aujourd'hui*.
Blanchot, Maurice, *Faux Pas*. Gallimard.
Belaval, Yvon, *Henri Michaux, Une Magie Rationnelle, Temps Modernes*, sept. 1951.
Renéville, Rolland de, *Univers de la Parole*, Gallimard.

(preface to an *Anthologie poétique*, Stock, 1946)

Poets travel, but they are not possessed by the adventure of travel.

The passion for travel has no liking for poems. It allows, if need be, a romance to be written about it. It allows a mediocre and a bad style, and is even pleased with that, but it doesn't like a poem. It is ill at ease in rhymes.

Even in exuberant times when enthusiasm homogenized man and made poems more "unified," in the period of the romantics, it preferred their prose to their poems.

If it takes on a grand air in Chateaubriand or in some other prince of literature, it discovers more often its real tone, which rings true, in a merchant, an adventurer, a jack-of-all-trades, who transpires it and reveals it in some naïve speech which he receives as a sovereign gift.

Doubtless it is not separable from poetry, but it doesn't behold *its* poetry in poems. It prefers bad company, in a word.

And one can't say it even chose the French, although it has made some of them work hard. But in terms of their poetry, it says that they don't submit easily enough.

Since everything, except mountains, meets finally, the poem and the voyage have met, and the meeting hasn't been generally speaking joyous, nor profitable, I would say.

Poetry wanted the voyage to be considered at leisure. And the voyage was embarrassed at this. Poetry (she) wanted to feel ecstasy over voyage (him). But does he care for ecstasy to that degree? She met him in nostalgia, but that isn't his preference. In refined, unusual and heightened qualifications. But wealth often does him harm. Or in relation to other enchanting figures. But what can he really do with them?

She would like to have seen him as you see love. But the voyage is not a woman. He doesn't want contemplation. His style is rather the male's. His passion is action.

Yet there has been one memorable exception:[1] Cendrars. He and his poems had voyage in their blood.

Still today, *Le Panama ou les aventures de mes sept oncles* and *Prose du Transsibérien et de la petite Jeanne de France* remind you of an express train carrying you off, of a hydroplane alighting on a gulf in the Tropics. A voyaging virtue still inhabits them after twenty years of turmoil, a marvellous compulsion to visit foreign countries and peoples.

What about the others? It is curious, but they were perhaps more important. If Jules Verne made voyaging popular for the French, Baudelaire's *Invitation au Voyage*, with a few perfect poems of men who had never stepped outside of Europe, have been best remembered.

It is too bad, and it is not too bad. Inclination is the lot of the poet. It is by imperishable inclinations that periodically humanity and its hordes of new adolescents rediscover themselves in men who had learned to live by inclinations and not by actions.

Exciting for the young in a state of pre-realization for the old in a state of post-realization, poets are eternally giving the signal for "departure."

The impulse makes their will felt, the cryptic with profundity find their deepest meaning in others, the lovers without a mistress inspire love, the voyagers without leaving call up cruisers.

Yet poetry which didn't begin with this modest role, couldn't cherish indefinitely the role of poor relative or vehicle.

For years it had been looking for its own adventure, hesitatingly at first, and then excitedly. It learned that, in terms of voyage, it needed no one, since it possessed everything itself.

What boundless power it had for displacement, transformation, evasion! Why travel, when a rhyme levels off a mountain, when an adjective peoples a country, when an assonance causes the whole earth to swing out?

The poem was a sky, and the poet held the broomstick.

Yes, he can create for himself many restrictions.

All that changed.

---

1. A second exception, if you count Rimbaud. Yet his real life was not there.

For their first readers, *Au 125 du boulevard Saint-Germain* of Benjamin Péret and the *Chants de Maldoror* of Lautréamont were remarkable voyages. Nothing could hold them back now. Neither distances nor walls, obstacles of the real and of experience. Metamorphoses, transubstantiations, rentings, physical impossibilities became apparently the easiest thing in the world.

The pleasure was so intense and so liberating that hundreds of surreal voyages in that many minds were accomplished in very little time. There was so much hope that we could almost see the "communion of genius."

Yet people yawned over poems of surreal voyages as they had yawned over poems of voyages. All the elements of the voyage were there. But there was no route.

That is why they are still waiting, or waiting all over again, for the poem of the real voyage . . . and the poems about the call to voyage persist.

Mes Occupations

Je peux rarement voir quelqu'un sans le battre.
D'autres préfèrent le monologue intérieur. Moi,
non. J'aime mieux battre.
Il y a des gens qui s'asseoient en face de moi au restaurant et ne
disent rien, ils restent un certain temps, car ils ont décidé
de manger.
En voici un.
Je te l'agrippe, toc.
Je te le ragrippe, toc.
Je le pends au porte-manteau.
Je le décroche.
Je le repends.
Je le redécroche.
Je le mets sur la table, je le tasse et l'étouffe.
Je le salis, je l'inonde.
Il revit.

Je le rince, je l'étire (je commence à m'énerver, il faut en finir),
je le masse, je le serre, je le résume et l'introduis dans mon verre,
et jette ostensiblement le contenu par terre, et dis au garçon:
"Mettez-moi donc un verre plus propre."
Mais je me sens mal, je règle promptement l'addition et je m'en
vais.

Mes Propriétés

Chant de Mort

La fortune aux larges ailes, la fortune par erreur m'ayant
emporté avec les autres vers son pays joyeux, tout à coup, mais
tout à coup, comme je respirais enfin heureux, d'infinis petits
pétards dans l'atmosphère me dynamitèrent et puis des couteaux
jaillissant de partout me lardèrent de coups, si bien que je re-
tombai sur le sol dur de ma patrie, à tout jamais la mienne main-
tenant.

La fortune aux ailes de paille, la fortune m'ayant élevé pour
un instant au-dessus des angoisses et des gémissements, un groupe

My Occupation

I can seldom see anyone without beating him up.
Others prefer the stream of consciousness. That's not for me.
    I like fighting better.
There are men who sit down opposite me in the restaurant and
    say nothing. They stay there for a while because they
    have decided to eat.
Here's one.
I grab him, tap.
I grab him again, tap.
I hang him up on the coat-hanger.
I unhook him.
I hang him up again.
I unhook him again.
I put him on the table, I squeeze him and stifle him.
I mess him up and drown him.
He recovers.

I rinse him, I stretch him (this begins to get on my nerves, I
must bring it to a close), I massage him and press him, I sum him
up and put him into my glass, and obviously throw the contents
on the floor, and say to the waiter: "Give me a clean glass."
But I feel sick, pay my check immediately and go off.

Death Chant

    Fortune with big wings, fortune erroneously having carried
me off with the others toward her happy land, suddenly but
suddenly, as I was joyfully breathing at last, infinitely small
firecrackers in the air dynamited me and then knives coming
from everywhere rained blows on me, so that I fell back on the
hard ground of my country, which was mine forever now.
    Fortune with wings of straw, fortune having raised me for
a moment above sufferings and moanings, a group formed by a
thousand, hidden by my distraction in the dust of a high moun-
tain, a group made by the death struggle for a long time, sud-

formé de mille, caché à la faveur de ma distraction dans la poussière d'une haute montagne, un groupe fait à la lutte à mort depuis toujours, tout à coup nous étant tombé dessus comme un bolide, je retombai sur le sol dur de mon passé, passé à tout jamais présent maintenant.

La fortune encore une fois, la fortune aux draps frais m'ayant recueilli avec douceur, comme je souriais à tous autour de moi, distribuant tout ce que je possédais, tout à coup, pris par on ne sait quoi venu en dessous et par derrière, tout à coup, comme une poulie qui se décroche, je basculai, ce fut un saut immense, et je retombai sur le sol dur de mon destin, destin à tout jamais le mien maintenant.

La fortune encore une fois, la fortune à la langue d'huile, ayant lavé mes blessures, la fortune comme un cheveu qu'on prend et qu'on tresserait avec les siens, m'ayant pris et m'ayant uni indissolublement à elle, tout à coup comme déjà je trempais dans la joie, tout à coup la Mort vint et me dit: "Il est temps. Viens." La Mort, à tout jamais la Mort maintenant.

Plume précédé de *Lointain Intérieur*

Destinée

Déjà nous étions sur le bateau, déjà je partais, j'étais au large, quand, m'arrivant tout d'un coup, comme l'échéance d'une dette, le malheur à la mémoire fidèle se présenta et dit: "C'est moi, tu m'entends, allons, rentre!" et il m'enleva, ce ne fut pas long, et me ramena comme on rentre sa langue.

Déjà sur le bateau, déjà l'océan aux voix confuses s'écarte avec souplesse, déjà l'océan dans sa grande modestie s'écarte avec bonté refoulant sur lui-même ses longues lèvres bleues, déjà le mirage des terres lointaines, déjà . . . mais tout à coup. . . .

Quand le malheur prenant son panier et sa boîte à pinces, se rend dans les quartiers nouvellement éclairés, va voir s'il n'y a pas par là un des siens qui aurait essayé d'égarer sa destinée. . . .

Quand le malheur avec ses doigts habiles de coiffeur empoigne ses ciseaux, d'une main, de l'autre le système nerveux d'un homme, frêle échelle hésitante dans des chairs dodues, tirant des éclairs et des

denly falling on us like a meteor, I fell back on the hard earth of my past, a past forever now the present.

Fortune once again, fortune with fresh sheets, receiving me with gentleness, as I smiled at all those around me, distributing all I owned, suddenly, caught by something coming from below and behind, suddenly, like a pulley which is unhooked, I swung out, it was a huge leap, and I fell back on the hard earth of my destiny, destiny forever mine now.

Fortune once more, fortune with its tongue of oil, having washed my wounds, fortune like a hair you take and might braid with your own, having taken me and having indissolubly united me with her, suddenly as already I was entering upon joy, suddenly Death came and said to me: "It is time. Come." Death, forever Death now.

Fate

Already we were on the boat, already I was sailing, I was in the open sea, when, falling on me suddenly like the date of payment of a debt, misfortune of faithful memory came and said: "It's I, you know, come now, come back!" and he took me away in no time at all, and he drew me in as you pull in your tongue.

Already on the boat, already the ocean with its confused voices withdraws with suppleness, already the ocean in its great modesty withdraws with kindness pressing back on itself its long blue lips, already the mirage of distant lands, already . . . but suddenly . . .

When misfortune taking its basket and its box of pincers, goes into the newly lighted parts of the city, goes to see if there isn't over there one of its own who might have tried to lose its destiny. . . .

When misfortune with its skillful fingers of a hair-dresser takes hold of its scissors in one hand, and in the other the nerve system of a man, that frail hesitant ladder in the plump flesh,

spasmes et le désespoir de cet animal de lin, épouvanté. . . .

Oh, monde exécrable, ce n'est pas facilement qu'on tire du bien de toi.

Celui qui a une épingle dans l'oeil, l'avenir de la marine à vapeur anglaise ne l'intéresse plus. Dormir, s'il pouvait seulement dormir. Mais la paupière recouvrant son mal comme une brosse. . . .

Sur un oeil, pour peu qu'on le sorte convenablement, on peut aussi faire tourner magnifiquement des assiettes.

C'est merveille de voir ça, on ne se lasserait pas de regarder. Mais celui qui en souffre, de cet oeil, prend à ce jeu une part qu'il revendrait volontiers, oh! il ne se ferait pas prier. . . . Oh non, ou du moins pas longtemps.

Difficultés

Un Homme Paisible

Etendant les mains hors du lit, Plume fut étonné de ne pas rencontrer le mur. "Tiens, pensa-t-il, les fourmis l'auront mangé. . . ." et il se rendormit.

Peu après sa femme l'attrapa et le secoua: "Regarde, dit-elle, fainéant! pendant que tu étais occupé à dormir on nous a volé notre maison." En effet, un ciel intact s'étendait de tous côtés. "Bah, la chose est faite," pensa-t-il.

Peu après un bruit se fit entendre. C'était un train qui arrivait sur eux à toute allure. "De l'air pressé qu'il a, pensa-t-il, il arrivera sûrement avant nous" et il se rendormit.

Ensuite le froid le réveilla. Il était tout trempé de sang. Quelques morceaux de sa femme gisaient près de lui. "Avec le sang, pensa-t-il, surgissent toujours quantité de désagréments; si ce train pouvait n'être pas passé, j'en serais fort heureux. Mais puisqu'il est déjà passé . . ." et il se rendormit.

—Voyons, disait le juge, comment expliquez-vous que votre femme se soit blessée au point qu'on l'ait trouvée partagée en huit morceaux, sans que vous, qui étiez à côté, ayez pu faire un geste pour l'en empêcher, sans même vous en être aperçu. Voilà le mystère. Toute l'affaire est là-dedans.

drawing forth flashes and spasms and the despair of that flaxen animal, terrified. . . .

Oh! loathsome world, it wasn't easy to draw good from you.

For him who has a pin in his eye, a future in the English navy is no longer interesting. If only he could sleep. But the eyelid covering his sore like a brush . . .

On an eye, if you push it out just a bit for the purpose, you can flip plates magnificently.

It is marvellous to see that. You never tire watching. But the man who suffers from that eye, has a part in this game he would sell willingly, without being urged. Or at least not for long.

A Peaceful Man

Stretching his hands out of the bed, Plume was amazed at not touching the wall. "Well," he thought, "the ants must have eaten it . . ." and he went back to sleep.

Soon after, his wife took hold of him and shook him: "Good-for-nothing," she said, "Look! while you were busy sleeping, they stole our house from us." It was true. Wherever he looked, he saw the sky. "Bah! it's done now," he thought.

Soon after, he heard a noise. It was a train rushing at them. "With all that haste," he thought, "it will certainly get there before us," and he went back to sleep.

Next, the cold woke him up. He was drenched in blood. A few pieces of his wife lay near by. "With blood," he thought, "there are always a great many annoyances. I'd be very happy if this train hadn't really passed. But since it's already passed by . . ." and he went back to sleep.

—Well, said the judge, how do you explain that your wife was wounded and found cut into eight pieces and you who were beside her couldn't do anything to stop it. You didn't even see it. That's the mystery. The whole trouble is right there.

—I can't help him with that story, thought Plume, and he went back to sleep.

—Sur ce chemin, je ne peux pas l'aider, pensa Plume, et il se rendormit.

—L'exécution aura lieu demain. Accusé, avez-vous quelque chose à ajouter?

—Excusez-moi, dit-il, je n'ai pas suivi l'affaire. Et il se rendormit.

Un certain Plume

Plume Voyage

Plume ne peut pas dire qu'on ait excessivement d'égards pour lui en voyage. Les uns lui passent dessus sans crier gare, les autres s'essuient tranquillement les mains à son veston. Il a fini par s'habituer. Il aime mieux voyager avec modestie. Tant que ce sera possible, il le fera.

Si on lui sert, hargneux, une racine dans son assiette, une grosse racine: "Allons, mangez. Qu'est-ce que vous attendez?"

"Oh, bien, tout de suite, voilà." Il ne veut pas s'attirer des histoires inutilement.

Et si la nuit on lui refuse un lit: "Quoi! Vous n'êtes pas venu de si loin pour dormir, non? Allons, prenez votre malle et vos affaires, c'est le moment de la journée où l'on marche le plus facilement."

"Bien, bien, oui . . . certainement. C'était pour rire naturellement. Oh oui, par . . . par plaisanterie." Et il repart dans la nuit obscure.

Et si on le jette hors du train: "Ah! alors vous pensez qu'on a chauffé depuis trois heures cette locomotive et attelé huit voitures pour transporter un jeune homme de votre âge, en parfaite santé, qui peut parfaitement être utile ici, qui n'a nul besoin de s'en aller là-bas, et que c'est pour ça qu'on aurait creusé des tunnels, fait sauter des tonnes de rochers à la dynamite et posé des centaines de kilomètres de rails par tous les temps, sans compter qu'il faut encore surveiller la ligne continuellement par crainte des sabotages, et tout cela pour . . ."

"Bien, bien. Je comprends parfaitement. J'étais monté, oh, pour jeter un coup d'oeil! Maintenant, c'est tout. Simple curi-

—The execution will take place tomorrow. Accused, do you have anything to add?

—Excuse me, he said, I haven't followed the case. And he went back to sleep.

Plume Travelling

Plume cannot say that he has been paid great respect while travelling. Some pass right over him without a word of warning, and others placidly wipe their hands on his coat. He grew accustomed to this. He prefers to travel modestly. As long as he can, he will behave thus.

If some one cross serves him a root on his plate, a big root, "Come now, eat. What are you waiting for?"

"Of course, right away." He doesn't want to become involved uselessly.

And if at night they refuse him a bed: "You don't mean you come from so far just to sleep? Come, take your bag and your things. This is the best part of the day for walking."

"Why yes, certainly! I was just pretending. My little joke." And he sets out in the dark of night.

And if you throw him out of the train. "So you think we fired this locomotive for three hours and attached eight cars to transport a young fellow of your age, in good health, who may be of great service here, and who has no need of going that far, and that it's for that reason they dug out tunnels, dynamited tons of rock and laid hundreds of miles of rails in all kinds of weather, without forgetting that we still have to guard the tracks continually for fear of sabotage, and all that for . . ."

"Of course, of course. I understand. I came inside just to look. And now that's over. I was just curious, you understand. Many thanks." And he goes back to the road with his bags.

And if at Rome he asks to see the Coliseum: "No, Sir! It's already in a terrible condition. You'll want to touch it, lean against it or sit down. That's why there are ruins everywhere. It's been a lesson for us, a hard lesson, but from now on, nothing doing, do you understand?"

osité, n'est-ce pas. Et merci mille fois." Et il s'en retourne sur les chemins avec ses bagages.

Et si à Rome, il demande à voir le Colisée: "Ah! non. Ecoutez, il est déjà assez mal arrangé. Et puis après Monsieur voudra le toucher, s'appuyer dessus, ou s'y asseoir . . . c'est comme ça qu'il ne reste que des ruines partout. Ce fut une leçon pour nous, une dure leçon, mais à l'avenir, non, c'est fini, n'est-ce pas."

"Bien! Bien! c'était. . . . Je voulais seulement vous demander une carte postale, une photo, peut-être . . . si des fois . . ." Et il quitte la ville sans avoir rien vu.

Et si sur le paquebot, tout à coup le Commissaire du bord le désigne du doigt et dit: "Qu'est-ce qu'il fait ici celui-là? Allons, on manque bien de discipline là, en bas, il me semble. Qu'on aille vite me le redescendre dans la soute. Le deuxième quart vient de sonner." Et il repart en soufflotant, et Plume, lui, s'éreinte pendant toute la traversée.

Mais il ne dit rien, il ne se plaint pas. Il songe aux malheureux qui ne peuvent pas voyager du tout, tandis que lui, il voyage, il voyage continuellement.

"Je Vous Écris d'un Pays Lointain"

I

Nous n'avons ici, dit-elle, qu'un soleil par mois, et pour peu de temps. On se frotte les yeux des jours à l'avance. Mais en vain. Temps inexorable. Soleil n'arrive qu'à son heure.

Ensuite on a un monde de choses à faire, tant qu'il y a de la clarté, si bien qu'on a à peine le temps de se regarder un peu.

La contrariété pour nous dans la nuit, c'est quand il faut travailler, et il le faut: il naît des nains continuellement.

2

Quand on marche dans la campagne, lui confie-t-elle encore, il arrive que l'on rencontre sur son chemin des masses considérables. Ce sont des montagnes et il faut tôt ou tard se mettre à plier les genoux. Rien ne sert de résister, on ne pourrait plus avancer, même en se faisant du mal.

MODERN FRENCH POETS / MICHAUX

"Excuse me! It was only to . . . I only wanted to ask for a postcard, a photograph, perhaps . . . if by chance. . . ." And he leaves the city without seeing anything.

And if on the boat the Purser points him out and says, "What's that fellow doing here? I don't think there's very good discipline down below. Quick! take him down to the storeroom. The second watch has just rung." And he goes off whistling, and Plume, throughout the crossing, has a hard time of it.

But he says nothing, and doesn't complain. He thinks of the poor wretches who can't travel at all, while he travels, and travels continuously.

"I Am Writing You from a Distant Land"

I

Here, she says, we have only one sun a month, and for a very short time. You rub your eyes for days in advance. No use. The weather doesn't change. The sun comes by appointment.

Then there are a million things to do while the light lasts, so that we hardly have time to look at one another.

The annoyance for us at night is when you have to work, and you have to, dwarfs are always being born.

2

When we walk in the country, she confides to him, we often come upon tremendous masses. They are mountains, and sooner or later you have to bend your knees. No point in resisting. You couldn't advance even in hurting yourself.

I don't want to disturb you with this. I could say other things if I really wanted to disturb.

3

The dawn is gray here, she told him. It wasn't always that way. We don't know whom to accuse.

At night the cattle give great bellows, long and flute-like at the end. People are compassionate, but what is there to do?

Ce n'est pas pour blesser que je le dis. Je pourrais dire d'autres choses si je voulais vraiment blesser.

3

L'aurore est grise ici, lui dit-elle encore. Il n'en fut pas toujours ainsi. Nous ne savons qui accuser.

Dans la nuit le bétail pousse de grands mugissements, longs et flûtés pour finir. On a de la compassion, mais que faire?

L'odeur des eucalyptus nous entoure: bienfait, sérénité, mais elle ne peut préserver de tout, ou bien pensez-vous qu'elle puisse réellement préserver de tout?

4

Je vous ajoute encore un mot, une question plutôt.

Est-ce que l'eau coule aussi dans votre pays? (je ne me souviens pas si vous me l'avez dit) et elle donne aussi des frissons, si c'est bien elle.

Est-ce que je l'aime? Je ne sais. On se sent si seule dedans quand elle est froide. C'est tout autre chose quand elle est chaude. Alors? Comment juger? Comment jugez-vous vous autres, dites-moi, quand vous parlez d'elle sans déguisement, à coeur ouvert?

5

Je vous écris du bout du monde. Il faut que vous le sachiez. Souvent les arbres tremblent. On recueille les feuilles. Elles ont un nombre fou de nervures. Mais à quoi bon? Plus rien entre elles et l'arbre, et nous nous dispersons gênées.

Est-ce que la vie sur terre ne pourrait pas se poursuivre sans vent? Ou faut-il que tout tremble, toujours, toujours.

Il y a aussi des remuements souterrains, et dans la maison comme des colères qui viendraient au-devant de vous, comme des êtres sévères qui voudraient arracher des confessions.

On ne voit rien, que ce qu'il importe si peu de voir. Rien, et cependant on tremble. Pourquoi?

The smell of eucalyptus trees is all about: kindness, serenity, but it can't protect us from everything, or do you think it really can protect us from everything?

4

Let me add one more word, or rather a question.

Does water flow also in your country? (I don't remember whether you told me) and it makes you shudder if it is really water.

Do I like it? I don't know. I feel so alone in it when it's cold. It is something else when it's warm. So, how can I judge? How do you judge, tell me that, when you speak of it frankly, without subterfuge?

5

I write to you from the end of the world. I want you to know that. Often the trees tremble. We gather the leaves. They have a tremendous number of veins. But what is the point? There is nothing between them and the tree, and we disperse awkwardly.

Couldn't life continue on the earth without the wind? Or must everything tremble for ever?

There are also subterranean stirrings, and in the house waves of anger coming up to you like serious individuals who want to extract confessions from you.

We see nothing, except what matters little to see. Nothing, and yet we tremble. Why?

Clown

Un jour.
Un jour, bientôt peut-être.
Un jour j'arracherai l'ancre qui tient mon navire loin des mers.
Avec la sorte de courage qu'il faut pour être rien et rien que rien,
Je lâcherai ce qui paraissait m'être indissolublement proche.
Je le trancherai, je le renverserai, je le romprai, je le ferai dégrin-
     goler.
D'un coup dégorgeant ma misérable pudeur, mes misérables com-
     binaisons et enchaînements "de fil en aiguille."
Vidé de l'abcès d'être quelqu'un, je boirai à nouveau l'espace
     nourricier.

A coups de ridicules, de déchéances (qu'est-ce que la déchéance?),
     par éclatement, par vide, par une totale dissipation-déri-
     sion-purgation, j'expulserai de moi la forme qu'on croyait
     si bien attachée, composée, coordonnée, assortie à mon
     entourage et à mes semblables, si dignes, si dignes mes
     semblables.

Réduit à une humilité de catastrophe, à un nivellement parfait
     comme après une intense trouille.
Ramené au-dessous de toute mesure à mon rang réel, au rang
     infime que je ne sais quelle idée-ambition m'avait fait
     déserter.
Anéanti quant à la hauteur, quant à l'estime.
Perdu en un endroit lointain (ou même pas), sans nom, sans
     identité.

CLOWN, abattant dans la risée, dans l'esclaffement, dans le
     grotesque, le sens que contre toute lumière je m'étais fait
     de mon importance,
Je plongerai.
Sans bourse dans l'infini-esprit sous-jacent ouvert à tous,
ouvert moi-même à une nouvelle et incroyable rosée
à force d'être nul
et ras . . .
et risible. . . .

Peintures

Clown

One day.

One day perhaps soon.

One day I will pull up the anchor which holds my boat far
from the sea.

With the kind of courage you need to be nothing and less than
nothing.

I will let go of what seemed to be indissolubly close to me.

I will cut it off, capsize it, break it, make it fall down.

Suddenly discharging my wretched modesty, my wretched
combinations and consequences "slowly and surely."

Relieved of the abscess of being someone, I will drink anew the
nourishing space.

By strokes of ridicule and downfalls (what is a downfall?), by
bursting apart and emptiness, by a total dissipation-deri-
sion-purgation, I will expel from me the form they thought
so well attached, composed, coordinated, matching my
entourage and men like me, so worthy, so worthy the men
like me.

Reduced to a humility of catastrophe, to a perfect levelling as
after an intense fright.

Brought back below all measure to my real rank, to the minute
rank which some ambition-idea had made me desert.

Annihilated in terms of height and esteem.

Lost in a distant spot (or not even that), without name, with no
identity.

CLOWN, tumbling down into laughter, gaffaws, grotesquerie,
the meaning which, contrary to all light, I had made of
my importance,

I will dive.

Without pouch into the spirit-infinite lying below opened to
all

myself opened to a new and unbelievable dew

by dint of being no one

and shorn

and laughable. . . .

PIERRE EMMANUEL

IN EARLY 1946 two volumes of Pierre Emmanuel were published in Montreal. Pierre Seghers had first published them in Paris. This was one of the youngest voices to reach America at the close of the war. It was the voice of an authentic poet whose language, in its explosion of images, in its struggle between life and death, testified to the suffering of a very tense, very dramatic nature. It was not difficult to see that behind the immediate passion of the world, Emmanuel was referring to another Passion, that of the Gospels. He belongs to the line of cataclysmic poets and revolutionaries, those men who are tormented by the demands of Christ, who live with the daily paradox of God-in-man and the Man-God. With such a faith as this poet possesses he is able to consider and explore all the experiences of man, those related by a Catholic Claudel and those of a more Freudian Jouve. He even recalls the surrealist revolution in his will to destroy everything in order to start afresh and rediscover life in its origins and in its purity.

Few poets have written so much in so short a time, and evolved so rapidly as Pierre Emmanuel. In 1947, he published in Paris an autobiographical essay, *Qui est cet homme*, which is a valuable document on the poet's formation.

Soon after his birth his parents moved to America where Emmanuel lived from the age of three to six. He was sent back to France for his education and grew up there without knowing his parents, who continued to live in America. His first ten years were supervised by relatives: an aged aunt, a grandmother and a great-aunt. He was a lonely boy, so apt a pupil that he was suspected by his comrades of playing the favorite. After primary school, he was entrusted to an uncle in Lyon and sent to a church school, a "pensionnat des Lazaristes," taught by Brothers. The emphasis of his studies was on science. Emmanuel's uncle believed that literature was a superfluous subject. His teachers insisted upon a letter-perfect knowledge of their subjects, and the boy memorized easily the text books and was head of his class for six years. The solitude of his childhood years continued. Until eighteen he had no friend, no sense of belonging to a group, no real human experiences. His scholarly triumphs were easy for him and joyless.

During the last two years at school, Emmanuel prepared and passed the two baccalaureat examinations. He had been raised by the Brothers at school and by his uncle, in the strictest fashion. At eighteen he was caught reading *La Rose Publique* of Eluard, and the book was confiscated by his uncle under the pretext that it was immoral. The religious and moral training to which he was subjected was narrow and severe. Only one priest, Abbé Devert, inspired him with confidence and opened his eyes to the spiritual meaning of the confessional.

Three books especially influenced him profoundly in the early years: selections from the writings of Nietzsche, which today have little appeal to Emmanuel; *Les Nourritures Terrestres* of Gide, the book which seemed to love him (*Il me semblait que ce livre m'aimait*), and which taught him a new way of enjoying words and possessing them; and thirdly, *Les Pensées* of Pascal, whose jansenism liberated Emmanuel from the jansenism of his teachers and confessors. Pascal helped him to see himself and to take cognizance of his state of mind. One of his teachers of mathematics, Abbé Larue, initiated him to the poetry of Valéry by reading some passages from *La Jeune Parque.* What held the young listener was especially the rhythm of the verses and the language itself in the contradictions it seemed to create with ordinary logic.

The summer, after receiving his degree, when Emmanuel was tutoring for the October examination, he came upon the work of a poet which was to have on his vocation a lasting influence. It was *Sueur de Sang* by Pierre-Jean Jouve. He was attracted first by the appearance of the page, the unusual typography, and bought the book for that reason. In the preface, Jouve defined poetry as a fundamental operation of the mind, as a spiritual necessity of life without which we would lack some essential aspects of knowledge. This preface, called *Inconscient, Spiritualité et Catastrophe,* was a revelation to Emmanuel. On reading it and the poems, he had the impression of plunging into matter itself, a form of matter where the mind, the body and the elements were all one. Through this book he began to see in a new perspective the conflicts of the world. He wasn't able to understand all the texts but he lived them. The meaning of a literary work became clearer to him. This book of Jouve provided a setting for his meditation, a spiritual uplift. Although later he realized that his poetic means and methods were not the same as Jouve's, he has acknowledged the debt his own work owes to the older poet.

At the end of the summer—he was nineteen—he returned as teacher to the school where he had been a student. Everything changed for him with this change of situation. The mediocrity and the suspicious hostility of the Brothers grew more apparent. His success as teacher was resented. There were minor campaigns to separate him from the pupils attracted to him. He fell ill and left the *collège* in March, and went to live in the country outside of Lyon. He had begun preparing a higher degree (*agrégation*) at the University of Lyon where he remembers especially the philosophy course of Jean Wahl. This philosopher was a poet also and became for Emmanuel the supreme type of dialectician.

In the fall of 1938, just before leaving for Cherbourg, where he was to teach, Emmanuel called on Jouve in his Paris apartment and showed him large numbers of poems. He had confidence in the judgment and honesty of the older man, and accepted the critical analysis of the poems. The advice was excellent. Jouve, who believes that real poetry begins with the maturity of the poet, counselled greater slowness in writing, and greater willingness to wait until the experience itself becomes the language. After a six months silence, Emmanuel wrote a long poem, the first of his work which he has kept, *Christ au Tombeau*. It was different from everything he had written previously, but the poet himself on rereading it was puzzled by its meaning. He sent it to Jouve who found power and beauty in the poem. A new phase in Emmanuel's life and vocation had begun.

Selected Bibliography of Emmanuel

1944   *Cantos*, Ides et Calendes, Neuchatel.
1945   *Jour de Colère*, Ed. Charlot.
1942   *Combats avec tes défenseurs*, Poésie 42, Seghers.
1944   *Tombeau d'Orphée*, Poésie 44, Seghers.
1946   *La liberté guide nos pas*, Poésie 46, Seghers.
1947   *Qui est cet homme*, Egloff.

The function of the poet—of the creator of values, to speak more generally—is to reveal the mortal malady of the period, before it has openly declared itself; to denounce, behind the equivocal symptoms, the profound malaise of energy; to prevent the latter from flourishing in the great body which no longer supports it; to turn it away from the seductions of anarchy, from that morbid exuberance you see in rotting organisms, and which is the diminishing of vital power. His function is, on the contrary, to center it anew in man reassembled, reassured, reinvigorated by his limitations. (p. 152)

From all the teachings I have derived from the Bible, the highest seems to me to come from the nature of human language. . . . I learned to respect in words, not the image of things, but the very substance of man. (p. 227)

The readers of the Bible will understand that it made me realize the truth of aesthetics: the search for the beautiful, in which the artist finds his reason for existence, is inseparable from the word which every man has received as a vocation; inseparable, therefore, from the moral communion which true Beauty manifests in all its domain. (p. 228)

My great force, in my art, was first and foremost: ignorance. I fell in love only with what spoke to me. Belonging to no school, I had no prejudice before any meeting: no *a priori* on language hindered my reflection. Eluard's voice was not mine: my disappointment helped me to understand this; I was wrong about myself, and that borrowed language, false as it was, participated in my error. Our language is made from ourself, and what is not yet defined can only imitate, and learn to speak with the disguise of another word. When abruptly our life, which advances ahead of us, calls us back to itself, we measure the distance of language between borrowed and real experience: but without this borrowed image we would still be invisible to ourselves; it is by stages that we find our differences, that our life becomes a word, and our word life. (p. 258-9)

. . . One day I wrote—not knowing how nor why—a poem in-
spired by the three days between Good Friday and Easter.
There were two parts: in the first, Christ lying in the tomb was
suffering a state of extreme anguish between death and life
equally impossible. In the second, the Word was concentrated
in him, his wounds began again to bleed, and he was resurrected
by the power of the word which was at the same time his own
blood.

I didn't understand this poem, but it seemed real to me, and
unified, whereas everything I had written up to then was only
a clutter of images quickly dissolved. It was from that great
symbol that all my future poetry was to come. I was in the
center of a need and a hope which every man darkly bears within
him. I foresaw them without explaining them to myself. By
the coherent development of a system of images stemming
from that original symbol, I was to succeed in making them in-
telligible. This took a great deal of time, and if the filiation of
major themes is quite clear in my work, it is true that there are
also frequent relapses into the imaginary chaos which preceded
the discovery I have referred to.

I will try to translate that symbol into common language.
Modern man has the feeling of being walled up in his history:
his values, the civilization on which he lived, are dead, and he
has gone down with them into the tomb. But eternal man in
him, the prisoner of a corpse, suffers at being neither dead nor
living. But it is in him, through that force of creation which
was given him to triumph even over triumphant death, where
the one hope for the future is found. This great symbol, for
a Christian, is true only because it was verified once and for
all in history by the resurrected Christ.

The experience of the war years and those which followed
has allowed me to adjust this symbol to the form of history
unfolding before our eyes. For quite a long time it did turn me
away from myself through the consideration of the event and
its general spiritual meaning. But such a consideration, without
the parallel relationship between myself and the world, ended

by creating an inner loss of equilibrium, all the more serious because the Creator tends to justify himself by what he says rather than by what he is. To be precise, he takes his ideal images for the expression of universal man, but he is satisfied to be that universal man and forgets to be an individual man, a man like everyone else, subordinated to the same moral law as they are. He forgets to know himself and judge himself.

Printemps des morts! je m'irritais de sa douceur,
de ses tendres coulées de honte sur mes membres
de cette soif d'un néant vert au fond du temps
qui me prenait à voir les monts naissants, humides
du vert prodigieux des éternelles eaux. . . .
Des bouffées d'un oubli sauvage m'emplissaient
de quelle odeur de terre ou de bête mouillée
et je me débattais à même le limon
—mêlé à l'ombre végétale, et déjà moite
sous l'effort des chimies profondes
       mais ô vie
ô lassitude de la chair insidieuse
abandonnée au plaisir traître de la Mort,
je n'ai point perdu pied dans ta vase, je fus
debout parmi les morts et ferme sur la roche
où la Croix est fichée de toute éternité.

N'ayant d'autre saison que l'humaine agonie,
ni d'autre ciel que l'âme humaine écartelée
que Dieu marqua du grand midi de Sa Colère,
je restai sourd à l'infini consentement:
insensible au fluide appel des courbes lentes
quand l'harmonie se baigne nue au sein des blés,
aveugle au soir exquis des tombes, où la pierre
un instant attisée par le couchant s'éteint
et redevient cendreuse aux pas, jeune et légère,
je voyais l'affre des mourants mordant la terre,
et sentais l'homme mutilé grandir en moi
rigide, monstrueux de clameur retenue,
un strict bandeau de ciel opaque sur les yeux
et des haillons d'honneur sur ses moignons atroces.
En butte au rire épais des hommes, discordant
et seul! il résonnait de plaintes, harpe amère
offerte au comble du mutisme au vent du sang.

Le charnier me fixait de son oeil sans mémoire,
l'horreur du sang battait mon corps comme la mer

Good Friday Rhapsody

Springtime of the dead! I was uneasy with its mildness
with its tender hands of shame over my body
with that thirst for a green void in the depths of time
which seized me when I saw the nascent mountains, moistened
with the rich green of eternal waters. . . .
Gusts of a wild forgetting filled me
with that smell of earth or of a wet animal
and I struggled in the mud itself
—mingled with the shade of plants already moist
under the effort of hidden chemistry
                              but O life
O weariness of insidious flesh
abandoned to the treacherous pleasure of Death,
I didn't lose footing in your slime, I was
standing among the dead and strong on the rock
where the Cross is driven in for all eternity.

Having no other season than human agony,
no other sky save the human soul quartered
which God marked with the great heat of His Wrath,
I remained deaf to the infinite consent:
insensitive to the fluid call of slow curves
when harmony bathes naked in the heart of the wheat,
blind to the delicate evening of graves, where the stone
a moment lighted by the setting sun goes out
and turns ashes again under our steps, young and light,
I saw the torture of the dying men on the earth,
and felt the mutilated man growing in me
rigid, monstrous by withheld clamor,
a severe band of opaque sky over his eyes
and tatters of honor over his terrible stumps.
A butt to the thick laughter of men, discordant
and alone! he resounded with complaint, bitter harp
offered to the extreme of silence in the blood wind.

The charnel house looked at me without memory,
the horror of blood like the sea beat my body

et là-haut un vautour rythmait à grands coups d'aile
l'âpre marée du désespoir: je l'entendais
ce battement de l'Ombre implacable! mon coeur
était l'ombre de ce vautour sur la durée,
l'immense pulsation d'abîme refoulait
mon sang jusqu'aux plus véhémentes plaies de l'homme
couché en croix la face à la merci du ciel

O Croix! squelette déchirant de la Colombe
à jamais consumée au zénith des douleurs
tu maintiens la vigile ardente, tu mesures
de tes bras vigoureux la folie des humains,
de ton sublime vol la liberté de l'homme,
et ton raidissement vertical, redressant
le faix d'un innombrable fruit (si lourd d'années
que l'absolu jamais n'y parvient à mûrir)
l'empêche de succomber à son mutisme
au désespoir irrémissible de l'oubli. . . .

Ce fruit, que de soleils à le mûrir s'usèrent
et que de nuit, à méditer ses sucs futurs!
Et quel travail fit la substance douloureuse
pour atteindre à ce point d'extase où trop pesant
tomber dans le pardon sans borne, être léger
de tout le temps enfin devenu liberté
pur, de toute la faute enfin sanctifiée
heureux, de toute la souffrance enfin comprise.

Mais l'Arbre ravagé sans cesse par les vents
voit pourrir dans l'humus noirâtre des batailles
sur les routes givrées de famine et de sang
ou dans l'eau des paroles mortes, croupissante
sous un ciel de nuées somnambules, son fruit

Son christ véreux, son christ que les canons dévorent,
son christ sinistre en des postures foudroyées
son christ déchiqueté par l'appétit des bombes
son christ suant de haine et de terreur, son christ
acharné sur sa propre image! O créatures
voyez en vous le christ obscène se salir

MODERN FRENCH POETS / EMMANUEL

and in the air a vulture with great wings gave movement
to the harsh tide of despair: I heard it
that beating of the implacable Dark! my heart
was the shadow of this vulture over time,
the immense pulsation of the sea forced down
my blood to the most vehement wounds of man
lying on the cross his face to the mercy of the sky

O Cross! tragic skeleton of the Dove
forever consumed at the zenith of grief
you continue the burning vigil, you measure
with your vigorous arms the madness of men,
with your sublime flight the liberty of man,
and your vertical stiffening, reerecting
the burden of so many fruit (so heavy with years
that the absolute never ripens on it)
prevents it from succumbing to its silence
to the irremissible despair of oblivion. . . .

How many suns were drained on ripening this fruit
and how many nights on meditating its future juice!
And what labor performed the sorrowing substance
to reach the point of ecstasy where too heavy
to fall into limitless pardon, to be light
with all time finally becoming freedom
pure, with all error finally sanctified
happy, with all suffering finally understood.

But the Tree ravaged ceaselessly by the winds
sees rotting in the black humus of battle
on the roads icy with famine and blood
or in the water of dead words, stagnating
under a sky of sleep-drunk clouds, its fruit

Its worm-eaten christ, its christ devoured by canon,
its sinister christ in death-striken postures
its christ slashed by the appetite of bombs
its christ sweating with hate and fear, its christ
attacking its own image! O creatures
see in yourselves the obscene christ soiling himself

regardez à vos pieds sa forme défoncée,
sa face à bout portant lorsque vous épaulez,
ses plaies rapaces qui tournoient dans le ciel blême
et paissent la morne charogne des vivants:
ce christ d'ordure intarissable vous submerge
vous putréfie debout, tyrans, esclaves, dieux,
ô pauvres monotones hommes! qu'épouvante
du blasphème l'immensité tangible enfin
et le cri de la damnation inéluctable
qui sort de cette bouche ignominieuse en vous

Puis contemplez la Croix! car le vrai fruit toujours
est intact sur la haute branche de ce monde
le Christ mûrit avec lenteur tout le péché
jusqu'au jour où fondue en gloire, la chair sombre
retrouvant la saveur limpide de l'Esprit
aura changé tout l'immondice de l'histoire
(l'homme, foyer de pourriture au coeur du temps
dieu, monstre d'injustice éternelle et d'absence
la Terre, éponge saturée d'une âcre Nuit)
en un jour pur, si transparent que dieu Lui-même
S'évanouira dans l'infinie dilection
le Chant de la douleur parfaite, Corps de l'homme
promu au tout-aimant silence! ô humble chair
justifiant enfin le Verbe dans le Père
Fais donc rage, Immobile Coeur de la détresse
ceux-là savent qui dans le Mal sont assurés
que Tu es la seule permanente catastrophe,
Christ, ô printemps unique ô chancre exubérant
                    Combats avec tes défenseurs

Les Noces de la Mort

I
Orgie de pierre!
Je buvais la haine en tes lieux bas
et baignais d'un sauvage été nos verts sépulcres
ô morte
et ma bouche animale s'altérait

see at your feet his collapsed form,
his face close when you take aim
his rapacious wounds which turn in the pale sky
and graze the dull carcass of the living:
this christ of inexhaustible filth submerges you
putrefies you standing, tyrants, slaves, gods,
O poor tedious men! terrified at last
by the tangible immensity of blasphemy
and the cry of inevitable damnation
which issues from that ignominious mouth in you

So, contemplate the Cross! for the true fruit always
is intact on the high branch of this world
Christ ripens slowly all sinning
until the day when changed to glory, the dark flesh
recovering the clear taste of the Spirit
will have changed all the filth of history
(man, rotting center in the heart of time
a god, a monster of eternal injustice and absence
the Earth, a saturated sponge of an acrid Night)
into a pure day, so transparent that god Himself
will vanish in infinite love
the Song of perfect grief, Body of man
raised to the all-loving silence! O humble flesh
justifying at last the Word in the Father
Rage then, Immobile Heart of distress
they who are assured in Evil know
that You are the one permanent catastrophe,
Christ, one spring time blossoming canker.

Death Wedding

I
Orgy of stone!
I drank hate in your low places
and bathed with a savage summer our green tombs
O dead one
and my animal mouth was made thirsty

sur les lèvres décomposées de quel jadis
étrange

Accablée de dieu que je t'aimais
dans les transfigurants étés ô madeleine
très nue les seins taris par tant d'âpre beauté
et tant d'impétueux soleil entre tes jambes
et à ton flanc deux larges plaies d'odeur

Je t'aimais ruisselante et dorée de fatigues
ô grappe de péché mûrie en mon regard
j'adorais tes chaudes montées buveuses d'ombre
et les maisons tes dents de gloire et tes jardins
tout humides le soir du rêve des putains
Ville nocturne aux murs de larmes crypte amère
que j'ai chanté de litanies obscènes que j'ai prié
tes madones de plaisir et d'épouvante
que d'ex-voto coupables j'ai taillés
en mes années hagardes!
Que j'ai prié pleuré chanté
que de ténèbres entonnées à ta louange
sur l'orgue des pluies d'hiver dans les tubas
vertigineux de l'ombre
et que j'ai marché!

Que j'ai suivi longtemps la Mort sous tes arcades
que de rues j'ai pétries de mon pas de souffrance
que de sang j'ai mêlé à l'huile des pavés
que j'ai cherché le crime pur atrocement
parmi les meurtres discordants les agonies
l'amour

Et svelte au noir vitrail que je l'aimais
si nue dans les parvis de la mémoire
qu'elle était claire à grands monceaux quand ses cheveux
te versant leurs graminées folles descellaient
tes marbres fiers ô taciturne
qu'elle était grave et sculptée de tes sueurs
la morte qui te baignait de ses bras tendres

on the decomposed lips of what strange
yesterday

How I loved you in your love of god
in the transfiguring summers O madeleine
very naked your breasts dried up by so much harsh beauty
and so much impetuous sunlight between your legs
and on your side two wide odorous wounds

I loved you wet and golden with fatigue
O grape ripened with sin before me
I worshipped your warm slopes drinkers of darkness
and the horses your teeth of glory and your gardens
all moist at night with the dream of whores

Night city with walls of tears bitter crypt
how many obscure litanies I sang how I prayed
to your madonnas of pleasure and fear
how many guilty votive plaques did I carve
in my wild years!
How I prayed wept sang
how my tenebrae intoned for you praise
on the organ of winter rain in the dizzying
trumpets of darkness
and how far I walked!

How long I followed Death under your arcades
how many streets I pounded with my suffering steps
how much blood did I mix with the oil of pavements
how madly I looked for the pure crime
among the discordant murders agonies
love

And slender on the black window how I loved her
so naked in the courtyards of memory
how clear she was in large heaps when her hair
pouring over you their mad grasses unsealed
your proud marble O silent one
how solemn she was and graven with your sweat
the dead woman who bathed you with her tender arms

qu'elle était haute comme l'aube au fond des lacs
et que tes fleuves étaient doux sur son ivoire

Qu'elle était dure hostie de larme où crucifiée
tu paraissais
trahie d'en-bas par la ténèbre

Qu'il était noir superbement ce lourd calice
élevé par deux mains de sang sur ton péché

Laquelle
      de l'autre à jamais inutile
            est la tombe

II

Seigneur Tu me cherchais
dans les eaux désertes d'une femme
sous les myrtes déchirants Tu l'étreignais
la jeune morte toute en pleurs! Et Tu criais
plus désespérément que la lumière
et Tu riais contre la terre on entendait
battre Ton coeur féroce au sein des pierres

Père de ma douleur! Tu déchires ma mort
mais pourquoi tuer le cadavre puisque Tu veux
le sang? et pourquoi le vide? et pourquoi
me laisses-Tu cette victime?

Les mains souillées de nuit suis-je le meurtrier
suis-je le prêtre mauvais de cette morte

ai-je mangé la pain sur elle et bu le vin
ai-je pleuré Ton sang sur elle
                   ai-je inventé
son corps croix de volupté pour m'y clouer
O dieux jaloux quel est mon crime?
                      je l'aimais
Elle était une épée de fureur entre nous
jadis,
mais morte qu'a-t-elle encore à ma semblance
cette roche d'oubli meurtrie par les baisers?

how high she was like dawn in the bottom of lakes
and how gentle your rivers were over her ivory

What a hard host of tear she was where crucified
you appeared
betrayed from below by the darkness

How gloriously black was that heavy chalice
raised by two hands of blood over your sin

Which one
            of the other forever useless
                                    is the tomb

II

Lord You sought me
in the abandoned waters of a woman
under the sorrowing myrtles You embraced
the young woman dead in tears! And You cried out
more desperately than light
and You laughed against the earth they heard
Your wild heart beating in the midst of stones

Father of my grief! You tear my death
but why kill the corpse since You wish
the blood? and why the void? and why
do You leave me this victim?

My hands soiled with night am I the murderer
am I the bad priest of this dead woman
have I broken bread over her and drunk wine
have I wept for Your blood over her
                              did I invent
her body cross of pleasure to nail myself to it
O jealous gods what is my crime?
                          I loved her
She was a sword of fury between us
long ago,
but dead what does she still have in my resemblance
this rock of oblivion wounded by kisses?

Est-ce blasphème
que ces rites d'un coeur pieux
un duvet sous l'aile des pierres
un noir soleil en ses cheveux
une gorgée d'ombre à ses lèvres
un peu d'automne dans sa main
une herbe

Mais O
Tu n'es point trompé par ces contrées
aux allées de sommeil tranquille: et Tu veux
que je sois nu dans la bataille!
Me voici
en gloire, un grand drapeau de paysage aimé
la Mort
à la plus haute tour de l'impossible,
pour elle déployé!
Je suis la forteresse de regards
bâtie sur la colère nue de la mémoire
hymne de pierre et tombeau retentissant
où se dresse gardée de Toi Pâque adorable
Celle qui fut la morte
                    ô délivrée
Toi Seigneur, marche au crime!
                    parmi
les détonations de l'âme et les géants
éclatements de profondeur,
hâte le dénouement profane ou la ténèbre
ou la résurrection qu'importe! et ne va point
lever les yeux vers le rideau de ce théâtre.

Tombeau d'Orphée

Are these rites of a pious heart
blasphemy
a down under the wing of stones
a black sun in her hair
a throatful of darkness at her lips
a little autumn in her hand
a grass

But O
You are not deceived by this country
with its paths of quiet sleep: and You want
me naked in battle!
Here I am
in glory, a great flag of cherished landscape
Death
at the highest tower of the impossible,
unfurled for her!
I am the fortress of glances
built on the nude anger of memory
hymn of stone and resounding tomb
where rises up guarded by Your adorable Pasch
She who was dead
                    now delivered
You Lord, onward to crime!
                              amid
the firings of the soul and the giant
blasts of the depths,
hasten the profane ending darkness
or resurrection it matters little! and do not
raise your eyes toward the curtain of that theatre.

Nada

Mon dieu qui es absent infiniment
des montagnes et des fleuves et des arbres
de la mer et du ciel et des yeux qui les créent
et des astres où se forment les pensées
et de la vie et de la mort et de l'absence

Mon dieu qui es ailleurs infiniment
en des yeux sans regard des mains sans étendue
en des âmes inhabitées depuis toujours
en des clartés vides et vertes de silence
où l'on n'atteint jamais par naissance ni mort

Mon dieu pressentiment de ma gaîté captive
fruition et liberté pure dans le rien
jamais jamais ma prison en toi n'est assez dure
mes paupières assez murées jamais jamais
pour enfermer l'ombre de ton néant

Mon dieu

Jour de Colère

Nada

Lord who are infinitely absent
from mountains and rivers and trees
from the sea and the sky and the eyes which create them
and from the stars where thoughts are formed
and from life and death and absence

Lord who are infinitely elsewhere
in eyes without sight in hands without extent
in souls uninhabited forever
in lights empty and green with silence
which are never reached by birth or death

Lord foreboding of my imprisoned joy
richness and pure freedom in nothing
never is my prison in you severe enough never
my eyelids are never walled up enough never
to contain the darkness of your void

Lord

A CATALOG OF SELECTED
DOVER BOOKS
IN ALL FIELDS OF INTEREST

A CATALOG OF SELECTED DOVER
BOOKS IN ALL FIELDS OF INTEREST

DRAWINGS OF REMBRANDT, edited by Seymour Slive. Updated Lippmann, Hofstede de Groot edition, with definitive scholarly apparatus. All portraits, biblical sketches, landscapes, nudes. Oriental figures, classical studies, together with selection of work by followers. 550 illustrations. Total of 630pp. 9⅛ × 12¼.
21485-0, 21486-9 Pa., Two-vol. set $29.90

GHOST AND HORROR STORIES OF AMBROSE BIERCE, Ambrose Bierce. 24 tales vividly imagined, strangely prophetic, and decades ahead of their time in technical skill: "The Damned Thing," "An Inhabitant of Carcosa," "The Eyes of the Panther," "Moxon's Master," and 20 more. 199pp. 5⅜ × 8½. 20767-6 Pa. $4.95

ETHICAL WRITINGS OF MAIMONIDES, Maimonides. Most significant ethical works of great medieval sage, newly translated for utmost precision, readability. Laws Concerning Character Traits, Eight Chapters, more. 192pp. 5⅜ × 8½.
24522-5 Pa. $4.50

THE EXPLORATION OF THE COLORADO RIVER AND ITS CANYONS, J. W. Powell. Full text of Powell's 1,000-mile expedition down the fabled Colorado in 1869. Superb account of terrain, geology, vegetation, Indians, famine, mutiny, treacherous rapids, mighty canyons, during exploration of last unknown part of continental U.S. 400pp. 5⅜ × 8½. 20094-9 Pa. $7.95

HISTORY OF PHILOSOPHY, Julián Marías. Clearest one-volume history on the market. Every major philosopher and dozens of others, to Existentialism and later. 505pp. 5⅜ × 8½. 21739-6 Pa. $9.95

ALL ABOUT LIGHTNING, Martin A. Uman. Highly readable non-technical survey of nature and causes of lightning, thunderstorms, ball lightning, St. Elmo's Fire, much more. Illustrated. 192pp. 5⅜ × 8½. 25237-X Pa. $5.95

SAILING ALONE AROUND THE WORLD, Captain Joshua Slocum. First man to sail around the world, alone, in small boat. One of great feats of seamanship told in delightful manner. 67 illustrations. 294pp. 5⅜ × 8½. 20326-3 Pa. $4.95

LETTERS AND NOTES ON THE MANNERS, CUSTOMS AND CONDITIONS OF THE NORTH AMERICAN INDIANS, George Catlin. Classic account of life among Plains Indians: ceremonies, hunt, warfare, etc. 312 plates. 572pp. of text. 6⅛ × 9¼. 22118-0, 22119-9, Pa. Two-vol. set $17.90

ALASKA: The Harriman Expedition, 1899, John Burroughs, John Muir, et al. Informative, engrossing accounts of two-month, 9,000-mile expedition. Native peoples, wildlife, forests, geography, salmon industry, glaciers, more. Profusely illustrated. 240 black-and-white line drawings. 124 black-and-white photographs. 3 maps. Index. 576pp. 5⅜ × 8½. 25109-8 Pa. $11.95

THE BOOK OF BEASTS: Being a Translation from a Latin Bestiary of the Twelfth Century, T. H. White. Wonderful catalog real and fanciful beasts: manticore, griffin, phoenix, amphivius, jaculus, many more. White's witty erudite commentary on scientific, historical aspects. Fascinating glimpse of medieval mind. Illustrated. 296pp. 5⅜ × 8¼. (Available in U.S. only) 24609-4 Pa. $6.95

FRANK LLOYD WRIGHT: ARCHITECTURE AND NATURE With 160 Illustrations, Donald Hoffmann. Profusely illustrated study of influence of nature—especially prairie—on Wright's designs for Fallingwater, Robie House, Guggenheim Museum, other masterpieces. 96pp. 9¼ × 10¾. 25098-9 Pa. $8.95

FRANK LLOYD WRIGHT'S FALLINGWATER, Donald Hoffmann. Wright's famous waterfall house: planning and construction of organic idea. History of site, owners, Wright's personal involvement. Photographs of various stages of building. Preface by Edgar Kaufmann, Jr. 100 illustrations. 112pp. 9¼ × 10. 23671-4 Pa. $8.95

YEARS WITH FRANK LLOYD WRIGHT: Apprentice to Genius, Edgar Tafel. Insightful memoir by a former apprentice presents a revealing portrait of Wright the man, the inspired teacher, the greatest American architect. 372 black-and-white illustrations. Preface. Index. vi + 228pp. 8¼ × 11. 24801-1 Pa. $10.95

THE STORY OF KING ARTHUR AND HIS KNIGHTS, Howard Pyle. Enchanting version of King Arthur fable has delighted generations with imaginative narratives of exciting adventures and unforgettable illustrations by the author. 41 illustrations. xviii + 313pp. 6⅛ × 9¼. 21445-1 Pa. $6.95

THE GODS OF THE EGYPTIANS, E. A. Wallis Budge. Thorough coverage of numerous gods of ancient Egypt by foremost Egyptologist. Information on evolution of cults, rites and gods; the cult of Osiris; the Book of the Dead and its rites; the sacred animals and birds; Heaven and Hell; and more. 956pp. 6⅛ × 9¼. 22055-9, 22056-7 Pa., Two-vol. set $21.90

A THEOLOGICO-POLITICAL TREATISE, Benedict Spinoza. Also contains unfinished *Political Treatise*. Great classic on religious liberty, theory of government on common consent. R. Elwes translation. Total of 421pp. 5⅜ × 8½. 20249-6 Pa. $7.95

INCIDENTS OF TRAVEL IN CENTRAL AMERICA, CHIAPAS, AND YUCATAN, John L. Stephens. Almost single-handed discovery of Maya culture; exploration of ruined cities, monuments, temples; customs of Indians. 115 drawings. 892pp. 5⅜ × 8½. 22404-X, 22405-8 Pa., Two-vol. set $15.90

LOS CAPRICHOS, Francisco Goya. 80 plates of wild, grotesque monsters and caricatures. Prado manuscript included. 183pp. 6⅜ × 9⅝. 22384-1 Pa. $5.95

AUTOBIOGRAPHY: The Story of My Experiments with Truth, Mohandas K. Gandhi. Not hagiography, but Gandhi in his own words. Boyhood, legal studies, purification, the growth of the Satyagraha (nonviolent protest) movement. Critical, inspiring work of the man who freed India. 480pp. 5⅜ × 8½. (Available in U.S. only) 24593-4 Pa. $6.95

ILLUSTRATED DICTIONARY OF HISTORIC ARCHITECTURE, edited by Cyril M. Harris. Extraordinary compendium of clear, concise definitions for over 5,000 important architectural terms complemented by over 2,000 line drawings. Covers full spectrum of architecture from ancient ruins to 20th-century Modernism. Preface. 592pp. 7½ × 9⅜. 24444-X Pa. $15.95

THE NIGHT BEFORE CHRISTMAS, Clement Moore. Full text, and woodcuts from original 1848 book. Also critical, historical material. 19 illustrations. 40pp. 4⅝ × 6. 22797-9 Pa. $2.50

THE LESSON OF JAPANESE ARCHITECTURE: 165 Photographs, Jiro Harada. Memorable gallery of 165 photographs taken in the 1930's of exquisite Japanese homes of the well-to-do and historic buildings. 13 line diagrams. 192pp. 8⅜ × 11¼. 24778-3 Pa. $10.95

THE AUTOBIOGRAPHY OF CHARLES DARWIN AND SELECTED LETTERS, edited by Francis Darwin. The fascinating life of eccentric genius composed of an intimate memoir by Darwin (intended for his children); commentary by his son, Francis; hundreds of fragments from notebooks, journals, papers; and letters to and from Lyell, Hooker, Huxley, Wallace and Henslow. xi + 365pp. 5⅜ × 8. 20479-0 Pa. $6.95

WONDERS OF THE SKY: Observing Rainbows, Comets, Eclipses, the Stars and Other Phenomena, Fred Schaaf. Charming, easy-to-read poetic guide to all manner of celestial events visible to the naked eye. Mock suns, glories, Belt of Venus, more. Illustrated. 299pp. 5¼ × 8¼. 24402-4 Pa. $7.95

BURNHAM'S CELESTIAL HANDBOOK, Robert Burnham, Jr. Thorough guide to the stars beyond our solar system. Exhaustive treatment. Alphabetical by constellation: Andromeda to Cetus in Vol. 1; Chamaeleon to Orion in Vol. 2; and Pavo to Vulpecula in Vol. 3. Hundreds of illustrations. Index in Vol. 3. 2,000pp. 6⅛ × 9¼. 23567-X, 23568-8, 23673-0 Pa., Three-vol. set $41.85

STAR NAMES: Their Lore and Meaning, Richard Hinckley Allen. Fascinating history of names various cultures have given to constellations and literary and folkloristic uses that have been made of stars. Indexes to subjects. Arabic and Greek names. Biblical references. Bibliography. 563pp. 5⅜ × 8½. 21079-0 Pa. $8.95

THIRTY YEARS THAT SHOOK PHYSICS: The Story of Quantum Theory, George Gamow. Lucid, accessible introduction to influential theory of energy and matter. Careful explanations of Dirac's anti-particles, Bohr's model of the atom, much more. 12 plates. Numerous drawings. 240pp. 5⅜ × 8½. 24895-X Pa. $5.95

CHINESE DOMESTIC FURNITURE IN PHOTOGRAPHS AND MEASURED DRAWINGS, Gustav Ecke. A rare volume, now affordably priced for antique collectors, furniture buffs and art historians. Detailed review of styles ranging from early Shang to late Ming. Unabridged republication. 161 black-and-white drawings, photos. Total of 224pp. 8⅜ × 11¼. (Available in U.S. only) 25171-3 Pa. $13.95

VINCENT VAN GOGH: A Biography, Julius Meier-Graefe. Dynamic, penetrating study of artist's life, relationship with brother, Theo, painting techniques, travels, more. Readable, engrossing. 160pp. 5⅜ × 8½. (Available in U.S. only) 25253-1 Pa. $4.95

PLANTS OF THE BIBLE, Harold N. Moldenke and Alma L. Moldenke. Standard reference to all 230 plants mentioned in Scriptures. Latin name, biblical reference, uses, modern identity, much more. Unsurpassed encyclopedic resource for scholars, botanists, nature lovers, students of Bible. Bibliography. Indexes. 123 black-and-white illustrations. 384pp. 6 × 9. 25069-5 Pa. $8.95

FAMOUS AMERICAN WOMEN: A Biographical Dictionary from Colonial Times to the Present, Robert McHenry, ed. From Pocahontas to Rosa Parks, 1,035 distinguished American women documented in separate biographical entries. Accurate, up-to-date data, numerous categories, spans 400 years. Indices. 493pp. 6½ × 9¼. 24523-3 Pa. $10.95

THE FABULOUS INTERIORS OF THE GREAT OCEAN LINERS IN HISTORIC PHOTOGRAPHS, William H. Miller, Jr. Some 200 superb photographs capture exquisite interiors of world's great "floating palaces"—1890's to 1980's: *Titanic, Ile de France, Queen Elizabeth, United States, Europa,* more. Approx. 200 black-and-white photographs. Captions. Text. Introduction. 160pp. 8⅞ × 11¾. 24756-2 Pa. $9.95

THE GREAT LUXURY LINERS, 1927–1954: A Photographic Record, William H. Miller, Jr. Nostalgic tribute to heyday of ocean liners. 186 photos of Ile de France, Normandie, Leviathan, Queen Elizabeth, United States, many others. Interior and exterior views. Introduction. Captions. 160pp. 9 × 12. 24056-8 Pa. $10.95

A NATURAL HISTORY OF THE DUCKS, John Charles Phillips. Great landmark of ornithology offers complete detailed coverage of nearly 200 species and subspecies of ducks: gadwall, sheldrake, merganser, pintail, many more. 74 full-color plates, 102 black-and-white. Bibliography. Total of 1,920pp. 8⅝ × 11¼. 25141-1, 25142-X Cloth. Two-vol. set $100.00

THE SEAWEED HANDBOOK: An Illustrated Guide to Seaweeds from North Carolina to Canada, Thomas F. Lee. Concise reference covers 78 species. Scientific and common names, habitat, distribution, more. Finding keys for easy identification. 224pp. 5⅜ × 8½. 25215-9 Pa. $6.95

THE TEN BOOKS OF ARCHITECTURE: The 1755 Leoni Edition, Leon Battista Alberti. Rare classic helped introduce the glories of ancient architecture to the Renaissance. 68 black-and-white plates. 336pp. 8⅜ × 11¼. 25239-6 Pa. $14.95

MISS MACKENZIE, Anthony Trollope. Minor masterpieces by Victorian master unmasks many truths about life in 19th-century England. First inexpensive edition in years. 392pp. 5⅜ × 8½. 25201-9 Pa. $8.95

THE RIME OF THE ANCIENT MARINER, Gustave Doré, Samuel Taylor Coleridge. Dramatic engravings considered by many to be his greatest work. The terrifying space of the open sea, the storms and whirlpools of an unknown ocean, the ice of Antarctica, more—all rendered in a powerful, chilling manner. Full text. 38 plates. 77pp. 9¼ × 12. 22305-1 Pa. $4.95

THE EXPEDITIONS OF ZEBULON MONTGOMERY PIKE, Zebulon Montgomery Pike. Fascinating first-hand accounts (1805–6) of exploration of Mississippi River, Indian wars, capture by Spanish dragoons, much more. 1,088pp. 5⅜ × 8½. 25254-X, 25255-8 Pa. Two-vol. set $25.90

CATALOG OF DOVER BOOKS

A CONCISE HISTORY OF PHOTOGRAPHY: Third Revised Edition, Helmut Gernsheim. Best one-volume history—camera obscura, photochemistry, daguerreotypes, evolution of cameras, film, more. Also artistic aspects—landscape, portraits, fine art, etc. 281 black-and-white photographs. 26 in color. 176pp. 8⅜ × 11¼. 25128-4 Pa. $13.95

THE DORÉ BIBLE ILLUSTRATIONS, Gustave Doré. 241 detailed plates from the Bible: the Creation scenes, Adam and Eve, Flood, Babylon, battle sequences, life of Jesus, etc. Each plate is accompanied by the verses from the King James version of the Bible. 241pp. 9 × 12. 23004-X Pa. $9.95

WANDERINGS IN WEST AFRICA, Richard F. Burton. Great Victorian scholar/adventurer's invaluable descriptions of African tribal rituals, fetishism, culture, art, much more. Fascinating 19th-century account. 624pp. 5⅜ × 8½. 26890-X Pa. $12.95

FLATLAND, E. A. Abbott. Intriguing and enormously popular science-fiction classic explores the complexities of trying to survive as a two-dimensional being in a three-dimensional world. Amusingly illustrated by the author. 16 illustrations. 103pp. 5⅜ × 8½. 20001-9 Pa. $2.50

THE HISTORY OF THE LEWIS AND CLARK EXPEDITION, Meriwether Lewis and William Clark, edited by Elliott Coues. Classic edition of Lewis and Clark's day-by-day journals that later became the basis for U.S. claims to Oregon and the West. Accurate and invaluable geographical, botanical, biological, meteorological and anthropological material. Total of 1,508pp. 5⅜ × 8½. 21268-8, 21269-6, 21270-X Pa. Three-vol. set $26.85

LANGUAGE, TRUTH AND LOGIC, Alfred J. Ayer. Famous, clear introduction to Vienna, Cambridge schools of Logical Positivism. Role of philosophy, elimination of metaphysics, nature of analysis, etc. 160pp. 5⅜ × 8½. (Available in U.S. and Canada only) 20010-8 Pa. $3.95

MATHEMATICS FOR THE NONMATHEMATICIAN, Morris Kline. Detailed, college-level treatment of mathematics in cultural and historical context, with numerous exercises. For liberal arts students. Preface. Recommended Reading Lists. Tables. Index. Numerous black-and-white figures. xvi + 641pp. 5⅜ × 8½. 24823-2 Pa. $11.95

HANDBOOK OF PICTORIAL SYMBOLS, Rudolph Modley. 3,250 signs and symbols, many systems in full; official or heavy commercial use. Arranged by subject. Most in Pictorial Archive series. 143pp. 8¼ × 11. 23357-X Pa. $6.95

INCIDENTS OF TRAVEL IN YUCATAN, John L. Stephens. Classic (1843) exploration of jungles of Yucatan, looking for evidences of Maya civilization. Travel adventures, Mexican and Indian culture, etc. Total of 669pp. 5⅜ × 8½. 20926-1, 20927-X Pa., Two-vol. set $11.90

CATALOG OF DOVER BOOKS

DEGAS: An Intimate Portrait, Ambroise Vollard. Charming, anecdotal memoir by famous art dealer of one of the greatest 19th-century French painters. 14 black-and-white illustrations. Introduction by Harold L. Van Doren. 96pp. 5⅜ × 8½.

25131-4 Pa. $4.95

PERSONAL NARRATIVE OF A PILGRIMAGE TO ALMANDINAH AND MECCAH, Richard Burton. Great travel classic by remarkably colorful personality. Burton, disguised as a Moroccan, visited sacred shrines of Islam, narrowly escaping death. 47 illustrations. 959pp. 5⅜ × 8½. 21217-3, 21218-1 Pa., Two-vol. set $19.90

PHRASE AND WORD ORIGINS, A. H. Holt. Entertaining, reliable, modern study of more than 1,200 colorful words, phrases, origins and histories. Much unexpected information. 254pp. 5⅜ × 8½. 20758-7 Pa. $5.95

THE RED THUMB MARK, R. Austin Freeman. In this first Dr. Thorndyke case, the great scientific detective draws fascinating conclusions from the nature of a single fingerprint. Exciting story, authentic science. 320pp. 5⅜ × 8½. (Available in U.S. only) 25210-8 Pa. $6.95

AN EGYPTIAN HIEROGLYPHIC DICTIONARY, E. A. Wallis Budge. Monumental work containing about 25,000 words or terms that occur in texts ranging from 3000 b.c. to 600 a.d. Each entry consists of a transliteration of the word, the word in hieroglyphs, and the meaning in English. 1,314pp. 6⅜ × 10. 23615-3, 23616-1 Pa., Two-vol. set $35.90

THE COMPLEAT STRATEGYST: Being a Primer on the Theory of Games of Strategy, J. D. Williams. Highly entertaining classic describes, with many illustrated examples, how to select best strategies in conflict situations. Prefaces. Appendices. xvi + 268pp. 5⅜ × 8½. 25101-2 Pa. $6.95

THE ROAD TO OZ, L. Frank Baum. Dorothy meets the Shaggy Man, little Button-Bright and the Rainbow's beautiful daughter in this delightful trip to the magical Land of Oz. 272pp. 5⅜ × 8. 25208-6 Pa. $5.95

POINT AND LINE TO PLANE, Wassily Kandinsky. Seminal exposition of role of point, line, other elements in non-objective painting. Essential to understanding 20th-century art. 127 illustrations. 192pp. 6½ × 9¼. 23808-3 Pa. $5.95

LADY ANNA, Anthony Trollope. Moving chronicle of Countess Lovel's bitter struggle to win for herself and daughter Anna their rightful rank and fortune—perhaps at cost of sanity itself. 384pp. 5⅜ × 8½. 24669-8 Pa. $8.95

EGYPTIAN MAGIC, E. A. Wallis Budge. Sums up all that is known about magic in Ancient Egypt: the role of magic in controlling the gods, powerful amulets that warded off evil spirits, scarabs of immortality, use of wax images, formulas and spells, the secret name, much more. 253pp. 5⅜ × 8½. 22681-6 Pa. $4.50

THE DANCE OF SIVA, Ananda Coomaraswamy. Preeminent authority unfolds the vast metaphysic of India: the revelation of her art, conception of the universe, social organization, etc. 27 reproductions of art masterpieces. 192pp. 5⅜ × 8½.

24817-8 Pa. $5.95

CHRISTMAS CUSTOMS AND TRADITIONS, Clement A. Miles. Origin, evolution, significance of religious, secular practices. Caroling, gifts, yule logs, much more. Full, scholarly yet fascinating; non-sectarian. 400pp. 5⅜ × 8½.
23354-5 Pa. $6.95

THE HUMAN FIGURE IN MOTION, Eadweard Muybridge. More than 4,500 stopped-action photos, in action series, showing undraped men, women, children jumping, lying down, throwing, sitting, wrestling, carrying, etc. 390pp. 7⅞ × 10⅝.
20204-6 Cloth. $24.95

THE MAN WHO WAS THURSDAY, Gilbert Keith Chesterton. Witty, fast-paced novel about a club of anarchists in turn-of-the-century London. Brilliant social, religious, philosophical speculations. 128pp. 5⅜ × 8½.
25121-7 Pa. $3.95

A CEZANNE SKETCHBOOK: Figures, Portraits, Landscapes and Still Lifes, Paul Cezanne. Great artist experiments with tonal effects, light, mass, other qualities in over 100 drawings. A revealing view of developing master painter, precursor of Cubism. 102 black-and-white illustrations. 144pp. 8¾ × 6⅜.
24790-2 Pa. $6.95

AN ENCYCLOPEDIA OF BATTLES: Accounts of Over 1,560 Battles from 1479 B.C. to the Present, David Eggenberger. Presents essential details of every major battle in recorded history, from the first battle of Megiddo in 1479 B.C. to Grenada in 1984. List of Battle Maps. New Appendix covering the years 1967–1984. Index. 99 illustrations. 544pp. 6½ × 9¼.
24913-1 Pa. $14.95

AN ETYMOLOGICAL DICTIONARY OF MODERN ENGLISH, Ernest Weekley. Richest, fullest work, by foremost British lexicographer. Detailed word histories. Inexhaustible. Total of 856pp. 6½ × 9¼.
21873-2, 21874-0 Pa., Two-vol. set $19.90

WEBSTER'S AMERICAN MILITARY BIOGRAPHIES, edited by Robert McHenry. Over 1,000 figures who shaped 3 centuries of American military history. Detailed biographies of Nathan Hale, Douglas MacArthur, Mary Hallaren, others. Chronologies of engagements, more. Introduction. Addenda. 1,033 entries in alphabetical order. xi + 548pp. 6½ × 9¼. (Available in U.S. only)
24758-9 Pa. $13.95

LIFE IN ANCIENT EGYPT, Adolf Erman. Detailed older account, with much not in more recent books: domestic life, religion, magic, medicine, commerce, and whatever else needed for complete picture. Many illustrations. 597pp. 5⅜ × 8½.
22632-8 Pa. $8.95

HISTORIC COSTUME IN PICTURES, Braun & Schneider. Over 1,450 costumed figures shown, covering a wide variety of peoples: kings, emperors, nobles, priests, servants, soldiers, scholars, townsfolk, peasants, merchants, courtiers, cavaliers, and more. 256pp. 8⅜ × 11¼.
23150-X Pa. $9.95

THE NOTEBOOKS OF LEONARDO DA VINCI, edited by J. P. Richter. Extracts from manuscripts reveal great genius; on painting, sculpture, anatomy, sciences, geography, etc. Both Italian and English. 186 ms. pages reproduced, plus 500 additional drawings, including studies for *Last Supper, Sforza* monument, etc. 860pp. 7⅞ × 10¾. (Available in U.S. only) 22572-0, 22573-9 Pa., Two-vol. set $31.90

THE ART NOUVEAU STYLE BOOK OF ALPHONSE MUCHA: All 72 Plates from "Documents Decoratifs" in Original Color, Alphonse Mucha. Rare copyright-free design portfolio by high priest of Art Nouveau. Jewelry, wallpaper, stained glass, furniture, figure studies, plant and animal motifs, etc. Only complete one-volume edition. 80pp. 9⅜ × 12¼. 24044-4 Pa. $9.95

ANIMALS: 1,419 COPYRIGHT-FREE ILLUSTRATIONS OF MAMMALS, BIRDS, FISH, INSECTS, ETC., edited by Jim Harter. Clear wood engravings present, in extremely lifelike poses, over 1,000 species of animals. One of the most extensive pictorial sourcebooks of its kind. Captions. Index. 284pp. 9 × 12.
23766-4 Pa. $9.95

OBELISTS FLY HIGH, C. Daly King. Masterpiece of American detective fiction, long out of print, involves murder on a 1935 transcontinental flight—"a very thrilling story"—NY Times. Unabridged and unaltered republication of the edition published by William Collins Sons & Co. Ltd., London, 1935. 288pp. 5⅜ × 8½. (Available in U.S. only) 25036-9 Pa. $5.95

VICTORIAN AND EDWARDIAN FASHION: A Photographic Survey, Alison Gernsheim. First fashion history completely illustrated by contemporary photographs. Full text plus 235 photos, 1840–1914, in which many celebrities appear. 240pp. 6½ × 9¼. 24205-6 Pa. $8.95

THE ART OF THE FRENCH ILLUSTRATED BOOK, 1700–1914, Gordon N. Ray. Over 630 superb book illustrations by Fragonard, Delacroix, Daumier, Doré, Grandville, Manet, Mucha, Steinlen, Toulouse-Lautrec and many others. Preface. Introduction. 633 halftones. Indices of artists, authors & titles, binders and provenances. Appendices. Bibliography. 608pp. 8⅜ × 11¼. 25086-5 Pa. $24.95

THE WONDERFUL WIZARD OF OZ, L. Frank Baum. Facsimile in full color of America's finest children's classic. 143 illustrations by W. W. Denslow. 267pp. 5⅜ × 8½. 20691-2 Pa. $7.95

FOLLOWING THE EQUATOR: A Journey Around the World, Mark Twain. Great writer's 1897 account of circumnavigating the globe by steamship. Ironic humor, keen observations, vivid and fascinating descriptions of exotic places. 197 illustrations. 720pp. 5⅜ × 8½. 26113-1 Pa. $15.95

THE FRIENDLY STARS, Martha Evans Martin & Donald Howard Menzel. Classic text marshalls the stars together in an engaging, non-technical survey, presenting them as sources of beauty in night sky. 23 illustrations. Foreword. 2 star charts. Index. 147pp. 5⅜ × 8½. 21099-5 Pa. $3.95

FADS AND FALLACIES IN THE NAME OF SCIENCE, Martin Gardner. Fair, witty appraisal of cranks, quacks, and quackeries of science and pseudoscience: hollow earth, Velikovsky, orgone energy, Dianetics, flying saucers, Bridey Murphy, food and medical fads, etc. Revised, expanded In the Name of Science. "A very able and even-tempered presentation."—The New Yorker. 363pp. 5⅜ × 8.
20394-8 Pa. $6.95

ANCIENT EGYPT: ITS CULTURE AND HISTORY, J. E Manchip White. From pre-dynastics through Ptolemies: society, history, political structure, religion, daily life, literature, cultural heritage. 48 plates. 217pp. 5⅜ × 8½. 22548-8 Pa. $5.95

SIR HARRY HOTSPUR OF HUMBLETHWAITE, Anthony Trollope. Incisive, unconventional psychological study of a conflict between a wealthy baronet, his idealistic daughter, and their scapegrace cousin. The 1870 novel in its first inexpensive edition in years. 250pp. 5⅜ × 8½.　24953-0 Pa. $6.95

LASERS AND HOLOGRAPHY, Winston E. Kock. Sound introduction to burgeoning field, expanded (1981) for second edition. Wave patterns, coherence, lasers, diffraction, zone plates, properties of holograms, recent advances. 84 illustrations. 160pp. 5⅜ × 8¼. (Except in United Kingdom)　24041-X Pa. $3.95

INTRODUCTION TO ARTIFICIAL INTELLIGENCE: SECOND, EN-LARGED EDITION, Philip C. Jackson, Jr. Comprehensive survey of artificial intelligence—the study of how machines (computers) can be made to act intelligently. Includes introductory and advanced material. Extensive notes updating the main text. 132 black-and-white illustrations. 512pp. 5⅜ × 8½.　24864-X Pa. $8.95

HISTORY OF INDIAN AND INDONESIAN ART, Ananda K. Coomaraswamy. Over 400 illustrations illuminate classic study of Indian art from earliest Harappa finds to early 20th century. Provides philosophical, religious and social insights. 304pp. 6⅜ × 9⅜.　25005-9 Pa. $11.95

THE GOLEM, Gustav Meyrink. Most famous supernatural novel in modern European literature, set in Ghetto of Old Prague around 1890. Compelling story of mystical experiences, strange transformations, profound terror. 13 black-and-white illustrations. 224pp. 5⅜ × 8½. (Available in U.S. only)　25025-3 Pa. $6.95

PICTORIAL ENCYCLOPEDIA OF HISTORIC ARCHITECTURAL PLANS, DETAILS AND ELEMENTS: With 1,880 Line Drawings of Arches, Domes, Doorways, Facades, Gables, Windows, etc., John Theodore Haneman. Sourcebook of inspiration for architects, designers, others. Bibliography. Captions. 141pp. 9 × 12.　24605-1 Pa. $7.95

BENCHLEY LOST AND FOUND, Robert Benchley. Finest humor from early 30's, about pet peeves, child psychologists, post office and others. Mostly unavailable elsewhere. 73 illustrations by Peter Arno and others. 183pp. 5⅜ × 8½.　22410-4 Pa. $4.95

ERTÉ GRAPHICS, Erté. Collection of striking color graphics: *Seasons, Alphabet, Numerals, Aces* and *Precious Stones.* 50 plates, including 4 on covers. 48pp. 9⅜ × 12¼.　23580-7 Pa. $7.95

THE JOURNAL OF HENRY D. THOREAU, edited by Bradford Torrey, F. H. Allen. Complete reprinting of 14 volumes, 1837–61, over two million words; the sourcebooks for *Walden,* etc. Definitive. All original sketches, plus 75 photographs. 1,804pp. 8½ × 12¼.　20312-3, 20313-1 Cloth., Two-vol. set $125.00

CASTLES: THEIR CONSTRUCTION AND HISTORY, Sidney Toy. Traces castle development from ancient roots. Nearly 200 photographs and drawings illustrate moats, keeps, baileys, many other features. Caernarvon, Dover Castles, Hadrian's Wall, Tower of London, dozens more. 256pp. 5⅜ × 8¼.　24898-4 Pa. $6.95

AMERICAN CLIPPER SHIPS: 1833–1858, Octavius T. Howe & Frederick C. Matthews. Fully-illustrated, encyclopedic review of 352 clipper ships from the period of America's greatest maritime supremacy. Introduction. 109 halftones. 5 black-and-white line illustrations. Index. Total of 928pp. 5⅜ × 8½.
25115-2, 25116-0 Pa., Two-vol. set $17.90

TOWARDS A NEW ARCHITECTURE, Le Corbusier. Pioneering manifesto by great architect, near legendary founder of "International School." Technical and aesthetic theories, views on industry, economics, relation of form to function, "mass-production spirit," much more. Profusely illustrated. Unabridged translation of 13th French edition. Introduction by Frederick Etchells. 320pp. 6⅛ × 9¼. (Available in U.S. only)
25023-7 Pa. $8.95

THE BOOK OF KELLS, edited by Blanche Cirker. Inexpensive collection of 32 full-color, full-page plates from the greatest illuminated manuscript of the Middle Ages, painstakingly reproduced from rare facsimile edition. Publisher's Note. Captions. 32pp. 9⅜ × 12¼.
24345-1 Pa. $4.95

BEST SCIENCE FICTION STORIES OF H. G. WELLS, H. G. Wells. Full novel *The Invisible Man*, plus 17 short stories: "The Crystal Egg," "Aepyornis Island," "The Strange Orchid," etc. 303pp. 5⅜ × 8½. (Available in U.S. only)
21531-8 Pa. $6.95

AMERICAN SAILING SHIPS: Their Plans and History, Charles G. Davis. Photos, construction details of schooners, frigates, clippers, other sailcraft of 18th to early 20th centuries—plus entertaining discourse on design, rigging, nautical lore, much more. 137 black-and-white illustrations. 240pp. 6⅛ × 9¼.
24658-2 Pa. $6.95

ENTERTAINING MATHEMATICAL PUZZLES, Martin Gardner. Selection of author's favorite conundrums involving arithmetic, money, speed, etc., with lively commentary. Complete solutions. 112pp. 5⅜ × 8½.
25211-6 Pa. $2.95

THE WILL TO BELIEVE, HUMAN IMMORTALITY, William James. Two books bound together. Effect of irrational on logical, and arguments for human immortality. 402pp. 5⅜ × 8½.
20291-7 Pa. $7.95

THE HAUNTED MONASTERY and THE CHINESE MAZE MURDERS, Robert Van Gulik. 2 full novels by Van Gulik continue adventures of Judge Dee and his companions. An evil Taoist monastery, seemingly supernatural events; overgrown topiary maze that hides strange crimes. Set in 7th-century China. 27 illustrations. 328pp. 5⅜ × 8½.
23502-5 Pa. $6.95

CELEBRATED CASES OF JUDGE DEE (DEE GOONG AN), translated by Robert Van Gulik. Authentic 18th-century Chinese detective novel; Dee and associates solve three interlocked cases. Led to Van Gulik's own stories with same characters. Extensive introduction. 9 illustrations. 237pp. 5⅜ × 8½.
23337-5 Pa. $5.95

Prices subject to change without notice.
Available at your book dealer or write for free catalog to Dept. GI, Dover Publications, Inc., 31 East 2nd St., Mineola, N.Y. 11501. Dover publishes more than 175 books each year on science, elementary and advanced mathematics, biology, music, art, literary history, social sciences and other areas.